The Left in History

The Left in History

Revolution and Reform in Twentieth-Century Politics

Willie Thompson

Pluto Press
LONDON · CHICAGO, ILLINOIS

First published 1997 by Pluto Press
345 Archway Road, London N6 5AA
and 1436 West Randolph, Chicago, Illinois 60607, USA

British Library Cataloguing in Publication Data
A catalogue record for this book is available from the British Library

ISBN 0 7453 0892 9 hbk

Library of Congress Cataloging in Publication Data

Designed and produced for Pluto Press by
Chase Production Services, Chipping Norton, OX7 5QR
Typeset from the author's disk by Stanford DTP Services
Printed in the EC by J.W. Arrowsmith, Bristol

Contents

Acknowledgements   vi

Introduction   1

PART I   Mainstreams

1   The Matrix: Roots of the Catastrophe   15

2   Leninism and Stalinism   42

3   'Actually Existing Socialism'   76

4   The Fragments   110

5   Social Democracy   127

PART II   Alternatives

6   Trotskyism, Maoism, Eurocommunism   159

7   New Left, New Social Forces and Others   186

Conclusion – The Winter Landscape   222

Notes   232
Bibliography   253
Index   257

Acknowledgements

I would like to record thanks and appreciation to the people, too numerous to list, whose assistance and knowledge have made this book possible. In the first place the students, colleagues and friends with whom I have discussed and argued about the ideas contained in it. I am also enormously grateful for help in tracking down particular texts, especially to Stephen Brasher of the *New Statesman*. *New Left Review* and *Socialist Register*, journals without which our understanding of the contemporary left would be much poorer, have been particularly valuable sources. Especial thanks are due to Anne Beech of Pluto Press for her unfailing perceptiveness and encouragement.

Introduction

What was the Left?

When I was a teenager in the 1950s our history teacher spoke of a left-wing 'ratchet effect' operating in modern public life, by which he meant that any change made in a 'progressive' direction – extended franchise, improved welfare, humane penal codes – became irreversible and the starting point for yet further and better transformations. What had been the outrageously left-wing positions of one generation then became the middle-of-the-road ones of the next and in due course ended up as the conservative end of the political spectrum. His remark summed up a fairly general perception of the time, even among those who disliked the direction in which the country and the world were heading. The embittered reactionary Evelyn Waugh complained that the problem with British conservative governments was that they never put the clock back a single second.

'The left' is a very slippery term and not easily pinned down. My dictionary simply gives up, and defines 'left-wing' circularly as 'the political left'. It is however closely allied to, though not identical with, the idea of historical and social *progress*. In socialist jargon the terms 'left-wing' and 'progressive' have been virtually synonymous. The notion of progress as the dominant theme of historical development was culturally very prevalent in the West between 1850 and 1914, although never quite as universal as is sometimes assumed. Regressive notes sounded from certain quarters, warning of cultural decadence, racial degeneration, herd instincts, the servile state, yellow peril and suchlike. Nevertheless, 'progress' represented the prevailing assumption among educated opinion which foresaw the values of the civilisation it represented broadening across the unenlightened populations beneath the imperial sway of Western governments and deepening down through the underclasses within their own societies. Disease, destitution, ignorance remained acknowledged evils but certain to yield (albeit not always painlessly) to the application of science and enlightened social policy. The presuppositions of progress were shared no less vehemently, if from a different political angle, by the emergent labour and socialist movements of the period. It was not uncommon for the concepts of biological evolution to be misapplied to social

1

development, with a benign outcome expected in the shape of all-round moral betterment.[1]

The events of 1914–45 did a lot to shake such confident optimism, uncovering as they did instances of human depravity unparalleled in the historical record, but it was rekindled for a time in Western culture during the continuous years of unprecedented productive growth and expanding welfare of the 1950s and 1960s. Although the menace of global annihilation then hung over everything, that did not derail the collective psyche any more than the certainty of eventual death does to an ordinary individual. While a prodigious waste of resources went into the nuclear arms race and the Cold War, more than sufficient remained to eliminate structural unemployment, raise the living standard of the average Western family to previously unimaginable heights and make the abolition of poverty, in Western Europe at least, look for a time like a realisable goal.

The confident optimism of the early century was perhaps no longer present (in the era of Mutual Assured Destruction how could it be?) but the vista of indefinite technological and material progress was well reinstated. Cultural pessimists continuing to lament the good old days still existed but were on the defensive. A very popular and renowned text published in 1962 (and still in print), entitled *What is History?* by the historian of Soviet Russia and maverick pillar of the English academic establishment, E. H. Carr, eloquently conveyed the prevailing sense of advance. The theme of this short book is historiography, but Carr takes space to mock intellectuals who bemoan the alleged deterioration in civilised standards during the twentieth century, remarking that these gripes have more to do with the difficulties Oxbridge academics have in hiring servants than with the actual experiences of ordinary people. In addition he commits himself unreservedly to the idea of progress and long-term historical improvement. In this he reflected the elite *and* popular perception that the outcome and lessons of the Second World War had definitively overcome the causes of economic and political collapse that racked the world during the interwar decades. Leaving aside the question of the Soviet bloc, the era of the late 1950s, though presided over, paradoxically, by formally right-wing governments in all the major states, may certainly be viewed historically as the hour of the left. Carr, the more so because he was not identified with any specific political party or grouping, can be seen as representative of a general left-wing ethos. His text emphasises the left's status as a historical current closely associated with modernity, and which would indeed be meaningless in any other circumstances. The left's distinctive feature in the landscape of modernity however is its identification, rhetorically at least, with social improvement and regulation of economic structures in the interests of the masses – the 'ratchet effect' previously referred to.

If the values of the left implicitly dominated the language of politics in the 1950s, the language of the left came to dominate the discourse of politics and culture in the succeeding decade. The 1960s are traditionally regarded as the high tide of left-wing ascendancy in the public domain – era of hope or devil's decade depending on your point of view. Alongside the established traditions of the left, which continued to flourish and spread up till that point, emerged also a proliferation of new ones, influencing social levels hitherto scarcely touched by its outlook.

The subsequent collapse was by any historical standard astonishingly rapid. In just a little over two decades an entire modern culture appeared to wither and perish. Mighty institutions fell apart and expired almost without a struggle. Systems of belief were abandoned by millions practically overnight, even where, in governments or parties, institutional continuity and outward symbols were preserved. It is difficult to suggest any parallel in history: the only analogy which comes to mind is the uprooting of European paganism by Christianity – and that was a much more prolonged process, as well as the conquest of the old by the new rather than vice-versa. Barely two hundred years after the term first appeared in political usage it has begun to look as though 'the left', both culturally and institutionally, might well prove a transitory historical episode or even, in a breathtakingly ambitious formulation, that its catastrophe has marked 'the end of history'.

The Terminology

There is of course a sense in which the terms 'right' and 'left' may not refer to political entities or specific standpoints but simply differentiate positions within individual political movements or structures, a crude measuring instrument for mapping the spectrum of modern politics. A conservative party will possess its left and right wings – and so likewise will fascists, anarchists and communists.[2] In the crisis of communism the concept became even more blurred and ambiguous – was the 'left' of the ruling CPs made up of the reformers who tried to make the system more pluralist and market orientated or the hardline conservatives who fought to preserve it unchanged?[3] Was the 'left' in Eastern Europe in 1989 the regimes of the ruling communist parties or the democratic oppositionists who overthrew them? Was the Pol Pot regime of the extreme left or the extreme right or can it simply not be fitted into any such dimension? Where do the Greens of the present day find their place, or the nationalism represented by organisations such as ETA or the IRA?

In spite of these difficulties the notion of 'the left' does have a determinate meaning, but one which can only be understood historically rather than by definition, however complex. The use of the terms 'right' and left' as markers of political identity derives quite specifically from the French Revolution, but from a perfectly random circumstance. In the regime of the Revolutionary Convention the most politically radical deputies – in the sense of favouring popular democracy and greater egalitarianism – sat on the high benches to the chairman's left, whereas the more cautious, traditionalist, property-conscious and moderate took up position to the right. These contingent designations were to enjoy a momentous future.

Initially, to be on the left implied commitment at least to political rights for the majority of – or possibly for all – male citizens. The extreme left of the Convention envisaged the ideal political future as a democracy composed of families enjoying a more or less even distribution of small property, with pauperism and excessive wealth both eliminated, and a cultural environment in which symbols of inequality such as hereditary titles or deferential modes of address would be outlawed. The Revolution was viewed, rightly, both by its friends and enemies not merely as the overthrow of a particular regime but a revolt against the universal human order that had prevailed up to that point[4] and which, since the emergence of literate state systems five millennia earlier, had been founded upon extreme differentiation in wealth, power and culture: thin strata of elites and craft workers resting upon the backs of agricultural producers.

Social banditry and desperate revolt by the unprivileged were a perennial feature of these systems, and just as perennial was their inevitable defeat. Supernatural religion or its like providing the natural cultural framework of such societies, the demands and objectives of these rebellions, such as the English Peasants' Revolt of 1381 found their expression in religious idiom – 'When Adam delved and Eve span ... '. By the late eighteenth century religion was in retreat and the language of natural rights replaced it as the central element in the future discourse of politics. The American Declaration of Independence spoke in ringing sentences of 'rights' to 'life, liberty and the pursuit of happiness' (though 'endowed' by the Creator and not intended to apply to black slaves or Amerindians). The French revolutionaries improved matters with a 'Declaration of the Rights of Man' which dropped the 'Creator' and his 'endowments', merely citing the 'Supreme Being' as a witness.

The right-wing against which the French revolutionaries and their early imitators contended was defined in opposition to the concept of natural rights and admission of the masses (or rather their male half) to the 'political nation' by means of representative government. The right-wing stood for the perpetuation of traditional relationships in politics and society – hierarchy and subordination justified primarily by ancient lineage and rights over land, the form of property which counted for most in a pre-industrial economy. As its doctrines were formulated from 1790 onwards in reaction to what was occurring in France, the right's literary exponents – Burke, de Maistre, Bonald, Chateaubriand – adopted tones of greater or lesser intransigence. However, all were concerned to maintain privilege and inequality in power, property, status and education as a central principle of society; to assert the rightfulness and moral acceptability of some humans being permanently subordinated and exploited to the advantage of others.

A major problem for this right was that by trying to defend prescriptive privilege on rational or pragmatic grounds it virtually surrendered the argument in advance. The best that can be made of such defence is that society is some sense represents an organic totality, in which the ascendancy of privileged elites corresponds to the rule of the brain over the limbs, the lower orders fulfil necessary but subordinate functions, and any drastic tampering with the structure will only disrupt the organism and increase the sum of unhappiness.[5] However this is such a manifestly ideological construction as to lack all credibility and anyway the alleged organic order was from the late eighteenth century being revolutionised not merely and perhaps avoidably by political action, but inescapably by technology and market forces.

It is much better if the questions can never be asked in the first place and the social order be generally accepted as a timeless fact of nature instituted by God or whomever, equivalent to the seasons or the climate. The ultra-reactionary Spanish authorities of the 1790s, who banned Edmund Burke's *Reflections on the Revolution in France*, the classic statement of conservative integralism, knew what they were doing – for even to defend the old order by argument was to acknowledge the existence of unwanted questions and risk stimulating thought about the ideas being denounced.

Language and Reality

Like so much else of modern politics, the terminology of left and right was a legacy of the French Revolution to subsequent centuries. Meanings however became, in response to changing realities, if not transformed, at least substantially altered. Between the Revolution and the celebration of its centenary (which produced both the Eiffel Tower and the Statue of Liberty) human existence altered more profoundly than it had done in all of recorded or unrecorded history. By 1889 the globe had been networked with steam-driven transport systems and communications facilities using electric power. Photography was a routine process, the internal combustion engine was already in operation, cinema, radio and powered flight just around the corner. Technology and the application of capital to the productive process generated urbanisation, mass production and hitherto unimagined forms of social relationship,[6] above all the relations between owners of mobile capital and a propertyless, mobile workforce concentrated for the most part into the new conurbations.

The left came to be identified with the politics of the latter, who were regarded, though superficially, as the successors of the revolutionary *sansculottes*. The real situation of the propertyless wage-earners (or unemployed) was however very different from that of their presumed predecessors of the 1790s, and the new meaning which 'the left' came to assume in this century reflected that difference as well as new configurations of property and political power within the dominant classes.

Individualism and the free market, which in the days of petty production and land-based big property had been left-wing aspirations, became in the nineteenth century by and large the dominant ideologies of capital and were supplemented with Malthusian notions of demography, the source of destitution and misery for the masses. Collectivism and anti-individualism by contrast had been, in the form of the organic metaphor and the doctrine of mutual obligations between rich and poor, a standby of the earlier right. It was this which underpinned the 'one-nation conservatism' of such as Disraeli or the 'feudal socialism' ridiculed by Marx in the *Communist Manifesto*. Partly because it was manifestly impossible to divide great concentrations of industry among petty producers (unlike great concentrations of land) and, partly out of the importance of solidarity discovered in industrial conflict, common ownership, mutuality and collectivism developed as objectives and guiding principles of the nineteenth-century left.

A similar though somewhat less conclusive migration of concepts across the political spectrum occurred with nationalism. That too was initially associated with the left. Partisans of the French Revolution (and of earlier populist uprisings) liked to refer to themselves as 'patriots', emphasising that their attachment was to the nation rather than the monarch. When the left's enemies were predominantly dynastic states and aristocracies, national sentiment constituted an important weapon in its armoury. Following the defeated revolutions of 1848 however, conservatives and reactionaries learned that nationalism, and beyond it imperialism, could provide the identification between rulers and subjects – the ideological and social glue required to cement an unequal and hierarchical society – once religion and simple deference could no longer do so. Nationalism was played as the trump card against the left by politicians like Disraeli in Britain, Louis Bonaparte (Napoleon III) in France, Cavour in Italy, Bismarck in Germany. The Slavophil reactionaries in Russia worked to develop their own indigenous version. The left learned to be suspicious of nationalism, though continuing to uphold the rights of certain notoriously oppressed nations, especially Poland and Ireland.

The Great Schism

By the year of the revolutionary centenary the socialist left, though nowhere in possession of state power, was expanding, confident and convinced that the future belonged to it. The dominant state formations of the time were varieties of liberalism or conservatism which strove to maintain the existing structures of property relations with programmes of populist concessions. The right's ideological defences were a disarticulated compound of all the different stances which had characterised it over the course of a hundred years – prescriptive deference, of which large reservoirs still survived; economic individualism; nationalist jingoism and imperialism, with emphasis shifting to the latter. Unprecedented increases in output, in agriculture as much as industry, had generally discredited Malthusianism and its central claim that iron laws of demography rendered impossible any permanent improvement in the living standards of the labouring poor. However the right was about to discover a fresh weapon of great force and versatility in the work of Friedrich Nietzsche, which neither accepts unthinkingly nor defends apologetically the existence of subordination and exploitation. It celebrates them as the due destiny and reward of superior individuals exercising their will to power – although it is only in the late twentieth century that commerce, finance and the corporate boardroom have come to be viewed as an arena of heroic struggle.

The overall shape of the twentieth-century left was fixed between 1914 and 1918 by world war and the self-proclaimedly socialist revolution in Russia. The impact of these events was to turn the members of a supposedly fraternal movement into irreconcilable and deadly enemies, separated into camps of mutual hostility and hatred. The principal line of division, marked in blood, lay between those whose national loyalty and constitutional sentiments had determined their actions during the conflict, and the proponents of international class war as the paramount duty of a socialist. This corresponded closely with the divide between the part of the left

which applauded the Bolshevik Revolution as the transfer of class
power to the workers, the realisation of socialism's proper objectives,
worthy of imitation abroad, and the part which viewed it as the
triumph of barbarism and utter negation of democracy. This basic
divide was soon to be supplemented with others, no less or
sometimes even more, hate-filled.

The two decades which followed, whichever angle they might
be viewed from, appeared to end calamitously for the left. Its
position in 1939–40 is reminiscent in certain respects of the early
1990s. The Soviet Revolution did not spread beyond the borders
of the former Russian Empire; the regime founded in its name
degenerated into a bloody despotism and by the end of 1939 was
virtually allied to the fascist enemy. Throughout most of continental
Europe and the much of the world as well the left of whatever shape,
together with the industrial and political organisations of the labour
movement, had been destroyed and driven underground by
ascendant fascism or equivalent sorts of ultra-right dictatorship.
Where it survived it did so mostly as a weak and ineffectual minority.
The limited and mildly left experiment of the 1930s in the US had
proved an indifferent success and was reaching the end of its
potential. The more clear-cut success in Sweden was too marginal
and peripheral to count for much.

Nonetheless, the dramatic revival which took place after 1945,
deeply influencing also the right of the period, was testimony of
the extent to which the left continued to represent the hopes and
aspirations of hundreds of millions. The Soviet regime expanded
significantly in territory and communism grew gigantically in
influence and credibility. The most populous country on earth gave
birth to an indigenous communist revolution. Elsewhere, social
democracy entered its heyday. On the other hand, these
developments once more hardened, this time in the shape of the
Cold War, the antagonistic division between the universes of the
communist left on the one hand and an alliance of the non-
communist left and the mainstream right on the other. Once more
too, changing circumstances induced a migration of terminologies.
The defeat of fascism had made 'democracy' into a term of nearly
universal approbation: both sides fought for possession and
endeavoured to attach it to their regimes. The USSR operated an
elaborate electoral system. New communist regimes normally had
the word 'democratic' or 'people's' in the formal title of their
states, but the West had little difficulty in demonstrating the
profoundly undemocratic character of its rival and consequently
the banner of democracy was seized by the right – which prior to
the Second World War had scorned and despised it – and turned
into its principal ideological asset.[7]

The Contemporary Crisis

Apart from the two principal and rival versions of the mid-century left, communism and social democracy, there existed a number of peripheral and currently insignificant groupings inherited from previous eras – surviving pockets of anarchists and Trotskyists, for example. Some of these were to discover a renewed role during the 'long boom' of the 1950s to early 1970s and other formations were to make their appearance in that period. Taken together, the above constituted the left on the eve of the great collapse. The concept and the purpose of extensive and *deliberate* social improvement, and beyond that, social transformation in the interests of the unprivileged, were intrinsic to the identity of all of them and served as the emblem of the political left in general.

As Perry Anderson has expressed it: 'It is the modern labour movement that has really given birth to this quite new conception of historical change [a fully popular agency desiring and creating new social conditions of life for itself].'[8] Since these notions also tended to constitute the conventional wisdom of developed societies from roughly the early nineteenth century to the 1980s, the left, broadly defined, tended, except for the the years of fascist ascendancy between 1933 and 1942, to be swimming with the cultural tide and making the political running; the right, however many successful rearguard actions it fought, seemed to be permanently on the defensive, or, after 1945, forced to adopt the stance that 'if you can't beat them, join them'. The belief that history is on one's side may be a consolatory myth, but it is significant it was only to the left that this form of consolation was available, while the right had to make do with nostalgia.

What has evaporated at the close of the twentieth century is the expectation that it is possible for human collectives at the level of states or larger units to take their social fate into their own hands and consciously direct the enhancement of material wealth or social amenity. Rather the ruling presumption now is that such things, if they are to occur, can only be a fortunate but by no means inevitable by-product of free market operations, the latter being viewed as the only foundation upon which societies at any level of development can viably stand.

With this shift in outlook the central cultural citadel of the left has fallen into the hands of its enemies and with consequences far more disabling than any of the specific routs that the left has suffered upon the political field. The trend of current developments is viewed with horror and dismay, but no confident alternative to the anarchy of uncontrolled market forces and desperation of their victims is available. In short, no component of the left has any idea, beyond the barest glimmerings, of how a 'feasible socialism', the

term coined by Alec Nove, could actually work, let alone the
beginnings of a strategy for actually bringing it into being.

It might be thought odd and surprising that the exhaustion of
the postwar settlement in the West, that complex of international
monetary structures underpinned by extensive welfare provision
and/or full employment, should have resulted, not in the suppression
of market priorities or at least the emergence of new forms of
Keynsian organisation, but a swift regression to the discredited
formulae of nineteenth-century laissez-faire economics. The
phenomenon can be explained in terms of social differentiation
combined with economic, political and cultural pressures in the West,
but it gained incalculable reinforcement from the contemporaneous disintegration of the Soviet bloc which had purported to
embody the 'actually existing' socialist alternative and which was
confirmed on its collapse to have been a very shabby and ramshackle
alternative indeed.

The two traditions which had, for better or worse, historically
dominated the left through most of the twentieth century, Soviet
Marxism-Leninism and European social democracy, with its cognate
of US liberalism, thus encountered their nemesis at roughly the same
time;[9] and much as the latter repudiated the former with abhorrence,
the discredit of its rival adversely affected European social democracy
as well, for the right had contrived to taint it by association. A loss
of historic confidence, a loss of nerve, resignation to the terms and
agendas set by the free-market right,[10] a world of unconstrained
international capital embodied in corporations and institutions
unfettered by any form of social or political control – such are the
conditions under which the left approaches the millennium.
Pessimism is underscored by the ensemble of assumptions which
have come to be termed postmodernism, a cultural phenomenon
which has cast into disrepute all 'grand narratives' of progress,
including most emphatically those of the 'forward march of labour'.
It has ridiculed every expectation inherited from the eighteenth-
century Enlightenment about the possibility of human growth and
emancipation. The left's prospects have never looked bleaker since
the 1930s. 'The old century is not ending well ', as Eric Hobsbawm
writes in *Age of Extremes*.

For adherents of the left in any of its forms (apart from the few
who write of 'unprecedentedly favourable circumstances'[11]) it is
an unavoidable temptation to speculate and enquire whether the
turn of events was a product of accident and contingency, an
outcome of wrong decisions and mistaken strategies; whether the
right's global triumph might have been avoided and socialism,
with or without a human face, been by now in the ascendant. That
is certainly worth investigating, though unlikely to be answered with
any certainty, but it is more important to understand the chain of

developments through which matters actually got to this pass and to try to evaluate the position at which the left now stands around the world and trace the interconnections which may exist between its situation in different areas. That is what this book tries to undertake. A further temptation would be to begin to assess the prospects for the left's recovery and begin to specify what its adherents should do to start that process. That however, apart from some very few sketchy hints at the very end, I am concerned to avoid – analysis and interpretation seem to sufficiently fill the agenda in the meantime although I make some attempt to evaluate the current condition of the left in the long view and comment upon the cultural climate in which it faces its future – supposing it to have any.

Certainly from my own point of view I continue to hope that it does, but that hope can be justified only by acknowledging that almost exactly two centuries after its name first appeared in political discourse, the left has reached its nadir. The aim of this volume will be to examine the process through which this culmination was arrived at, to take into account the present situation of the left's surviving fragments and, very briefly, to enquire whether any potential still exists for its regrowth and the reformulation of its tradition. In this I make unashamed use of hindsight, being convinced that the development of any reality is only fully comprehended in the light of its eventual outcome.

PART I

MAINSTREAMS

CHAPTER 1

The Matrix: Roots of the Catastrophe

Historical divisions are always arbitrary, and there are a variety of timescales through which the evolution of 'the left' can be interpreted – although the years 1792–4, 1848, 1871 and 1917 would mark turning points in any such scheme. However, one way of envisaging this career is to consider it in two almost exactly equal phases lasting a century in each case. The first stretches from the appearance of the concept in the era of the French Revolution to the foundation of the Socialist International in 1889. These decades represented a period of flux, during which philosophies challenging the entrenched power of social and political conservatism competed on relatively equal terms. Ideologies (within an almost exclusively European crucible) were in the process of formation and organisations embodying them emerged and disappeared with regularity and rapidity. The tide underlying all these individual currents and eddies was that of demographic growth, urbanisation, expanding industrialisation and marketisation,[1] all disrupting age-old patterns of life among handicraft producers and peasants (whose numbers increased nonetheless) while generating new classes and class divisions; above all the class of propertyless wage labourers in the new technologically-orientated enterprises, concentrated in massive conurbations.

The 'working class', Marx's proletariat, was a creation of the nineteenth century, although the identifiable line of socio-economic development leading to its appearance stretched back several centuries. The banking techniques pioneered in thirteenth-century Italy constituted the indispensable starting point for the economic revolutions which brought into being a world dominated by machine industry and commodity production. However they certainly could not have played that role without the transformation which was effected in the sixteenth century by the emergence of a worldwide economy – still in its initial stages – thanks to European subjugation of the Americas and seaborne contacts established with the societies of southern and eastern Asia.

Through detours and fluctuations of greater or lesser violence, revolution, slump and war, three interlinked trends have asserted themselves in the evolution of the world regarded as a single market: firstly a demographic explosion; secondly constant expansion and deepening of productive capacities in this economy as a unit

15

(though not necessarily in all of its component sectors); and, thirdly
the steady extinction of subsistence production or insulated local
markets in favour of sucking an ever-rising proportion of the
expanding world population into the global circuits of exchange.
At all times however, the global economy has been dominated from
a single centre, by a particular political unit,[2] each of which can
be identified with a specific regime of accumulation, of which
historically there have been three – the Spanish, the British (in two
separate phases)[3] and the American. '… every step forward',
according to Giovanni Arrighi, 'involves a change of guard at the
commanding heights of the world capitalist economy and a
concomitant "organisational revolution" in processes of capital
accumulation'.[4]

During the first three centuries of the world economy the basic
producers overwhelmingly (though there were some exceptions[5])
remained either agriculturalists or handicraft workers – often
enough the same persons. It was however among urban handicraft
producers – and on occasion their female dependants – that an
ideological ferment was generated in such a manner as to provide
a numerous and receptive audience for notions that the social
world might – and should – be turned upside down.[6] These
individuals however were no homogeneous mass, rather they were
minutely differentiated by employment, income, age status and,
in Britain, religion.[7] Yet on certain occasions, England in the
seventeenth century and France in the eighteenth, they proved able,
when seized by an all-encompassing idea, amalgamating the
abstractions propounded by publicists and agitators with their own
social experience, primarily as regards the authoritarian arrogance
they received from their betters,[8] to combine into a political force
potentially or actually capable of toppling governments.

The Working Class

By the early years of the nineteenth century this social stratum was,
throughout the economically advanced states of Western Europe,
increasingly disciplined by the whip of market forces. These
producers, beneath the guise of contractual independence, were
in effect being turned into outworking wage labourers but loathed
having to acknowledge the fact. They faced severe, sometimes
catastrophic, reductions in income along with loss of independence
and status. They tended to be relatively well educated,[9] to possess
informal networks which could transmit and transform ideas, to
have leisure to read and think and to be conscious of the example
of the French Revolution which demonstrated that the powers
that be were not unchallengeable. On both the continent and

Britain it was among circles like these, rather than in the newly formed factory proletariat or the men who constructed and operated the emergent railway networks, that notions of political revolutionism with social overtones first took root and where the concept of the working class as a distinct social entity eventually found acceptance.[10] Wilhelm Weitling is described as 'the most important utopian socialist thinker within the early German labour movement', his ideas to be 'based completely upon a vision of craft production in small workshops'.[11] This was the proletariat which rose in revolt in Paris in 1848 and 1871 and which Marx and Engels took as the political model for the yet more recent working class of machine industry and concentrated production.

The latter, more novel still, was a class that had arrived on the scene with unprecedented speed and suddenness and whose emergence always transformed the age-old character of political and social relations. Wherever it formed it began – or at least its adult male component did – to pursue *organisation*: whether in educational circles aiming at basic literacy or expanded knowledge; friendly insurance societies as frail protection against the rigours of the job market; co-operative societies to abate the rigours of the nineteenth-century consumer market; or protective associations against the employer. The ultimate embodiment of such organisation was that of a political movement to either influence the state at its topmost level or to aim at its total overturn.

All of such developments were made possible only by the fact that the new industrial proletariat was as a class positioned differently from any of its predecessors. The individuals who composed it were not only in very large part pushed together in close proximity as operatives in factories and as dwellers in urban conurbations,[12] they also inhabited cultures of general literacy, mass periodical circulation, rapid transport and communication and a general weakening (if far from extinction) of religious influences – in short mass societies of an increasingly secular bent. The evolving labour movements had built their organisational structures after many experiments, trials and failures, often in desperate and precarious circumstances, to conform with the social and cultural principles of such societies. In Western Europe, as political legitimacy increasingly came to rest on a concept of universal citizenship exemplified by the electoral franchise, their political weight and leverage was correspondingly strengthened.

In the event Britain was the laboratory, as equally it was the pioneer of machine industry. E. P. Thompson's *The Making of the English Working Class* is, famously, only marginally concerned with the factory proletariat and concludes in the 1830s, at which time it might be considered that the classic British labour movement and working-class culture had scarcely begun to be formed. Indeed the book's subject is the late eighteenth and early nineteenth-century 'labouring poor' of the pre-factory era and the manner in which decades of bitter exploitation and political repression brought into being the consciousness of a working-class identity – which, rather than 'objective' relation to the mode of production, Thompson regarded as constituting the essence of class being.

It is possible to criticise *The Making* for an implicit presumption that the formation of mature class consciousness was the outcome to which all the preceding developments were striving with a greater or lesser degree of clarity. In this conception the experiences of the years 1793–1819 supplied the historical raw material out of which people like Cobbett and the primitive socialists articulated an outlook which had become the common sense of the workers by the 1830s of a fundamental if not irreconcilable conflict of interest between capital and labour.[13] Whether or not the classic can be faulted on those grounds, what its author certainly demonstrates beyond any question and in voluminous detail is the extent to which the collective institutions, practices and outlooks of an artisan and handicraft workforce were adapted and reconstructed into those of the new class and provided the underpinning also for real innovations. In the mutual benefit club, reaching back centuries, can be identified the embryo both of social insurance and the co-operative movement. Masonic forms of organisation and even ritual served as the model for early trade unionism; traditions of artisan self-education were carried right over into proletarian self-improvement associations. Religious forms of organisation – not to speak of ideology – were copied and made their contribution as well.[14] In the Chartist movement of the late 1830s and 1840s these streams of development coalesced into an emergent political party – one which however failed to survive a combination of government repression and antagonisms arising out of the different strata of the labouring population from which the movement was composed. Thereafter British nineteenth-century working-class political action assumed other forms.

With important variations in detail, of which their formal ideology and relation to political society is the most significant, the model pioneered in Britain was copied by the workers' movements in Europe and further afield and the transition from primitive industrial workforce to articulate labour movement rendered much shorter and more straightforward. The phraseology of a title like 'The Making of the German Working Class' would sound rather odd and forced. However it has to be acknowledged that whatever their pre-industrial antecedents, the forms of organisation arrived at by the various labour movements were ones which the structures of capital-labour relations and social divisions prevailing in nineteenth-century industry and society might have been expected to produce. Social insurance, co-operative marketing, collective bargaining, educational and cultural uplift, political petitioning and pressure are, after all, forms of action which have a certain evident logic and would certainly sooner or later find their place in any emergent working class's repertoire. It is quite a different matter with ideology and political consciousness.

Movements and Individuals

It has been a persistent vice of the left to mistake the formal positions adopted by its institutions – political parties, trade unions or whatever – for the unanimous outlook of the members, and that therefore winning formal endorsement of a programme from the meeting of a congress or executive is equivalent to achieving ardent commitment at the grassroots. In reality it has never been more than a small minority who are continuously thinking about or active in politics or projects of social change and who, also because of their special concerns and interests, tend to be in some degree alienated from the general culture of their class; and only very occasionally and in special circumstances that the masses are gripped by and become active participants around political issues.

Social consciousness in other words is for most people (of all classes, ethnic origins and sexual orientation) only very indirectly a matter of class, unless there are formal types of discrimination based explicitly upon it.[15] What people are concerned with in the main is getting on with their lives at the micro level. They are more likely to be exercised by the placings of the football league than the outcome of the municipal elections, though they may well have voted in the latter. Class, although an excellent conceptual tool to analyse economic and other forms of exploitation, is a rather poor predictor of social, let alone political consciousness.[16] Autobiographical recollections of British working-class socialist activists from the pre-1914 era make it clear how far they tended to be isolated in their local communities, regarded as eccentrics of some sort who developed in response attitudes of elitist superiority. The renowned socialist novel from the same period, The Ragged Trousered Philanthropists, has this isolation as its theme, incorporating a bitter denunciation of the group of workers among whom the story is set for their unwillingness to raise their consciousness to the protagonist's understanding of class realities.

Britain was notoriously behind other major European states in giving birth to a socialist labour movement and a political labour party,[17] although the paradox of the oldest and most socially experienced labour movement showing exceptional reluctance to break with its liberal mentors – not to speak of mass support for conservatism and imperialism within the British working class at large – might in itself have cast doubt on the historic confidence of the early Socialist International. Their French, and more especially their German, counterparts appeared on the face of things to be far more politically advanced. Socialism in one or another form had captured by the 1880s the proletarian culture in those countries, along with other smaller ones. But that too could be simplistic, misrepresenting attachments which might range from fervent activist identification through to indifference or passive acquiescence because the most available culture in terms of association, reading matter entertainment and even consumption happened to derive from the socialist movement.

The distinction between the movement and the individuals which constituted it is therefore important, for the outlooks of the two do not necessarily coincide; the movement's leadership need not and seldom did represent a working-class general will. Not only did it have its own bureaucratic interests, well-examined by historians, but for the most part the leadership would simply be accepted as long as it continued to deliver the expected goods. Explorations into the *Alltagsgeschichte*, the history of everyday life, by historians of both French and German working classes confirm the substantial gap that existed between 'official' and grassroots working-class culture.[18] Moreover, even in the workplace itself the advance of the large enterprise and the second industrial revolution of the late nineteenth century, far from generating a more homogeneous working class as Marx and Engels implicitly expected, strengthened sectional differences inherited from the artisan era and bred innumerable new ones with their endless implications for rivalry and conflict.

Nevertheless, with all these facts taken into account and the momentous consequences they were to have for the subsequent history of the left, is is equally important that some variety of leftwing orientation, generally socialism, did become the official political culture of the labour movements in Europe and elsewhere.[19] That this was so must be attributed directly or indirectly to the impact of the totalising explanation which Marx and Engels advanced for the world of the late nineteenth century and the respective roles of labour and capital within it. The impact was experienced and was influential even where, as in the UK and the US, the revolutionary doctrine was explicitly rejected.

[Bernard Shaw] meant that Marx's picture of social exploitation, as well as the promise of decisive social change, remained more or less intact. 'Read Jevons and the rest for your economics,' he wrote in 1887, and 'read Marx for the history of their working in the past and the condition of their application in the present.

And never mind the metaphysics.' ... even Webb continued to see the 'class war' ... as the key to the confused history of all European progress.[20]

Socialism and Communism

'The bourgeoisie', notes *The Communist Manifesto*, 'is historically a most revolutionary class.' Indeed. From whatever angle the outcome is considered, nobody can seriously deny that it was this social layer, whether or not in political command, which presided over the establishment of modernity and modern times, the most profound transformation in human circumstances since the neolithic revolution and invention of agriculture 10,000 years earlier. Economic and demographic growth, urbanisation, on a scale surpassing all earlier experience, and not as a single burst of development but with an accelerating momentum and bringing in its wake volcanic upheavals in economic and social relationships; the appearance of instruments of production (and destruction) of unimaginable power and novelty: 'All that is solid melts into the air', to quote the *Manifesto* again.[21]

The dialectic of modernity burst upon the consciousness of the nineteenth century. The full meaning of the changes ocurring in economic growth and organisation since the sixteenth century was not such as to be recognised before the age of machine production.[22] Adam Smith's renowned analysis, published in 1776, presumed an economy dominated by handicraft production. The philosophers of the Enlightenment in a real sense looked to the past rather than the future, for they saw the essence of their project as ridding the educated European mind of accumulated medieval lumber. The French revolutionaries, notoriously, envisaged themselves as restoring the political world of classical purity they imagined had existed before barbarism took hold. But whether modernity consisted in politically rational republican institutions, scientific and rational modes of thinking or expanded productive capacity, the new century made it clear to all but the most complacent that modernity was a dramatically two-sided process – prodigiously multiplying destitution, immiseration, anomie and wretchedness even as it generated fabulous social wealth and the prospect of turning material utopia into reality for the first time in human history.

Early sketches for a socialist reordering of economic affairs, or schemes for co-operative production, were among the intellectual responses.[23] The fateful conjunction arrived when the ideas they embodied were interpreted as being the responsibility and the destiny of the new class of hereditary wage-workers central to the capitalist production process. Through the ideological lead provided by hitherto independent artisan producers faced by or in the process of reduction to the status of waged labour, the word 'communist' entered the political vocabulary.[24] Marx began his career as a university-educated radical journalist who moved intellectually towards a communist standpoint before being co-opted into the leadership of an international organisation of such artisans, the League of the Just, subsequently restyled the Communist League, on whose behalf the *Communist Manifesto* was written. The really revolutionary character of this document was to integrate the social and political role ascribed to the proletariat, now defined in the broader terms appropriate to a society founded on the power of steam rather than muscle, into a messianic historical drama encompassing the past, present and future. Not only was the proletariat capable of instituting the higher form of society based upon the abolition of private property, but the dialectic of history ensured that it could not fail to do so. Its own interest in establishing a regime of collectively-controlled production embodied at the same time a universal emancipatory project.[25] Its specific class interests were simultaneously those of humanity at large. The proletariat, Marx asserted, would find in philosophy its weapon of liberation, and philosophy would discover its realisation in the proletariat.[26]

Following the abortive revolutions of 1848–9 separate strands on the continental left began to define themselves. Surviving as a tradition from the later eighteenth century was neo-Jacobininsm, ideologically fixated on 'the people' but impatient of approaches which took class as their central concept; authoritarian and governmentally centralist in outlook. During the middle years of the nineteenth century its outstanding exponent was Auguste Blanqui, a prolific instigator of secret societies devoted to the overthrow of governments by sudden armed coup d'etat and the installation of his followers as the embodiment of popular power. Anarchism, was the almost inevitable response of agrarian smallholders and precariously surviving handicraft producers to the ravages of the centralising market when the state was identified as the promoter and guardian of these destructive relationships.[27] The violent edge which the movement acquired in the later part of the century, when its exponents came to be identified in the public consciousness with bomb-throwing and individualistic acts of terrorism, was influenced especially by the activities and example of the Russian Mikhail Bakunin.

The future of the left however lay with the movements which mirrored and adapted to the advance and spread of technology and industrialised production, the ones which mobilised the masses of wage labourers concentrated especially in centres dominated by the new productive forces, or in older forms of industry, such as coalmining, which had become interlinked with the new. Once organised into mass parties interlocked with trade union structures capable of forcing employers to modify their behaviour, exerting electoral muscle and generating a network of co-operative and cultural associations, the new class appeared at least as a pressure group whose claims could not be ignored and at worst as a threat which menaced the continuing survival of entrenched property and power.[28] For the first time since the French Revolution 'the left' in this fashion achieved a stable and lasting institutional embodiment.

Marx's Ascendancy

Even so, before the 1870s Marx's future status as the central influence on the continental labour movements was far from accomplished despite the impression which *The Communist Manifesto* had already made. Ferdinand Lassalle, though Marx's rival and political enemy, claimed to be able to recite it from beginning to end. It provided as no other perspective could have done the energy and confidence needed to inspire the activists of a pariah class struggling to create a movement, despised by official society and frequently persecuted, with conviction of their historic destiny.

But even more momentous was the publication of *Capital* (Vol. 1) in 1867. Its aim and purpose was to turn inside-out the categories of bourgeois economics. Its social significance was that by doing so it claimed to confer scientific legitimacy on the revolutionary aim of 'expropriating the expropriators' by demonstrating that the wage-labour relationship was *inherently* exploitative, and did not become so only in the hands of particularly exacting or rapacious employers; whether hours were short or long, wages high or low, conditions foul or optimum, the relationship in itself nevertheless constituted exploitation. The fact that for decades only the first volume (the only one Marx completed) was available and likely to be read in full only by a minority, did not mean that its conceptions and categories did not find a much wider resonance.

In the newly-unified German state the workers' movement which Lassalle had inaugurated fell apart; its components were reconstituted into one led by acolytes of Marx, which before long had attained (with all due reservations made as to how deeply its theoretical ideas really penetrated popular consciousness) an unparalleled hegemony over the lives and consciousness of the majority of the German working class. The Social Democratic Party of Germany, the SPD (it was initially entitled the Socialist Workers' Party) was far more than a political organisation, it was also a trade, economic, social and cultural union. It had attached to it in subordinate relationship the country's major trade unions, a network of co-operative shops,

organised bodies covering virtually every sphere of social and
cultural activity – for women, youth, sports, recreation, the arts.
It published several *daily* newspapers, alongside uncountable
numbers of journals and books.[29] In the popularisation of Marxism
it provided an alternative conceptual universe for its adherents, set
against the official imperial one of the *Kaiserreich*. Subject to
attempted suppression by Bismarck between 1878 and 1890, it easily
survived the persecution which only succeeded in adding an aura
of martyrdom and invincibility to the movement.

> However strong [Max] Weber's objections to Marxist theory
> were on scientific grounds, he was prepared to pay tribute to
> 'pioneer' Marxism as a heroic, albeit utopian, creed which had
> stimulated the workers' movement within a society that had
> utterly rejected their claims to the social product and a decent
> living. Furthermore he considered the *Communist Manifesto* ...
> which predicted an inevitable early demise of capitalism, as
> prophecies with considerable suggestive power.[30]

It is not surprising in these circumstances that the SPD supplied
the standard model for the workers' parties which began to emerge
throughout Europe in the 40 years prior to 1914. Not all adopted
the overt revolutionism of their prototype (a revolutionism however
which was adapted to co-exist with the German state), but all
were imbued with the Marxist understanding of private property
in productive resources as historically outdated (hence morally
illegitimate) and with the Marxist vision of a progressive course to
history of which the industrial proletariat was the predestined
inheritor and culmination.

These parties and movements were internationalist (although that
was not necessarily true of the everyday cultural attitudes of their
members, which might be nationalist, chauvinist or even racist).
Famously, Marx had proclaimed 'The workers have no country',[31]
and the Kaiser (who had presumably never got round to reading
The Communist Manifesto) agreed with him, at least so far as his
own Social Democrats were concerned, denouncing them as
'fellows without a fatherland'. Although there were individual
exceptions, nationalism was viewed among the late nineteenth-
century labour movements as constituting, in essence, a link in the
ideological manacles with which the bourgeoisie strove to bind the
consciousness of the masses in order to reinforce its political and
institutional domination. In the rhetoric of the new parties, the
worker's primary affinity and loyalty was declared to be that of fellow-
proletarians across state frontiers, and the segmentation of the
movement into national sections only a convenience dictated by
realities of state divisions.

Marx had attempted to create an International Workingmen's Association as early as the 1860s. Possessing a tiny membership, the contrast between this initial sketch with its short and troubled life,[32] and that of its well-grounded successor 15 years later is instructive. During these years the industrial labour movements of Europe (or at least northern Europe) had succeeded in establishing themselves organisationally. For the most part they found in Marx's perspectives a world-view which bound their members together with a vision of an oppressed community confident nevertheless that they would inherit the future. In a small way the potential of the new movement was shown in 1894, when the Belgian labour movement conducted a successful political general strike for the widening of the parliamentary franchise.

The Socialist International

The general pattern is clear from around 1870, with the marginalisation or disappearance of all the preceding variants of the left,[33] although that overall trend still left scope for enormous variation of belief and practice. The dramatic insurrection known as the Paris Commune in 1871, which succeeded in controlling the city for some weeks, marked both an end and a beginning. As a beginning it provided a model for revolution seriously adopted by the Bolsheviks in the next century; as an end it expressed the culmination of revolutionary endeavours by pre-industrial forms of labour, and politically exhausted them. The 'natural' channel of development thereafter was for the trade union or political representatives of industrial workforces to function as a pressure group vis-a-vis the authorities: to agitate, argue and press for reform of particular abuses, to demand that the state underwrite or at least refrain from obstructing the right of labour to advance its claims by industrial or political action, and finally that the state concern itself with the demands of the masses and the social dimension of public affairs – all presupposing of course that the state was in some degree responsive to popular pressure.

Such was the evolution followed, for example, by the British labour movement drawing upon rich traditions of struggle, ideological debate and cultural formation inherited from the era preceding the mid-nineteenth century which proved to be in the later decades capable of influencing the established political system. In its initial manifestation, when emerging in the 1860s under the leadership of Ferdinand Lassalle, German organised labour was likewise reformist in orientation and ready to make deals with the Bismarckian state – which however spurned it. The apparent much greater impregnability of the state in continental Europe is generally agreed to have been the prime reason for the greater readiness of European labour movements to adopt ostensibly revolutionary postures.

Although the date of 1889 and the founding of the Socialist International may be arbitrary to some degree, it does mark the institutionalisation of a certain conception of the left as the form of politics which it would thereafter be identified. Certainly it represented a historically novel phenomenon, an organisation established explicitly to advance the interests of a social class defined by its members' role as propertyless basic producers – and to do so across international frontiers. For a very long time – effectively seven decades – significant fresh developments would henceforth evolve out of this matrix rather than appearing as spontaneous new creations. The organised, centralised labour movement, with political party, associated trade unions and peripheral affiliated organisations was embodied as the norm, and rival conceptions of the left rendered peripheral (anarchists were excluded from 1896) although the International itself was far from centralised and had only consultative powers in due course, it was to be derisively termed a mere 'post office'.

It can be said that the general outlook prevailing within the labour movements by the end of the nineteenth century had come to dominate somewhat against the grain and was sustained by a tradition which had been implanted only after severe struggles and whose ascendency was on the face of things by no means inevitable or even particularly likely. Mature European socialism inherited the universalist traditions of the Enlightenment and the French Revolution. To some degree this might be attributed to the extent to which it was open to influences emanating from dominant bourgeois ideologies – or its use of bourgeois political rights discourse against the bourgeoisie. It is important to keep in mind that Marx and Engels were politically formed not only as theoreticians but as active revolutionists and that the bodies they were then associated with were created by the transplant of ideas arising out of later workers' insurgencies into organisations tracing a direct line of descent to the revolutionary era.[34]

To speculate briefly on different historical options: if the French Revolution had *not* taken the radical turn that it did, causing it to shake Europe and beyond with the rallying-cry of universal rights – and such a possibility is by no means fanciful – the continental process of industrialisation might have been retarded somewhat, but probably not very much, given the momentum it had already acquired by the 1790s. In which case labour movements, as workers responded to the circumstances of employer/labour relations and employer-friendly governments, would still have developed organisationally – but they would have have assumed a very different ideological complexion. They would never have seen themselves in a world-transforming role, nor would they have taken aboard a model of historical development (or 'law' as it was contemporaneously defined) which assigned to themselves the most momentous historical destiny of all time – to make the leap from the realm of necessity to that of freedom, to bring about the extinction of class society and the end of 'prehistory', no less – for these were hopes and expectations ultimately inspired by the Revolution.

In the absence of such a consolatory vision others would doubtless have been available. Even in the countries of the deepest Marxist penetration, such as Germany, there were workers who remained outside its orbit and attached to religiously inspired or liberal organisations. On the other hand, the essentials of this essentially Marxist vision spread far beyond the ranks of formal Marxists. In Britain, stolid trade unionists, Fabians or Labour Party apparatchiks like Ramsay MacDonald could adhere to it as their integrating perspective, after translation into suitable evolutionary terms.

This vision and this culture, as well as being international, was profoundly humanitarian. The socialists, being the heirs of the Enlightenment and its universalising moral values,[35] were democrats as well as social democrats and incorporated all the progressive aspirations the bourgeoisie had exhibited in its own revolutionary phase. They demanded civil liberties and equal citizenship rights for all, not only from a class but from a universal standpoint. Their parties stood for the emancipation and enfranchisement of women.[36] They were on the side of oppressed nationalities. Mostly they opposed imperialism, and even where, as among the Fabians or Bernsteinians, it was accepted in principle, their demand – however unrealistic – was that it should be administered humanely.[37] Anti-Semitism was denounced – censured by August Bebel as the 'socialism of the fools'; and indeed the prominence of Jews in the leadership of social democrat parties gave anti-Semites a convenient handle with which to attack them. Nor did any of the socialist movements, regardless of where they were placed on the revolutionary-reformist spectrum, envisage a day of blood and vengeance against their class enemies. They did not by any means preclude insurrection on principle, but it was presumed that the transfer of power would either be peaceful, with the bourgeoisie overawed by the mass discipline of the insurgent proletariat, or that the minimum degree of force would be employed to overcome isolated armed resistance. The excesses of the French Revolution were explicitly deplored.[38]

Challenges

Scarcely was this form of social outlook and action internationally endorsed however, than a challenger appeared from within its own structures. Syndicalism took its name from French trade union organisations in the last third of the nineteenth century. The movement was a diffuse one and not easy to pin down in a simple definition but in essence – although there were variations of emphasis between countries and groupings – it rejected totally the involvement of workers' organisations with the state in any shape or form, whether reformist or revolutionary. As in anarchist conceptions, the state was viewed as a parasitic and malign excrescence. Political power ought to follow economic and social power and be concentrated in the workplace, from where revolution would emerge in the form of direct action unmediated by political parties. Revolutionary industrial unionism is as near as can be got to a summing up of the syndicalist programme,[39] with the separate trade organisations dropping their craft particularities and barriers and merging finally into 'one big union' through which capitalist power would be overthrown by means of an apocalyptic general strike. Parliamentary assemblies were therefore naturally damned. Moreover, political parties in themselves, even if ostensibly revolutionary, were viewed in syndicalist eyes as a dubious accommodation to the bourgeois state, scarcely likely to avoid the accommodation to bourgeois principles termed 'parliamentary cretinism' and in any case divorced from the realities of the workplace and immediate class confrontation.

It is perhaps not surprising that attitudes of such a kind should have been prevalent among the French workforce. The Third Republic had been erected in the blood of the Communards of 1871, and though subsequently adopting less reactionary postures than it began with, continued to demonstrate intransigent hostility to labour or social demands. Understandably, it was viewed as offering nothing to the labour movement, being fit only for annihilation. Categories of belief were not however clearly drawn. Most French workers who were members of syndicalist unions also voted in parliamentary elections for one or other of the socialist political parties which sought their franchise.

During the late nineteenth and early twentieth centuries syndicalism was to become influential well beyond its point of origin. It flourished among unskilled and migrant workers in the US, giving rise to the Industrial Workers of the World or 'Wobblies'. It spread to Britain, where it put down strong roots among the miners, and from there to parts of the white empire, particularly Australia and Canada. Syndicalist perspectives also influenced certain small parties which regarded themselves as orthodox Marxists, such as the Socialist Labour Party formed in the United States and its British offshoot of the same name. More importantly, they influenced the Bolsheviks.

Syndicalism on account of its structural looseness and passionate rejection of social authority was not uncongenial to anarchists, and anarcho-syndicalism emerged as a recognisable trend in the early years of the twentieth century. Syndicalism as such however was not excluded from the International. To gain membership socialist parties had to recognise the necessity for political action, but trade unions were automatically eligible. The full model set by the SPD was neither obligatory nor universal – and if syndicalism represented one pole of its broad church the other could be identified with the British labour movement. The latter was an unusually heterogeneous phenomenon and culturally a very rich one. With no revolutionary source of origin to look back to, its foundation was the trade unions (enrolling only a minority of the workforce) whose traditions were emphatically non-Marxian (Marx might be accorded respect, but certainly not allegiance). Its dominant political principles were drawn from the heritage of liberalism, and only with great reluctance did the Trades Union Congress in the 1890s and individual unions even later, abandon the movement's formal political links with the Liberal Party. These traditions of class conciliationism and con-stitutionalism did not vanish when the movement's separate political expression, the Labour Representation Committee, retitled the Labour Party six years later, was instituted in 1900. Scarcely even a political party in the accepted sense, this comprised a loose confederacy of trade union representatives with two small labour parties and an intellectual society of doubtful socialist provenance. Its sole stated objective was to obtain independent parliamentary representation for the interests of labour.

The International had left the door open for the British trade unions even before they dropped their Liberal association; its strategy was to bring into its ranks as wide a spectrum as was feasible of representative workers' organisations, irrespective of their attitude to the state.[40] In behaving thus it enhanced its numbers, apparent strength and the alarm with which it was viewed by bourgeois Europe, but made for an extremely loose and unstructured organisation which would have been incapable of acting collectively and with direction in a crisis – even if its individual components had aspired to do so.

Thanks to its origins and the stature and prestige of the German Social Democrats, the International, despite being compounded of so many diverse tendencies and outlooks, assumed an unmistakably Marxist tone. In doing so it was carrying from an earlier era ideological baggage that was becoming increasingly inappropriate for an era of state consolidation, extending electoral franchises and the steady incorporation of a widening public into the representative machinery and symbolic rituals of bourgeois society. As Engels himself expressed it, the firepower and discipline of orthodox military forces in the 1890s made them invincible in barricade fighting, and the changing perception of the likely fighters behind the barricades – in the soldiers' eyes now an anti-social mob rather than 'the people' – made them much less likely to change sides.

Fissures

Thus from its creation as an institutional reality a potential fissure existed in the strata of the International, one which events would in due course widen into a chasm. On one side stood those who came to the conclusion from the above realities that the socialist agenda was achievable only through adaptation to the state-in-being – and were even prepared to detect expanding possibilities in the development of electoral and governmental systems. This was in contrast to a minority who took seriously the proposition that not only was capitalism and bourgeois society basically unreformable but neither could it be expected to be pushed off the stage by means of slow constitutional increments. In other words, a more or less violent rupture with legality was the necessary prelude to proletarian ascendancy in both economic and political spheres.

The most straightforward exponents of the former position were the British trade unions and, from the early years of the twentieth century, the Labour Party which they created.[41] Their standpoint derived from the peculiar stability of British social and political structures, themselves founded upon the success and size of the country's industrial economy and its domination of global commercial relations. It derived also from a lengthy tradition of acquiescence in the state and constitutional structures, from monarchy downwards; from the growing influence of imperial sentiment; from recent association and continuing collaboration with one of the long-established parties in the British political system, which applied no less to the 'left-wing' ILP than it did to the trade union mainstream. Such automatic and conditioned practice on the part of the British labour movement was articulated and theorised by the Fabian Society which made no bones about its constitutionalist and conservative positions and whose best remembered slogan was 'the inevitability of gradualness'. Its most eminent ideologues, the Webbs, had indeed commenced by viewing socialism as being primarily a matter of rational social administration (more in the tradition of Edwin Chadwick[42] than of Marx) and of having no particular relationship with the labour movement, to which they turned only because it came to appear the most likely vehicle to carry their agenda.[43]

Doctrinal considerations would have made any such approach unthinkable for the Marxist parties of the International, but they did not find it easy to reconcile their aspirations to revolution and the dictatorship of the proletariat with their practical impotence to secure any such aims or even to develop a convincing strategy for overcoming the contradiction. The SPD was, as usual, most representative in this respect. Its principal theoretical spokesperson, Karl Kautsky, resolved the dilemma verbally by asserting that the SPD was a *revolutionary* but not a *revolution-making* party. What this meant in practice was that it prepared endlessly either for the economic collapse of German capitalism, which would render the bourgeoisie helpless, or for the achievement of an SPD majority in the (largely impotent) Reichstag. Even preparation however did not mean discussion round a workable strategy in the event of either of those contingencies, but rather the constant widening of the party and its associated organisations, the strengthening of its organisational and propaganda apparatus, and the accumulation of Reichstag and other votes from election to election. According to principle, this was accompanied with refusal to participate in coalitions or to fight for participation in the governmental machine. The SPD universe therefore hung in isolation within the German political structure, protecting its Marxist integrity at the expense of any governmental leverage in the *Kaiserreich*.

Revisionism

The continuance of such a posture over two decades was a tribute to the strength of the frozen revolutionism imposed upon the SPD by the tensions between its Marxist heritage and the practical immovability of the German ruling class and elites. Unsurprisingly, it was challenged both from the left and the right of the party. From the left-wing, with Rosa Luxemburg emerging as its most prominent and able spokesperson, the demand was for the party to take its revolutionary objectives seriously and start concretely to think about how they might be attained. This challenge however was always easily blocked by the right and centre leaders who had the prestige of their record and the confidence of the grassroots.

The more articulate right, by contrast, urged the party to accept the implications of its real situation and accommodate its politics to the necessities of the constitutional and political structures as it found them, to accept domestic and overseas imperialism and the indefinite prolongation of the capitalist economy and bourgeois regime; to adopt what was in effect a strategy of reformism with consequent alterations in the party's political culture to involve participation where possible in the governmental system. The tendency found its most prominent advocate in Eduard Bernstein, Engels's literary executor, who was tactless enough to expound his

ideas openly in *The Presuppositions of Socialism*, published in 1899
and who had been influenced in his thinking by the Fabians. As
the underpinning for his argument Bernstein drew attention to a
variety of areas where Marx's forecasts had been or appeared to
be falsified and urged the necessity of 'revising' the doctrine to take
account of contemporary conditions – hence the name of
'Revisionists' applied to this school of thought. In fact Bernstein
was merely expressing in coherent form what was becoming the
actual orientation of some of the trade union leaders and local
leaderships of the SPD – who were not at all pleased to have the
unity of the party disturbed by such open explanation and
justification of what they had been quietly doing in any case.
Bernstein's initiative created a storm of outrage and his propositions
too were denounced and repudiated by the SPD leadership and
anathematised at congresses of the party and the International.

The debates were symptomatic. The experience of half a century
had made it clear enough that the social structures and political
systems of the 'civilised' nations of Europe were much more stable
than they had appeared to be during the revolutionary epoch 50
years earlier and that they contained sufficient flexibility to permit
a degree of modest material and cultural improvement for the
major part of the manual workforce – a process that would perhaps
be capable of indefinite extension. What then was the relevance of
revolutionary utopias, or even a radical-reformist one, that saw the
extinction of class society at the end of the line? In the main it was
as the foundation myth of the international labour movement, the
source of hope and inspiration that sustained the daily struggle and
provided the confidence that its scattered components added up
into a historically transforming whole.

By the first decade of the twentieth century the trend was
apparent everywhere – no labour movement in the International
was without its intransigent and its reformist wing, whether or not
the argument was conducted under the rubrics of Marxist doctrine.
In France (leaving aside the syndicalist outlook of the unions) the
division in the late nineteenth century was embodied in two rival
and evenly balanced socialist parties, popularly and revealingly
known respectively as the 'Possibilists' and 'Impossibilists' – they
united organisationally in 1905, but the political divisions persisted.

Bolshevism

Eric Hobsbawm has noted (*The Age of Empire*) that the most
renowned Marxist theorists of the Second International – even when
identified with the SPD – all originated in the Austro-Hungarian
Empire or points further east. Lenin, Luxemburg, Trotsky and

THE MATRIX: ROOTS OF THE CATASTROPHE   33

Kautsky were only the most prominent. Eastern Europe was composed of states and societies much less socially integrated or politically stable than those of the West or Germany, and consequently it was an area where Marxism in its revolutionary guise continued to hold a much greater living and immediate relevance. Revolution on a cataclysmic and bloody scale erupted in Russia in 1905 and triggered in the Austro-Hungarian monarchy a successful general strike for universal male suffrage.

The appearance in the 1890s of a labour movement in Russia on a recognisably European pattern originated both in the rapid expansion of machine production and associated industries in that country and from the example and inspiration of the now established international organisation in Europe. It was significantly influenced, in addition, by a centuries-long heritage of peasant revolt as well as the populist terrorist movement of the 1870s and 1880s, the narodniks of the People's Will, whose leading figures continued in the underground to be appreciated as revolutionary heroes even when their tactics were discarded.

In contrast to any other European state, the Russian labour movement was obliged to operate deep underground in an environment structured by the Tsarist autocracy, which rigorously outlawed both political opposition movements and oppositional labour organisations. It was to be expected that whatever labour movement emerged under such conditions would prove to be exceptionally combative and intransigent, and that if it adopted Marxism as its doctrinal outlook – as it was very likely to do – would be inclined to treat the revolutionary dimensions of the theory with the utmost seriousness. After all, even the Russian liberals of the time recognised revolution as being the only available option for achieving meaningful change in the absolutist political system.

Even so, it was only following considerable turmoil and infighting that social democracy on the German model emerged as the dominant trend within the emergent Russian labour movement, and even that position was somewhat precariously maintained. The first stage in the 1890s involved breaking with the traditions of the narodniks, not only politically in eschewing individualist terrorism, but conceptually in envisaging the industrial working class rather than the peasantry as the principal engine of social development.

> Accordingly, it is on the working class that the Social Democrats concentrate all their attention and all their activities. When its advanced representatives have mastered the ideas of scientific socialism, the idea of the historical role of the Russian worker, when these ideas become widespread, and when stable organisations are formed among the workers to transform the

workers' present sporadic economic war into conscious class
struggle – then the Russian WORKER, rising at the head of all
the democratic elements, will overthrow absolutism and lead
the RUSSIAN PROLETARIAT (side by side with the proletariat
of ALL COUNTRIES) *along the straight road of open
political struggle* to THE VICTORIOUS COMMUNIST
REVOLUTION. (Original emphasis)[44]

Nevertheless the narodnik-descended and largely non-Marxist
('only borrowed some miserable shreds', according to Lenin) Social
Revolutionary Party did not surrender its claims to lead the putative
bloc of workers and peasants, and remained a formidable political
competitor to the social democrats for the workers' allegiance.

Russian Marxism too generated its own disputes and schisms.
An important early trend was that of the 'Legal Marxists', a section
of the intelligentsia attracted by the theory, who preferred to
develop it as an academic discipline rather than a political weapon.
Shortly afterwards the proponents of 'economism' (in its original
meaning) advocated the confinement of labour struggles to economic
and labour relations issues, leaving political opposition to the
regime to liberal and bourgeois politicians.[45]

It was out of these disputes and the polemics around them,
carried on in the mostly underground press, that Marxist social
democracy finally found its institutional embodiment, and only as
late as 1903. The project of the (exiled) social democratic leaders
was to form out of scattered and uncoordinated local circles and
groupings an effective and centrally guided party capable of
presenting a real political challenge to tsardom. Prophetically, at
the very founding congress[46] of the new party a split developed.
Ostensibly, the occasion for the dispute was a relatively obscure
organisational issue relating to the conditions for party membership,
but it was one which reflected Lenin's determination to establish
a party of 'professional revolutionaries' to lead and give shape to
the spontaneous resistance and radicalism of the labour and peasant
movements. This in turn was a reflection of something even more
profound. It is worth noting in passing that not one of the principal
leaders in either faction of the new Russian Social Democratic and
Labour Party was in fact a worker, and that this continued to be
true down to the 1917 revolution[47] – they were without exception
drawn from the intelligentsia. The same even held good for nearly
all the second rank of leaders.

The split created two factions of what remained on paper for a
few more years a single party until Lenin declared a final break in
1912. The acquisition by the two groupings, of their respective titles,
Bolsheviks – majority people, and Mensheviks – minority people,
arose almost accidentally and it is by no means clear that the

Bolsheviks had the greater number of adherents among the Russian workforce. What Lenin's followers did possess, in excess of any other early twentienth-century socialists, was an unwavering revolutionary will to power – not power for its own sake, but to be exercised as the representatives of and in the interests of the Russian working class. The Mensheviks lacked such single-mindedness, and the temperamental difference corresponded to the parties' main difference of theoretical principle. The Mensheviks, regarding themselves as orthodox Marxists, remained convinced that the Russian working class was too small and too socially feeble to exercise undivided power in what was regarded upon all sides as the inevitably forthcoming Russian revolution, and so must content itself with being politically the junior partner of the bourgeoisie. Lenin wholly rejected this perspective and had what was – depending upon viewpoint – either a wholly bogus justification or a creative development of Marxism to substantiate his alternative.

In contrast to the traditional Marxist bloc of proletariat and bourgeoisie against feudalism, he envisaged a bloc of the working class and peasantry in which the working class, on account of its organisation and theoretical sophistication regardless of smaller numbers, and led by its Marxist party, would unfailingly form the dominant element. Whether this conception, termed 'the democratic dictatorship of the workers and peasants', was evolved[48] because it was attractive to an individual of Lenin's temperament or whether his intransigent and divisive practice followed from a theory worked out on purely rational grounds, it is clear that the overwhelming majority of Russian workers (let alone peasants), even the politically conscious ones, had not the faintest understanding of nor interest in the theoretical distinctions which so exercised the revolutionary exiles. The leaders of the International were also impatient of these apparently scholastic disputes and constantly urged Russian social democracy to cease dividing its paltry forces and to compose its differences in face of the common enemy.

That they had some cause to do so was vividly demonstrated in the Russian Revolution of 1905–6, when neither Bolsheviks nor Mensheviks turned out to be capable of channelling the forces of mass revolt which erupted throughout the empire, or of attaining a position of political leadership capable of directing events. Characteristically, Lenin (in *The Two Tactics of Social-Democracy in the Democratic Revolution*) was to blame the ultimate failure of the revolution on Menshevik vacillation. The same elemental popular insurgence however, brought into being the institutions of the soviets, the workers' councils which took over administrative power in cities where government authority collapsed. Lenin initially distrusted them as likely rivals to the party which had been created to lead just such a revolution, but, characteristically, changed his view once he appreciated their potential as organs of revolutionary authority and legitimacy.

The Forward March of Labour

Everywhere in Europe, from the Atlantic seaboard to the Balkans, industrial workforces at the beginning of the twentieth century were becoming organised in trade unions and political parties convinced of their historic mission, but if Europe remained the pivot of the labour movement, dynamic forces were also at work elsewhere. The failed revolution in Russia opened the first wave of twentieth-century revolutions and was succeeded by the nationalist and democratic upheavals in China in 1911 and Mexico shortly afterwards; a sign that beneath the equilibrium of expanding global communications and commerce maintained within an imperial balance of power, social lava of combined desperation and hope was heaving and boiling. The appearance of a new labour movement in Russia was followed by the beginnings of organisation in every centre of modern production – in the British settlement colonies, in Japan, in China and even, embryonically, in India, where a strike was recorded as early as 1877. In the US the trade union and socialist labour movement of the time, if retarded by German or French standards, was not much inferior to its British counterpart in terms of relative size, organisation or electoral credibility, while its conflicts with big capital were often incalculably more violent.[49]

From the perspective of, say, 1910 it is not too far away from the truth to regard the left on a world scale as coterminous with the labour movements of the period, committed with whatever differences of emphasis, strategy and tactics, to programmes of enlightened and humanitarian social transformation. It had grown simultaneously with the development of machine industry and compared with the few fragmentary and persecuted collectives of 40 years earlier, it was without question an impressive advance.

Needless to say, enlightened universalism did not universally prevail within labour forces – what is remarkable is the extent to which it did. The exceptions are specific, characteristic and highly revealing. The labour movement of the United States, in spite of the best efforts of socialists and syndicalists, remained permeated, indeed structured, by racism. The predominantly white workforce, itself subject to deep ethnic divisions resulting from the immigrant character of the country's population, saw in blacks only the threat of wage undercutting from pauperised, subservient and culturally isolated competitors in the labour market. White exclusivity became the norm in the skilled trades. On the other side of the Pacific the Australian labour movement, for similar reasons, upheld the 'White

Australia' policy, terrified by the notion of hordes of 'coolie' labourers descending from Asia and seizing their employment. An even more extreme, though similarly motivated, response to threats against job privilege occurred in South Africa in the aftermath of the First World War, when white miners resorted to armed insurrection under the slogan 'Workers of the World Unite: For a White South Africa!'

Although Europe did not in any measure lack ethnic and national frictions, except in Northern Ireland, nothing of the kind occurred on that continent. Ultra-right theorists in both France and Italy had begun to play with the notion of linking nationalism and socialism or syndicalism, but were at that stage getting nowhere. On Germany's eastern border tension existed between German workers and the lower-paid Polish immigrant labour which employers were only too eager to import.[50] It cannot be doubted that real racial animosity existed at the grassroots of the German workforce but it found no institutional expression. Further south, this time in the Bohemian province of the Habsburg Empire, an attempt was made to form a workers' party on nationally exclusive lines, aimed against lower-paid Slavonic competitors and the social democrats who worked to overcome ethnic divisions. The German Workers' Party was explicitly anti-Slav, anti-socialist and anti-Semitic; its aim to mobilise and exploit cultural jealousies, prejudices and hatreds stretching back a millennium.

> [The German speaking workers] who with their contributions had made Social Democracy powerful were in many areas pushed out of their jobs by the Slav comrades whom they had heartily welcomed. The German employer took the cheaper Slav worker; but the red organisation refused to give the German party veterans the protection to which they were entitled [thanks to] the perniciousness of international doctrines and the insincerity of social Democracy which is led by Jews and closely allied with mobile big capitalists.[51]

The significant point about the German Workers' Party, however, is that in spite of having apparent promising potential and a likely field of operation, it made virtually no impact at the time and would today be forgotten except that it constituted one of the rivulets that was later to flow into the formation of National Socialism. The essentially Enlightenment and democratic culture of the nineteenth-century socialist movement, though it might not correspond at all times to the everyday attitudes and prejudices of its individual members, nonetheless was accepted and structured their collective praxis.

Nationalism, Evasion and Debacle

Events were soon to demonstrate that the structure of the socialist movement was in fact an extremely fragile one and that the movement's ostensible ideology of opposition was built on much shallower foundations than anybody could have imagined. The fragility was concealed by obfuscation. The exact manner in which the overturn of bourgeois rule would supposedly come about was, in the mainstream of the movement, left purposely undefined – although the notion of the mass general strike had been adopted as the strategic aim of the syndicalists, it was reinforced as a possible option by the experience of the 1905 Russian Revolution, and attracted some left-wing Social Democrats, including Rosa Luxemburg. But of course actively to plan for revolution in any shape or form – at least outside Russia – was an intrinsic impossibility in view of the unpredictability of political circumstances and the solid public legitimacy of most governments, as well as the legal complications which would have arisen from such a project. Kautsky squared the circle, but only verbally, and 'followed a revolutionary concept with quietist conclusions'.[52]

Even more inexplicit was the presumed shape and character of the 'co-operative commonwealth' which would succeed the rule of capital. Refusal to speculate along such lines or produce any blueprint of the socialist society was more or less a point of principle with all trends within the International. Partly it was a reaction, forcefully justified by Marx himself, against the older traditions of utopian socialism, which in some versions had gone so far as to design the drainage systems to be used in the New Jerusalem. In more general terms it indicated, quite sensibly, a refusal to try to commit the future to particular formulae or courses of actions. It was presumed in effect that once the basis of collective property was established the circumstances would generate their own solutions. Nevertheless, this refusal to explore or debate options in advance meant that when socialist parties actually found themselves at the head of government following the First World War, whether they were the mildest reformists or the reddest revolutionaries, all were utterly devoid of any strategic vision of what actually to do with the socio-economic framework of which they had taken charge, and were obliged instead to stumble from expedient to expedient.

The shifts, compromises and evasions indulged in by its leaders and spokespeople at least held the International together as a broad church in which a range of theoretical perspectives and political emphases could compete and flourish without tearing the movement apart – although it has to be said that it is most unlikely that this balancing act could have been maintained forever even if war had not intervened. Tensions and stresses in regard to theory, to policy, to nationality and to interest groups were permanent features of the movement. Of the former, the uproar around 'revisionism' constituted by far the most important. The movement divided itself between Bernstein's supporters – mainly the British non-Marxist socialists – his implacable enemies such as the Bolsheviks and Luxemburg, who saw his notions as an intrusion of alien bourgeois ideology into the movement and wanted him expelled, and the majority, who were content to condemn his theses but permit him to continue and even occupy a prominent role in the SPD. By contrast the obscure theoretical quarrels of the Russian socialists were regarded by most of their colleagues as no more than an exotic and marginal phenomenon; a 'storm in a teapot' – as Stalin incautiously expressed it, though Lenin argued that Menshevism constituted the peculiarly Russian version of revisionism.

Disputes over policy formed a more material line of division and with rather more immediate consequences. The principal source of such division foreshadowed the future and in this instance did result in expulsions. The issue was one of the movement's relationship with bourgeois politics – specifically whether representatives of socialist parties should in any circumstances join governments formed by the parties of the class enemy. The prevailing attitude of the time was one of abhorrence of any such course and when in France the taboo was broken by Alexandre Millerand, who in the midst of the Dreyfus crisis entered an administration of republican unity to oppose the threat of clericalist reaction – where he found himself sitting round the same table as General Galliflet, a notorious butcher of the Communards in 1871. That was more than the French socialists of any description would tolerate, let alone the International, and Millerand, unlike Bernstein, was expelled – but it was clear that the problem was likely to recur. In the sphere of regional government, the south German organisation of the SPD was openly defying the Berlin headquarters by entering into coalition administrations – and getting away with it.

The unified French socialists of 1905 styled themselves the Unified Socialist Party of France, but also the SFIO – the French Section of the Workers' International. In spite of that assertion of internationalism, however, it was clear in the first decade of the century that national frictions were also adding to the tensions fomenting beneath the movement's surface. They emerged from time to time in rhetorical exchanges between the two largest parties of the International, the German and the French, located in the two states between which governmental tension was most frequently and seriously exhibited. Jean Jaurès, the French leader, did not fail to point out to his German counterparts the vacuity of their revolutionary pretensions,

Beneath the rigidity of your theoretical formulations which Kautsky will produce for you to the end of his days, you conceal from your own and from the international proletariat that you are incapable of action.[53]

His colleague Gustave Hervé put it even more bluntly, declaring that the SPD wanted 'to conquer the world with paper ballots', while the Germans for their part made it clear that their basic policies and strategy would be determined only by themselves, not by the International, some of their lesser spokespersons going so far as to express the point in positively chauvinist language. Proto-fascist chauvinism was resisted and excluded by the individual socialist movements, but nationalism of a more respectable sort made deep inroads into their constituencies.

Actual and potential divisions at the high levels of ideological discourse, Congress resolutions and inter-state relations were one thing, but they scarcely hinted at the depth of potential antagonism and conflict existing within workforces operating in a competitive labour market where mechanised transport systems supplied an unprecedented mobility to labour. Endless opportunities existed to incite craft against craft, skilled against unskilled, male against female labourers, sweated against better-paid, resident against incomer, gentiles against Jews, group against group, nationality against nationality. To Marxists the phenomenon was known as 'sectionalism', a recognised plague of the movement, but one they optimistically believed to be transient and historically conditioned, and which a combination of struggle and education would eliminate and replace with an all-embracing and international class loyalty. Indeed the practical efforts of Marx's short-lived IWMA (the First International) of 1863–72 were focused on overcoming the hatreds generated through employers' attempts to break strikes by importing foreign labour. There was therefore nothing naturally cohesive about the outlook of proletariats across Europe, let alone around the globe. It is likely that, together with the politic compromises noted earlier, nothing but the transforming vision of socialism, the workers' culture which was formed around it, and the institutional momentum acquired after a few years of existence could have held the International together.

The weaknesses and ambiguities proved to be fatal ones. None of that should conceal the fact that the internationally unified socio-political movement of the early century – global although patchy – was an exceptional creation. Its development might well be construed, in Edward Thompson's terms, as the making of the European working class, for it gave to what would otherwise have been an assortment of divided and divisive workforces the recognition of itself as a class, albeit fragile, unified by its perceived relation to capital and by its historic project. Although the movement was born from the conjunction of a tradition descending from the Enlightenment and revolution with the advancing processes of industrialisation and capital growth, it was also the product of a near half century's abstention from warfare between the great powers, an era when the major European states confined their military predation to the populations of what would now be termed the Third World.[54]

The activity and growth of the International and its component sections were premised upon the continuance of this state of affairs, upon the essentially peaceful if occasionally riotous conduct of relations between labour and capital. It was simply not fitted for an era of generalised total warfare and mass destruction, with all the implications and repressions that followed for civil populations caught up in the conflict, as Kautsky himself sorrowfully acknowledged. When the hurricane struck, the individual national movements, with a couple of exceptions, did what might have been expected in the circumstances – they abandoned their inter-nationalist postures and hastened to put themselves under the protection of their national governments, trading loyalty and dedication to the war effort for the acceptance or even goodwill of their respective authorities. Put to the test of real crisis, the movement failed abjectly. With the self-created universe of the international labour culture broken apart, an alternative focus of meaning was needed by its members, and that was most conveniently found in nationalism, which had the added advantage of bringing with it patriotic acceptance and recognition, a *union sacree* as the French put it, among all classes, the trancendance of class division and recreation of an organic community. Had the war been short, as according to precedent it should have been and nearly was, the Socialist International would nonetheless still have been utterly wrecked beyond hope of repair. As it was, the war was anything but short, and what had hitherto been marginal ideologies and parties in the International's configuration abruptly moved centre stage.

CHAPTER 2

Leninism and Stalinism

Leninism and the revolution with which it is associated have been indicted as the source of all evil in the twentieth century.[1] Apart from the horrors inflicted directly by the regimes inspired in one sense or another by Leninism, they have been held accountable for all the counter-revolutionary atrocities of the era – from the pogroms carried out by the anti-bolshevik generals of the Russian Civil War[2] to the existence of the Third Reich and the consequent extermination of European Jewry. The contention proceeds along two lines. Firstly, that the frenzied reaction of the threatened privileged groups and the support they gave to fascist movements was understandable, if not excusable, in the light of the fate that Bolshevism had in store for them. Secondly, that National Socialism copied its forms of rule and techniques of terror directly from a Bolshevik model.

The argument however, can be stood on its head. A case can be made just as plausibly that the motives and intentions of the Bolsheviks in 1917 and their imitators throughout the century were humane and emancipatory ones and would in fact have proceeded along such lines had they been left in peace to get on with them. Instead, an unrelenting campaign of terror, threat and physical destruction, absorbing during 70-odd years an incalculable percentage of their enemies' gross national product,[3] was from first to last directed against the revolutionary regimes. Civil war, blockade and foreign invasion were imposed upon the infant Soviet republic. 20 years later Nazi invasion, to be followed immediately by a US-sponsored Cold War deliberately designed to force it to extend its commitments and drain its resources.[4] Would the US have done any better under similar pressures? In other centres of successful revolutionary eruption the same principles were applied. The Chinese People's Republic was blockaded, starved and threatened until its regime was co-opted. Vietnam was, in the words of a US airforce general, bombed 'back into the stone age'. The island of Cuba has been isolated and blockaded with the explicit aim of wrecking its economy and reducing its population to destitution. In Mozambique, Angola and Nicaragua, armed counter-revolutionary gangs were trained, equipped and armed to destroy a promising but non-capitalist future by means of unrestrained massacre and destruction of economic and social facilities. In short, the descent into an authoritarian or totalitarian style – and some, like the Nicaraguan Sandinistas avoided that descent – was not intrinsic to Leninism but a hapless response to the relentless assault upon its embodiments. The revolutionaries declined, in Marcel Liebman's words, 'to answer the massive pressure exerted by the bourgeoisie (not to mention its violence) with the Franciscan virtues of renunciation, resignation and humility'.[5]

In fact neither of these cases will stand up to detailed historical examination (though the second does rather better than the first); for while the degeneration of the revolutionary regimes was certainly more of a response to circumstances than a question of betrayal or some intrinsic metaphysical flaw, it is equally evident in retrospect that the presumptions and expectations which underpinned the Bolshevik agenda were so far out of line with reality and so contradictory of their ostensible purposes that disaster was, if not certain, at any rate highly probable.

Marxism as a revolutionary doctrine was born out of a brief period of revolutionary turmoil in nineteenth-century Europe, in the late 1840s and early 1850s. There is no reason to believe that the founders of the doctrine, who lived on into the 1880s and 1890s and saw mass movements established under their inspiration, ever abandoned their revolutionary perspectives.[6] It was, however, the inevitable tendency of these same movements, regardless of their rhetoric to bend and adapt to the economically successful and socially stable societies in which they found themselves, to pursue the welfare of their adherents along the constitutional channels immediately available to them, rather than to try at enormous risk to blast through the rock face of the state and its apparatuses of armed coercion. German social democracy remained revolutionary on paper – we have already noted the reality. Russian Menshevism took its revolutionary mission more seriously than did the SPD but in essence it tended in a similar direction.[7] Bolshevism or Leninism at its birth was no more than a rather exotic component of international social democracy, with which it shared a great deal in ideological belief, political outlook and cultural practice. Ultimately more relevant was to be what distinguished it.

Russia had been one of the few European states, the only major one along with Britain, not to be shaken by political upheaval during the years 1848–51. Russian social democracy was nevertheless heir to a much more deep-rooted tradition of revolutionary violence than anything to be found in Western Europe, even in Spain, the nearest comparison. The Muscovite state succeeded in combining the worst traditions of Eastern despotism and Western feudal barbarism.[8] As autocratic as the former, it lacked any of the advanced material or literary culture of the great Asiatic empires; even more brutally oppressive than the latter, it failed to develop any compensating civil society or culture independent of the state.[9] At one and the same time a necessary framework for the continuance of social existence and a monstrous parasitic excrescence, from its foundation to the eighteenth century it was rocked by massive and desperate serf revolts. Under the descendants of Peter the Great (who built St Petersburg on a swamp and the bones of countless serf labourers, personally beheaded his victims and had his rebellious son tortured to death) the country acquired a superficial gloss of urban westernisation as well as a Western military arsenal and the status of a European great power.

By the late nineteenth century the empire was part of a global economy, with modern industry (some of it the most advanced in the world, thanks to Western investment) and the industrial working class upon which its social democracy was founded – as well as an overwhelmingly bigger peasant population still surviving under medieval conditions.[10] The nature of the autocracy forced all opposition or protest into revolutionary courses.

However the Bolsheviks shared this inheritance with the Mensheviks and the non-Marxist but populist Social Revolutionaries – it does not in itself account for Leninism's distinctive features. Nor does his party's rejection of political compromise and intransigent revolutionism, for they shared this with the left-wing of pre-war social democracy represented by individuals such as Rosa Luxemburg or Trotsky, not to speak of syndicalists and anarchists. Nor can it even be identified with a particular attachment to authoritarianism for, after some initial hesitation, the Bolsheviks recognised the soviets – whether in 1905 or 1917 – as the authentic embodiment of workers' power at a time when they had no apparent prospect of controlling them exclusively. *The State and Revolution*, the pamphlet Lenin wrote in 1917 at the nadir of his fortunes, in hiding from his enemies, facing what must have appeared like total defeat and which can therefore be regarded as his conscious political testament divorced from any tactical considerations, is a semi-anarchist tract celebrating what might be termed 'people power' and scarcely mentioning his party. Finally, it should not be forgotten that Lenin was far from being able to exercise tight control over his colleagues, let alone the Bolsheviks at large. The faction was constantly gripped with disputes and controversies in which Lenin by no means always had a majority. Bolshevism and Leninism are not entirely the same thing and moreover both underwent a constant process of change, adaptation and revision, attempting to draw new lessons both from historical trends and immediate events. As Marcel Liebman notes, two very anti-Soviet historians, at a symposium on the 50th anniversary of 1917, agreed that the Bolsheviks 'favoured a coalition of socialist parties and were forced to govern alone only because the other parties refused to co-operate'.[11]

What is usually taken to be Bolshevism's distinctive attribute – an inflexible revolutionary will to power – has to be understood against this background. The will to power was there all right, but there is no reason to believe that this was conceived in the first instance as a party dictatorship *over* the masses. Lenin's famous contention that the emergent labour movement in Russia would not spontaneously develop a socialist consciousness but would acquire one only through the activities of educated elements drawing out the links between workers' immediate struggles and wider political considerations was an observation of fact, not an intellectualist prejudice. The presumption was that once the party was established and rooted in the proletarian milieu it would become increasingly working class in composition and leadership. Lenin was prone enough to use workerist sentiments as a tactic in political debate and held a generally low opinion of intellectuals as a group. The party itself existed to provide Marxist education, inspiration, political and moral leadership, not to substitute itself for a politically conscious and autonomously organised working class. In 1917 Lenin was to declare that the masses were a thousand times more left than the Mensheviks *and a hundred times more left than the Bolsheviks.*

The unique character of pre-revolutionary Bolshevism is to be found not in any single feature but in a combination of traits, with which the revolutionary seriousness and will to power were combined. The others were the conviction that Marxism offered a comprehensive scientific account of reality[12] and guide to action and that it was imperative for the workers' party to maintain theoretical orthodoxy at all costs, even at the price of exclusiveness and, if necessary, isolation.[13] There followed on from that a historical super-confidence, total certainty in the fall of the bourgeoisie on a global scale and the triumph of socialist revolution, if not immediately then at no distant date.

However, while participating fully in the debates raging within the Second International in the early years of the century, the Bolsheviks' notions did not appear to have much relevance to the central current of European socialism with its broad-church Marxism and flexible and adaptive responses to contemporary social reality. Meantime, their practical attention prior to 1914 was fixed firmly upon Russia and the revolution which was their immediate concern. The central strategic conception, developed in the course of the abortive 1905 revolution, was termed by Lenin 'the democratic dictatorship of the proletariat and peasantry'. It was a clumsy theoretical cover for an unacknowledged recognition that the accepted Marxist scheme of bourgeois anti-feudal revolution

levelling the historic ground for subsequent proletarian revolution
was mistaken. Practical experience of the Russian bourgeoisie
revealed that it was devoid of revolutionary potential on French
lines and aspired to nothing better than political accommodation
with the regime.[14]

Lenin however had earlier argued that the agricultural and
commercial economy of the Tsarist empire was already capitalist
in nature even if its political system was still mired in feudal
inheritances – and so even riper for social overturn than France
had been in 1789. But since the industrial proletariat was manifestly
far too small and undeveloped to sustain the revolution on its own
(though it might aspire to lead it), the above formulation summarised
how a bourgeois revolution might be carried through without and
even against the bourgeoisie. It was a somewhat tortured attempt
to stretch Marxist categories to cover a novel reality. Trotsky's
conception of 'uneven and combined development', which placed
Russian developments within a world context, was a great deal more
realistic and convincing. Not surprisingly, Menshevik spokespersons
were able to accuse the Bolsheviks of revisionism as contrasted to
their own Marxist orthodoxy, which continued to envisage a
revolutionary role for the Russian bourgeoisie – or at least its more
radical sections.

Abstruse and abstract these debates may appear, but they guided
the strategies of the various actors in 1905–6 – although the
Bolsheviks then played anything but a leading role – and were to
reappear in an altered framework with much enhanced significance
in 1917. European war thrust Bolshevism from the margins of
international socialism to the centre of the historical stage. The events
of August 1914 marked the apparent end of Marxism's institutional
expression, not only in the sense that its parties reneged on their
solemn commitments and spurred on the working classes of the
continent to mutual slaughter, but, if anything more significantly,
they collapsed before the ruling classes' definition of reality, defined
their identity as primarily a national one and willingly accepted
subordination to their historic class enemy.

Lenin, from his Zurich exile, at first refused to believe that the
reports of the SPD's capitulation to its government were true, and
when they were confirmed suffered a nervous crisis – which might
suggest a certain naivety on his part, rather than the response of a
cynical power-broker. It is said that he actually considered
abandoning revolutionary politics. His further response, once he
had recovered his nerve, is suggestive as well as centrally important,
for it was the first link in the chain that was to connect together
the politics of the next 75 years and the starting point of a new
incarnation of the left.

Firstly, he identified the long-awaited general crisis of capitalism as having now explosively commenced, fitting the outbreak of war into a model of development that incorporated the previous decades of monopoly concentration and imperialist expansion. The room for cartel-style and diplomatic manoeuvre having been used up, the spoils were being forcibly divided. Secondly, Lenin discounted evidence of widespread popular enthusiasm and welcome for the war among workers and the complete absence of any disposition to 'turn the imperialist war into a civil war'. Instead he interpreted working-class acceptance of the bourgeois state's military compulsions as due to the malign influence of their treacherous leaders, allegedly bribed and corrupted out of imperialist super-profits – thus closing the theoretical circle. He predicted that once the realities of the conflict began to impress themselves then the masses in the trenches and the factories would dramatically change their attitudes. International socialist revolution was no longer a distant prospect but at the top of the immediate agenda.

The action which followed from this analysis was to re-establish as rapidly as possible an international Marxist organisation with the appropriate revolutionary perspectives – not to bring the war to an end by peace talks or compromise, but to use it to overthrow the warring governments. The project was immediately put in hand: anti-war socialists from around Europe who could be assembled across the battle-lines convened secretly in the obscure Swiss village of Zimmerwald, with Lenin at pains to weed out from the resulting collective any whose position was simply pacifist and failed to measure up to his revolutionary perspectives.[15] To an uninvolved observer the notion that such a tiny assemblage of isolated individuals representing little except themselves could have any bearing at all on the future of the states, armies and populations locked in mutual destruction must have seemed preposterous beyond belief.

Changing History

'It is useless to ask' writes Marcel Liebman, 'What would have happened in Russia, if in 1917, there had not been a party like the Bolshevik Party, and in it a man like Lenin, with as determined a revolutionary will as his, as persuasive and effective a leader as he was ... The pace of events is accelerated, and the impossible, or what has been thought to be impossible, suddenly becomes reality.'[16] Trotsky, conversely, expressed the view that if the Bolshevik revolution had not occurred, fascism would have had a Russian name – which, taking into account what happened elsewhere in Europe, appears to be a highly plausible speculation. It seems reasonably clear, not least from the evidence of Liebman's own volume, that in Lenin's absence the October Revolution would certainly *not* have taken place and the subsequent history of the twentieth century and of the left would have been very different.

Evidently the potential was there, generated by the forces of Russian and international history, but it required something like the Bolshevik party and someone of Lenin's peculiar abilities to bring it to fruition. The potential was a slender one however, and Lenin's revolution was carried out not with the tide of history but against it. The expected course of events, on the precedent of earlier European revolutions, would have been for the mass radicalism which erupted in February to have been dissipated, isolated and finally crushed – as was also soon to occur in Germany and Italy. Lenin was able against the odds to concentrate it and focus it successfully upon the eviction of a government tied to bourgeois property relations and the Entente side of the European conflict. A less determined and clear-sighted leader would never have succeeded, as he imagined, in thus launching the world revolution. Not only were the opposing forces formidable but the senior Bolsheviks in Russia at the time of the February revolution were virtually unanimous in opposing Lenin's strategy; his closest colleagues remained bitterly hostile to the eventual insurrection.

Was Lenin then, as Robert Service asks at the opening of his biography,[17] 'the demiurge of twentieth century world history'? In one sense the answer has to be 'yes' – because he was able to realise a highly unlikely outcome which did indeed have the effect of switching the tracks of the global future – but he and the state he founded were no less history's victims. In Russia, the perspectives adhered to by Lenin and Trotsky mobilised the energies of the masses, released incalculable hopes and aspirations and enabled their regime to prevail against all comers. Elsewhere they proved to be singularly inappropriate. It is scarcely too fanciful to suggest that after seven decades the world of the 1990s in broad outline looks rather as it might have done if the Russian Revolution had never happened.

This is not the place to rehearse that revolution's narrative. What is significant for our argument is that its actual course fitted exactly with the scenario Lenin had sketched for Europe as a whole from his Swiss exile. In just a little over two years the pathetic revolutionary fantasists of Zimmerwald village had seized power in Petrograd by a process corresponding precisely to Lenin's forecasts of how war was likely to turn into revolution. Another year and Central Europe was reverberating to the crash of empires and heaving with mass insurrection. It is hardly to be wondered at that the historical super-confidence already a part of the Bolshevik make-up was now reinforced beyond all measure and that Leninism

was judged to hold the key to history beyond any question. Nor is
it particularly remarkable that the eyes of nearly all revolutionaries
in the warring nations and beyond turned towards this beacon of
hope and promise.

The revolution had occurred in Russia and the workers' (and
peasants') state been precariously established there. The Bolsheviks'
strategy in 1917 had been informed to some degree by Lenin's
analysis in 1905, particularly in their total distrust of the country's
bourgeoisie – an analysis confirmed by the Provisional government's
insistence on maintaining participation in the imperialist war. But
the essential Bolshevik perspectives were not Russian any longer.
Now renaming themselves the Communist Party, they had taken
upon themselves the responsibility for leading or at least inspiring
the world revolution, a role which they judged their career up to
that point admirably equipped them to fulfil. While it is true that
they took steps to hurry the process along and try to accelerate
history, it is no less the case that they found an eager enough
response beyond their own frontiers.[18]

In consequence, there appeared on the world scene something
entirely new in historical experience: a global-wide revolutionary
institution backed by the power and resources of a major state –
indeed a state which was in geographical terms the largest in the
world and second in respect of population. Moreover, the Comintern
viewed itself as an international revolutionary army, subject to a
more-than-military discipline, with its central command in Moscow.
What had been done in Russia it would cause to happen around
the world – with the immediate strategic goal being Germany,
where prospects appeared to be most favourable and where success
would bring with it revolutionary control over the most economically
developed state in Europe and the one best placed to spread the
revolution west and southward.

The fate of both the International and the revolutionary state have
been analysed at great length – the latter exhaustively. 'Degeneration',
it would be fair to say, is the dominant thread which runs through
such accounts, and so far as the initial purposes of both are
concerned, that conclusion is difficult to avoid. It is interesting to
speculate on the outcomes which might have followed had the
expectations of Lenin and his colleagues been fulfilled and the
revolution actually had spread throughout Europe, or at least to
Germany. What in fact was the case was that their assessment of
the readiness of the European masses to rise against their masters
was wildly misjudged – though by no means absurd in the light of
what had happened between 1915 and 1919. The Russian case
turned out to be the exception, not the rule, and made possible
only by the circumstances of invasion combined with the utter
collapse of all instruments of state power, the disaffection of their

rank and file personnel and an elemental peasant revolt. The social
and cultural hierarchies of the industrialised European states were
much stronger. Although buckled by the war, they came nowhere
near to disintegration.

'The General Staff of the World Revolution'

The early Comintern was by no means a passive or unquestioning
instrument of the Soviet leaders' objectives. On the contrary, it was
an arena of passionate argument and disagreement between forceful
and independent-minded personalities with their own very decided
ideas about revolutionary strategy and perspectives. However, the
Russians' prestige, their control of the International's resources –
the International depended on Soviet funding and it's headquarters
was in Moscow – and the continuing lack of success elsewhere
ensured that they did ultimately have the last word. To a great extent
policy and strategy in the Comintern ceased to be determined on
its merits and even before Lenin's death had turned into a reflection
of differences and antagonisms in the Soviet Politbureau. The
Comintern was presided over by Zinoviev, who, following Lenin's
incapacitation in 1922, was desperate to assert his seniority over
Trotsky and did not scruple to use the International in pursuit of
that aim. Nonetheless, even without such an additional drag on its
efficacy, the leadership's perspectives and assumptions were
fundamentally flawed.

They had failed to learn what should have been for them the critical
lesson of abortive postwar revolutions in central Europe and the
absence of any revolutionary outbreak in the Western states. The
lesson was that in existing conditions their industrial working
classes – not to speak of other elements of the 'oppressed masses'
– remained simply unwilling, whatever their level of social dissatisfaction and resentment might be, to undertake the overthrow of
their electorally established regimes. Instead the Comintern
strategists – and Lenin here was as guilty as anyone – attributed
the problem to inadequate leadership, i.e. that the foreign communist
parties were insufficiently like the Bolsheviks, and tried to rectify
the deficiency by 'bolshevising' them and finding leaders willing
to act as yes-persons for the Comintern executive. The result, as
might have been expected, was to destroy initiative and stifle the
ability of the non-Soviet parties to react effectively to local
circumstances. Only after further debacles in 1921 and 1923 was
it accepted grudgingly that postwar capitalism had entered a period
of temporary stabilisation and that the CPs ought to withdraw
meantime from the offensive, consolidate their positions and try
to build bridges to the unregenerate sections of the working classes

– a strategy termed the 'united front'. Few among those involved doubted however that the revolutionary wave was certain to revive before long. In reality however the new turn was an expedient – the Comintern lacked any long-term strategy. It had been created on the presumption that European revolution was imminent and when that prospect failed to materialise the organisation could not hope to avoid becoming the creature of the state which had been formed out of the one successful revolutionary enterprise.

Prior to the revolution the Bolsheviks had given no thought whatsoever to the kind of state or economy they might establish in Russia. The assumption between March and November 1917 was that a combination of workers' power expressed through the Soviets and workers' control in industry would suffice until the victorious proletariats of more advanced states came to assist with raising the economic, social and cultural level of backward Russia. The reality of isolation, brutal civil war, famine, virtual collapse of productive industry, and flight from the main population centres meant that the bare survival of the regime became the overwhelming priority. The ultra-democratic forms of the initial weeks of Bolshevik rule had turned within a year into ultra-centralised and dictatorial ones. Workers' control in industry and transport proved to be an utter disaster and had to be replaced with 'one-man management' as fast as possible. 'In general, the factory committees refused to obey the instructions they received, and, often showing a corporatist spirit, sought to form alliances with the factory owners.'[19] That the Bolsheviks were able to win militarily against all the odds says something about the social energies and commitment released by their regime, but in a more profound sense they did in fact lose the civil war. They were forced amid the material and social wreckage of the country they governed[20] to rule with exceptional arbitrariness and violence, and to destroy or turn into empty husks the organs of popular representation through which they had climbed to power. Even before the civil war began they had lost their briefly enjoyed majority acceptance; by the time White armies and foreign interventionists had been cleared from Soviet territory they were deeply unpopular.

Not only had the soviets and other basic assemblies been deprived of all initiative and integrated into a bureaucratic dictatorship underpinned by an unaccountable secret police, but the Communist Party itself during the civil war had not merely passed from being a revolutionary party to a party of government but had itself been made into the bureaucratised apparatus through which the centralised government was exercised. In 1921, following the end of hostilities and after popular insurrection had compelled the party to loosen its iron straitjacket on the economy and society, centralised control of the party itself and its members was tightened still further lest its revolutionary virtue be contaminated by the greater relaxation about to be permitted in what, for a bourgeois polity, would be termed civil society.

Lenin's party by 1922 – when he was still its leader – was a wholly different entity from what it had been in 1917, or for that matter 1907. Elements of the vanguardist rhetoric inherited from its oppositional past and its role in the revolution could be utilised to obscure the difference. It would be unrealistic to expect that the party, after all that had transpired, should have acknowledged that it had lost the confidence of the masses and abdicated power. Had its leaders simply been a collective of power-seeking individuals indifferent to ideology and determined at any cost to hang onto their positions and privileges, the long-term outcome would have been far less damaging. In actuality they remained convinced that as the most advanced, successful and experienced revolutionary socialists anywhere on earth they embodied the real political will not merely of the Russian but of the world proletariat – a will which adhered to Marx's scheme of revolution even if the proletariat temporarily failed to realise it. Consequently they insisted that the communist parties of the International should be made in their own image – in structure, functioning and above all in outlook. The Comintern, it has often been emphasised, was not envisaged as an assemblage of national parties but as a single global party which would act in co-ordinated unity: 'the general staff of the world revolution', and of which the individual units were no more than sections.

It was a far cry from the perspectives of anybody prior to 1914, even of the Bolsheviks of that distant time, but the attractions of such a model should not be underestimated. What might repel some as a grotesque authoritarian parody of socialist practices and relationships might be taken by and appeal to others as a deadly serious commitment to revolution and an uncompromising hatred of the class enemy.[21]

German Revolution

The major non-Russian CP to be formed prior to the Comintern was the German, on new year's day 1919. It was in fact the Spartacus League, changing its title in the hope of emulating the Bolsheviks. It did so at a time when Germany was gripped by revolutionary and counter-revolutionary turmoil following defeat in war, the fall of the monarchy, and formation of soldiers' councils[22] and a government which actually called itself the Council of People's Commissars.

Such appearances were largely deceptive: the revolution was already lost. A doomed insurrection in Berlin later that month cost the lives of both Luxemburg and Liebknecht, and behind the facade of a Social Democratic administration the resurgent forces of the old regime easily mopped up the other insurrectionary centres before the end of the year. It was a definitive outcome, as well as predictable. The conditions which had permitted revolutionary success in Russia were altogether missing in Germany.[23]

For the leaders of the International the German deficiency plainly lay in the absence of a disciplined and tightly organised political force with an unbending revolutionary will to power comparable to the Bolsheviks – although this was a somewhat idealised image of what the Bolsheviks had been before and even after November 1917. It was taken for granted by these leaders that the objective conditions had been present for the German revolution and that its failure was to be explained by confusion, subjective error, and misguided tactics. The Comintern was designed as much as anything to ensure that the same thing should not happen in future when revolutionary opportunities again presented themselves in Germany or elsewhere – but especially in Germany – although the same presumption was made again, and equally erroneously, following the abortive KPD (Communist Party of Germany) insurrection of 1923.

Would a German revolution on Soviet lines have been possible? On a superficial reading it appears as though the old regime was so disorganised and demoralised that it might have been if the leaders of the Majority Socialists had been as bold and determined as Lenin, but in reality they were the opposite:

> One cannot avoid the suspicion that almost the last thing they wanted was to actually run a government of Germany. A lifetime in the Socialist movement had conditioned them only for a role of opposition. They had been neither trained nor emotionally prepared for a Socialist victory: in truth they had not really expected that it would come in their lifetime ... now they were in power, and it astounded and frightened them.[24]

To argue that a Soviet revolution was possible in Germany is therefore merely another way of saying that the men whom the German upheaval had propelled into authority were cut from the same cloth as their Menshevik and Social Revolutionary counterparts to the east. Their attitudes, as initially was the case in Russia, corresponded much better with mass feeling than did those of the revolutionaries. German events were never likely to develop in such a manner that the Russian scenario was capable of being repeated. Consequently the Sparticists were never going to have the opportunity to stand at the head of the masses. Luxemburg and Liebknecht were not elected to the National Congress of Workers' and Soldiers' Councils which met in Berlin on 16 December 1918 as the transitional sovereign body, and it refused them an honorary invitation. Only ten Sparticists were elected out of 489 delegates. '[The congress] represented the past, not the present; the backward small and middle-sized towns rather than the big industrial areas. In political character it was rather an Upper House than a People's Parliament', writes Frölich.[25] The Sparticists' strength in the streets of the big cities was enormously greater, but nowhere near enough to enable it to effect a workers' revolution against the entrenched forces of conservatism and the resistance of the majority socialists. The proposition that a socialist revolution in Germany might just have been possible – but only if Ebert had been willing to lead it – accurately reflects the balance of forces.[26]

The military apparatus and the established order in Germany were certainly badly shaken once defeat in the war became apparent. Mass disaffection spread through the army (and the navy) and a general collapse was averted only by bringing the troops back from the front as rapidly as possible. The aim of the rank and file soldiers however was to get home before Christmas rather than to conduct a revolution, and despite the existence of the *rate*, the workers' and soldiers' councils, a small but functional core remained under the authority of its right-wing officer corps, soon supplemented by the numerous well equipped and ferociously reactionary Freikorps. The civil administration continued to function; the German soviets did not encounter an administrative vacuum that they could fill, and were soon sidelined. The German peasantry -still the majority of the population despite the country's industrial capacity – represented a force for conservatism, not revolution.

Most significantly of all from a Marxist perspective, the German proletariat in its overwhelming majority, despite all the upheavals and traumas of the war, simply had no wish to embark on the enterprise of a social overturn on Russian lines – the modest political and social reforms identified with the early Weimar Republic represented the limit of their demands. When these were threatened in 1920 by the attempted Kapp Putsch the labour movement showed itself capable of a united, vigorous and effective response, but beyond this it would not collectively go. The revolutionary left were hopelessly isolated.[27] Lenin had remarked with reference to Russia in the middle of 1917 that the masses were politically a hundred times ahead of the Bolsheviks. The reverse was true in Germany in 1919. No doubt the SPD leaders both deliberately and unconsciously deceived and misled their followers but there is no doubt either that in the main they shared and mediated their outlook and that is why they remained in control of the situation. Had there been an experienced and effective communist party in Germany at the time the outcome would have been the same and it would have made no difference if it had been led by a dozen individuals all of Lenin and Trotsky's calibre. Even imagining the impossible, that Ebert and his colleagues had been real revolutionaries and installed Soviet power in Berlin, which they could certainly have done, the consequence (leaving aside how the Allies might have reacted in such circumstances) would have been a civil war which the left would almost certainly have lost.

Certainly, the Comintern was right in believing that Germany would be the paradigm for labour movements everywhere in the sense that they would tend to duplicate in a weaker form the example given by the former flagship of world socialism. However they got it the wrong way round – instead of picking up and developing the lead given in Petrograd, German socialism demonstrated in dramatic historical terms the inherent social conservatism of the working classes in developed Europe. In the course of the 1920s, with less expenditure of blood than in Germany, but often through dramatic enough industrial confrontations, the large, legal and well-established labour movements of Western and Central Europe all moved in a similar direction. Revolutionary postures would only be maintained in revolutionary circumstances. However the German events of 1918–19 are assessed, and supposing even that there was a missed revolutionary opportunity during those months, what is certain is that after its defeat the possibility of a European-wide revolution would never recur.

Stalinism

Thus Lenin's revolutionary hope and perspective, upon which everything had been gambled, was falsified and the Soviet state left isolated and shattered behind its enormous borders. In historical perspective, despite the the turmoil of the interwar years, the First World War can be more appropriately seen not as imperialism's debacle, but as releasing the tensions accumulating in the European state system and enabling world capitalism in the 1920s to find a new basis of stability: a world order in which the USSR, though an international pariah and the purported desperate enemy of this order, was nevertheless at the same time, and paradoxically, an integral part. It appeared as a very convenient negative 'other', against which capitalist states could gain legitimacy by defining themselves as everything it was not – but it also entered into significant economic and even military relationships within the international state system.[28]

After 1921, albeit with reluctance, the Comintern accepted that the revolutionary wave had broken and after another two years recognised that the tide had receded in the meantime – temporarily, it was confidently assumed. Although the sections of the Comintern were instructed to build bridges to the masses under social democratic influence, this was only so as to be better prepared for the next surge, when these masses would then be the more readily detached from their social democratic misleaders. These were tactical expedients which might or might not be justified by the realities of the times. What was more significant was that the failure of the basic analysis combined with the need to retain the claim to historical omniscience imbued the International and its constituent parties with a quasi-religious outlook in which the movement itself became effectively an object of worship, and errors could never be admitted. The party line by definition could never be wrong and if it failed to work that was only because it was incorrectly applied.

Developments of this sort were of course linked to the rise of Josef Stalin to supreme authority in the Soviet state itself. Stalin's ascendancy in Soviet Russia itself may be explained, if one so wishes, in terms of a bureaucratic caste led by the General Secretary imposing itself on the revolutionary institutions of the party and state. There is indeed an element of truth in this claim, though I believe it to be superficial, to ignore the real problems for Marxist concepts and in other aspects to be simply mistaken. What it does not begin to address is the question of how or why Stalinism, with only minimal struggle or opposition, took over *all* the parties of the International well before Stalin was acknowledged as a semi-divine figure or in any position to enforce his point of view by simple unquestioned declaration.

It makes a lot more sense to conclude that what became known as Stalinism, as a style of party management (as distinct from personal dictatorship in the state and more distinct still from relentless political terror), prevailed universally, not *mainly* because the Stalin-controlled Comintern directed all the member parties along such a course but because it actually fulfilled the requirements of revolutionary parties or revolutionary regimes functioning under varying degrees of siege condition, whether political or economic. The case of the Chinese communists in the 1930s reinforces the point. Without doubt the regime within the party and the areas it controlled in defiance of the Kuomintang government were Stalinist in all essentials. But there is no evidence that Mao Zedong and his colleagues paid much attention to Comintern emissaries or anything more than lip service to Stalin.

Stalinism outside the USSR represented rather a mind-set in which unquestioning conviction and relentless zeal, combined with an acute but narrowly-focused political understanding, were applied to political strategies that were for the most part designed to withstand political persecution and/or accommodate the reality that support for the communist parties' objectives were confined to a minority in any social class. It depended too upon an implicit and never to be avowed recognition, contradicting all formal communist belief, that the proletariat was not, or had ceased to be, a potentially revolutionary class in the Leninist sense. Again the Chinese example is pertinent – after the destruction of the party's urban base in 1927 the communist revolutionaries were entirely peasant in social composition.

In his biography of Stalin Isaac Deutscher comments that the General Secretary was effectively running the country at a time, not long after Lenin's death, when scarcely anybody outside the circle of leaders knew his name. This was certainly true, but only in the organisational sense. A further five years of consolidation, reworking of the party apparatus, manoeuvre and isolation of rivals at the top were necessary before he was the acknowledged leader in policy making, and even then he was still some way from having emerged as unchallenged dictator. Until 1928 the Comintern was led by Zinoviev and then Bukharin, as Stalin's allies, not his subordinates.

Socialism in One Country

Until the mid-1920s it seems likely that among the Comintern and Soviet leadership generally, a revival of the world revolutionary process was genuinely anticipated. Stalin, whatever his private opinions, was obliged to express himself in the same vein. The watershed was the Soviet debate over 'Socialism in One Country', which raged throughout 1925.[29] It marked a definite retreat and shift in strategic direction. The Bolsheviks, like other socialists of their time and beforehand, had possessed only the most sketchy notion of what a socialist society would actually be like or how it could be made to work. They had assumed that when the workers' revolution occurred in the advanced states it would all come out in the wash, so to speak, and in this they had followed Marx, who had consciously refused to draw up in advance prescriptions of how the post-revolutionary society should be run. He had been adamant that socialism and the dictatorship of the proletariat was not born out of the brain of this or that theorist – including himself – but represented the real historical movement in the process of coming into being.

In *State and Revolution* and other writings Lenin had expressed his conviction that monopoly capitalism had organised the industrial economy to such an advanced level that the victorious proletariat would find no difficulty in operating it for use rather than profit, by the application of simple accounting and administrative procedures. The experience and experiments of the infant Soviet Republic had not been exactly happy ones, though the problems might well be attributed to the desperation of the circumstances rather than any intrinsic failure. It has been noted above how utopian experiments in workers' control had to be rapidly abandoned. They were succeeded by the rigours of 'war communism', a regime of intense centralisation and authoritarian command where agricultural surpluses above subsistence were requisitioned by force from the peasantry; their distribution and that of such industrial production as still continued, with no functioning currency, made by administrative decision or barter.

There were some among the Soviet leaders, including Bukharin, who actually imagined that this system could represent the initial stage of a genuinely non-monetary economy, a form (albeit primitive) of socialised production. In reality, once the pressures of the White armies were off it provoked extensive peasant revolt and exhausted most of the genuine popular enthusiasm for Bolshevism. The New Economic Policy of 1921 summoned the forces of the market to cope with circumstances which had manifestly passed out of administrative control. It retained the commanding heights of the economy – heavy industry, foreign trade, banking – under tightly administered government control, turning over agriculture, consumer production and distribution to the market.[30] The sorts of social tensions which the system generated were the ones to be expected under such conditions. The regenerating industrial labour force bore most of the burdens and received fewest rewards, owing to the emphasis on lowering costs of production and the reality of unemployment with few welfare benefits, while fat cats in the shape of kulaks and Nepmen (petty capitalists and traders) flourished under the re-established market and were even encouraged by Bukharin to 'enrich yourselves'. Well might these workers ask whether they were not supposed to be the ruling class, and indeed what the Revolution had been all about.

Yet it was this same system which was identified as the necessary instrument of 'socialism in one country', which at that stage was *not* regarded as equivalent to forced-pace industrialisation, the latter indeed being damned as a Trotskyite heresy. The strategic conception was that Soviet power could insulate the USSR from the capitalist world market, while within its borders, surpluses generated by the agricultural market and siphoned off through taxation could provide the basis for industrial and social investment in a relatively painless fashion. Whether or not he was personally responsible for the idea, Bukharin emerged as its most committed enthusiast and prominent spokesperson. Superficially this position appeared to be in direct contradiction to the one he had occupied as the most passionate advocate of war communism – he seemed to have moved from the extreme left to the ultra-right of the party. In reality it was not so: there was a deeper consistency. Internationalist though he undoubtedly was, Bukharin betrayed in both stances attraction towards solutions which, though at opposite ends of the social spectrum, had in common a voluntarist reliance on the power of successful Bolshevism alone, disregarding the expectations of wider European or global revolution. Although a caricature of Leninism, it looked decidedly more convincing than Trotsky's alternative policy conception of 'permanent revolution'. The latter's defeat in this inner-party struggle[31] marked the definitive moment of his downfall; to be followed by isolation, persecution, expulsion from the party and shortly afterwards the country.

The slogan of 'socialism in one country', was popular in the party because it flattered the self-esteem of the CPSU's cadres and deployed prospects of the Soviet peoples being able to construct a socialist society on their own, just as they had earlier carried though the revolution without outside assistance. It fulfilled another function as well, implicit in the logic of events since 1917 and the failure of the European revolution. For any 'normal' state in the economic, political and international situation of the early USSR the expected ideological configuration would have been some form of great power nationalism. The pressure of circumstances and the attitudes which they bred among the ruling elite did indeed draw the state in such a direction. At the same time the state's international revolutionary credentials remained intrinsic to its political legitimacy and could not be abandoned. Its designation as a very special kind of state, the stronghold of workers' power awaiting the wider revolution, covered both the international and national dimensions, but was a formula which could not be sustained indefinitely in the absence of that wider revolution. 'Socialism in a single country' satisfactorily answered the dilemma, shifted the balance emphatically in a nationalist direction, and elevated yet further the importance of the Soviet state in historic perspective, paradoxically strengthening rather than diminishing its importance as a pole of attraction for the world movement.

Nonetheless it is hard to envisage for how long a Soviet regime functioning on New Economic Policy principles could have continued to inspire the loyalty of world communism. Imagine for a moment the impossible outcome of Bukharin proving the victor in his inner-party fight with Stalin in 1927–8 or (more plausibly) Stalin making the full Bukharinist programme his own. A further implantation of market relations would have occurred in the Soviet economy, more concessions would have been made to the better-off peasantry who controlled the grain surplus, the change would have been reflected in the composition and methods of the CPSU whose style and image would have been shifted in a pronounced rightward direction. The end result might well have been the old Bolsheviks evicted from power less bloodily than Stalin was to do, and international revolutionary pretensions publicly abandoned. It might well have meant a happier twentieth century both for the country's citizens and the world at large.

The NEP regime expressed the broad preference of the masses both in town and country (revealingly, its demise was never formally pronounced) both because of the material benefits with which it was associated – even workers' living standards were beginning to improve towards the end – and because it catered to national sentiment with its central assertion that the USSR could rely upon its own resources to achieve a beneficial social transformation unprecedented in human experience and at relatively minimal cost. The grain delivery crisis of 1927–8 might have been solved, as Bukharin favoured, by a further consolidation of the policy. That it was not was almost certainly because Stalin foresaw the kind of consequences sketched above and the implications for his own position.[32]

Stalin's Revolution

The 'Stalin revolution' which formed the alternative course of action relied not upon majority support in either the party or among the people, but upon the implacable determination, initially, of only part of his own apparatus; a layer of, mostly young, industrial workers and technical intelligentsia frustrated with the unheroic cautions and compromises of the NEP and the necessary middle-level administrative cadres without whom the project could not have been accomplished, a great many of them recently defeated party leftists and Trotskyists, convinced that Stalin was beginning to adopt the essence of their own policies.

This great turn was a product of internal Soviet developments and was designed in relation to specifically Soviet circumstances.[33] Stalin and the group ruling around him had long ceased to give serious weight to communism's international dimensions. The foreign parties and the Comintern, however inescapable as a heritage of the revolution, had become useful chiefly as a chorus to endorse and give added reinforcement to the victors in the Kremlin power struggles. It was by no means accidental that the new departure was marked culturally by fresh emphasis on nationalist rhetoric and rehabilitation of the 'great' tsars.[34] Even so communist internationalism could not be ostensibly abandoned, being part of the Soviet state's foundation charter – and so the Stalin revolution found its reflection within communist parties everywhere else.

The Soviet opponents of the new course had been branded as rightists, a relentless campaign of political denigration and abuse was aimed against them. Similar purges were directed at Bukharin's erstwhile supporters in the other CPs. Just as the Soviet state was expressing its self-reliance in economic construction so the CPs at large must express theirs in revolutionary attainment. They had to present themselves as the sole authentic representatives of their working classes and adopt postures of deadly enmity towards the treasonous social democratic lieutenants of capital, who were now to be marked out as objectively indistinguishable from fascism, 'social fascists' indeed. The new course, abandoning the standpoint of the 'united front', was encapsulated in the notion of the 'third period'. This asserted that after the revolutionary upsurge of 1917–23 and the following period of capitalist stabilisation, the world was now entering into a new third period of renewed capitalist breakdown and revolutionary advance. All that was needed was for communists to come out boldly, raise the standard of 'class against class' and give a lead to the masses now ready to repudiate the counter-revolutionary social democratic leaders. In actual fact there were substantial elements within the communist parties – though still a minority[35] – happy to respond to such a programme. In the event this position, insofar as it was sincere, represented a total misjudgment of the masses' mood in the industrialised countries. The result was universally calamitous, above all in Germany.

Nevertheless, through the occurrence of a bizarre historical contingency, it could for some years appear plausible. In October 1929 came the Wall Street stock market crash followed by an unprecedented collapse in the international capitalist economy – exactly according to Comintern forecasts. In the eyes of growing numbers of workers (and in some cases peasants and intellectuals), feeling the impact of the slump in their own lives, capitalism as a system was certainly discredited and doomed. In the European storm centre, Germany, the application of the 'class against class' strategy by the KPD did produce growing support and influence. At the last free elections, in November 1932, the KPD vote continued to rise while that of all other parties (including the Nazis) fell; in Berlin they overtook the Social Democrats. However, they were still far outstripped electorally by the Nazis, and the deadly animosity between the two working-class parties safeguarded, if it was not responsible for, Hitler's legal seizure of power in January 1933.

By any test of logic this ought to have brought discredit and reprobation on the heads of the Soviet leaders who had forced through the policies that had produced the debacle. In reality the opposite was the case. Collectivisation and the Five-Year Plan, breakneck industrialisation and the transformation of the balance between town and country imparted a wholly new meaning to the notion of 'socialism in one country'. For all but the poorest peasants the rural upheaval represented an unmitigated disaster. Collectivisation amounted to veritable civil war in the countryside, bringing mass famine in its train as the peasants, using the last mode of resistance that they possessed, destroyed livestock and farm equipment, while the Soviet authorities seized all the food stocks available. Resistance meant immediate death or consignment to labour camps. Even capitulation ensured no safety, for it could still mean starvation, while for anyone marked down as belonging to the kulak class (which might mean as little as the possession of a cow) victimisation was inevitable anyway. The kulaks were not permitted to join the collective farms and the unresisting ones, though they escaped the labour camps, were still deported to central Asia and ordered to recommence agricultural operations in hostile environments, where naturally they died *en masse*. The terrorised survivors, forcibly reorganised into agricultural collectives, lost every remnant of autonomy or their cultural heritage. Soviet agriculture never really recovered from the trauma, but the main objective, to bring the agricultural surplus under central control, was achieved.

For the industrial workforce the consequences were more ambiguous. The urban population was dramatically swollen by displaced peasants, for collectivisation was also designed to make them available as labour for the Five-Year Plan. The building industry could not keep up and pressure upon living space became extreme, with several families compelled to share a single inadequate room. Medical facilities were at an equivalent level. Labour shortages did result in wage drift,[36] for all the government's attempts to control it, but the calamitous shortage of every consumer good meant that they could purchase little. Even black bread was rationed. On the other hand, in the turmoil of a centrally-directed industrial revolution with severe labour shortages, a skilled and energetic worker could readily secure advancement and status. The attainment of skills was encouraged by programmes of education and technical training, while the Communist Party provided an accessible career ladder with potentially enormous rewards, albeit after 1935 a very dangerous one. There was of course no particle of independent self-activity available to the industrial workers. Since the Civil War the trade unions had functioned more as an instrument of government control over the workforce than as representative organisations and under the Stalin regime this relationship tightened immensely.

Only the more attractive sides of these realities found any reflection in the regime's self-presentation. The Soviet Union now stood forth as the example of an economy insulated by planning and public ownership from the impact of the world market catastrophe: one which grew and flourished while its rivals sank into apparently terminal crisis. The Five-Year Plan (basically successful, though not nearly to the extent that was pretended) was also presented as the triumph of heroic communist will over circumstances and history. If the Soviet state was no longer in reality the co-ordinator of world revolution it might still appear as its stronghold and model, and it wasn't difficult to present this claim to the world (inside the country it was an unquestionable article of faith, that *this* was what the Bolshevik revolution had originally intended).[37] As the focus of world admiration by sympathisers well beyond the ranks of communists,[38] it integrated Great-Russian nationalism with the Kremlin's unavoidable international role even more satisfactorily than the original NEP had done.

Anti-Fascism and After

The other reason for the idealisation of the USSR far beyond the circles of communist adherents was that with fascism on the march throughout and beyond Europe and aggressively triumphant in Germany, the Soviet state now portrayed itself as the leader of an anti-fascist coalition of all democratic elements. In the wake of the German catastrophe, the 'class against class' slogans were increasingly phased out and the entire concept buried at the seventh and last Comintern congress of 1935. Going into total reverse, and without hint of an apology or acknowledgment of blameworthiness, the leaders of the communist movement now summoned social democrats, democrats, liberals and even democratic conservatives to a joint crusade, a 'people's front' against the fascist menace. At the same time the USSR itself sought diplomatic and military alliances with the democratic states and supplied aid to the popular front government of Spain elected in 1936 and immediately challenged by a fascist-backed military revolt.

These features of the Soviet and international scene during the 1930s were powerful inducements to the left to regard the Soviet state in a positive or at least indulgent light and to promote some measure of unity between local communists and other left-wing elements. The Labour Party leadership in Britain was unusual in maintaining an attitude of uncompromising hostility – one that was rejected by considerable sections of its own membership who were moved by the imperative of anti-fascist unity. Anti-fascist unity covered over the bloodbath of oppositionists in particular and Soviet citizens in general upon which Stalin embarked from 1936 onwards. All the public victims of the show trials were linked by the prosecution to Trotsky, and so successfully had Soviet propaganda demonised him in the minds of communists after his rupture with the regime that preposterous accusations against virtually all of Lenin's surviving colleagues were swallowed without a murmur.[39] Non-communists sympathetic to the USSR and unacquainted with the history of the factional struggles between 1917 and 1929 swallowed them as well.

A lot of this credit was dissipated during the two years of the Hitler-Stalin Pact of August 1939, for if the justifications advanced for that action and the subsequent designation of the European armed conflict as an 'imperialist war' convinced established communists, they convinced few others.[40] The forced entry of the USSR into the war in the summer of 1941, and the spread of the conflict to world dimensions six months later, transformed matters. It was not so much the temporary popularity which accrued to Stalin and the Red Army among the English-speaking belligerents as the fact that in nearly all the occupied countries of Europe and Asia communist parties emerged as the backbone of the resistance movements.

With the entry of the US into the war in December 1941 Axis defeat became a certainty, confirmed beyond any doubt just over a year later following the German debacle at Stalingrad. For Stalin's regime the Grand Alliance with the Western democracies presented both exceptional opportunities and unprecedented dangers. On the one hand it held out the promise of military security through a recognised extension of Soviet borders with a ring of friendly and diplomatically subservient states west of the new frontier and the indefinite neutralisation of Germany as a state capable of making war. To this might be added, providing good diplomatic relations were maintained, access to US resources and goodwill for the prodigious work of reconstruction made necessary by wartime devastation. The dangers in such a course were no less apparent. It risked abandoning the self-sufficiency which the Soviet state had maintained (apart from the supply of US military equipment, mainly transport) ever since the failed attempt to attract Western capital in the early 1920s, and entering into a degree of reliance on US favour. It also risked affecting the hermetically sealed polity and culture through contamination from Western influences. The 'dialectics of victory', in Isaac Deutscher's words, might undo all that Stalin had spent a decade and limitless effusions of his people's blood in constructing.

In spite of frequent grievances and irritations with his wartime partners, particularly Churchill, this was the strategy to which the Soviet leader decided to adhere. In truth there appeared to be little obvious alternative so long as the war was being waged. The priority for the postwar era was to settle the future of Europe and beyond by inter-government agreement in which the USSR would act as an equal partner and, where its security interests were concerned, as the dominant voice. Accordingly in 1943 the Comintern was disbanded, on the grounds that it was expendable. The public justifications advanced for its dissolution were, naturally, vacuous. The real reason, as everyone realised, was that an international and purportedly revolutionary organisation claiming the primary allegiance of numbers of their citizens remained inherently offensive to the Western allies, and that therefore the organisation, in which such hopes and energies had been invested at the time of its creation, had become no more than a diplomatic embarrassment. Stalin in effect sacrificed nothing. He rid himself of the embarrassment but the Soviet hold over the other communist parties remained such that the formal demise of the Comintern made no difference whatever to their relations.

The close of the Second World War reproduced on an even broader stage the revolutionary atmosphere and expectations evoked among the fall of empires 25 years earlier. A European-wide passion prevailed for irreversible social transformation and for the removal of those malevolent political institutions which had given birth to fascism and war. Mass communist parties clothed in the lustre of their Resistance records emerged as the leading political forces in France, Italy, Finland, Czechoslovakia, Yugoslavia and Greece – and these were only the most spectacular. Where free elections were held in these states the communists headed the polls with never-to-be-repeated percentages of the vote.

Both Stalin and the Western allies had a joint interest in keeping these aroused and potentially volatile movements under control and ensuring that they were prevented from upsetting the diplomatic applecart by their unauthorised actions. To the Anglo-American power and its local adherents, anxious to preserve as much as possible of the pre-war social if not political structures, they were a nuisance where they were not a menace; from the Soviet viewpoint their existence contained more ambiguity. To a degree they represented an asset insofar as they upheld Soviet interests inside those European states where the Red Army was absent, or where its dominance was challenged internally as was the case in Poland. In the last resort the European communist parties could be employed as a lever to pressure the Western powers. In the Eastern European liberated nations where Soviet forces *were* in control of the situation, they functioned as a valuable supplement whether they had a respectable indigenous base, as in Bulgaria, or were largely post-1945 creations, as in Hungary. On the other hand the mass CPs represented forces that were less than completely under Stalin's authority, or at least where he had to work constantly to reassert it and could never take it entirely for granted. If they got out of line by attempting inappropriate revolutions under pressure of their rank and file or popular sentiment, relations with the West and Kremlin high policy might be seriously dislocated.

Cold War

In the immediate term solutions were arrived at to satisfy both the Western and Soviet sides of the great power duet. Churchill was determined to restore the corrupt pre-war, ultra-right royal regime in Greece, viewing this as an essential imperial interest because of the country's geographical proximity to the Suez Canal and the Middle East. The communist-led popular movement which had grown from the anti-Nazi resistance to dominate the country could not be reconciled to such a conclusion to their struggle. For Stalin, Greece was no vital concern and accordingly he looked the other way while, beginning in 1944, ELAS (the Greek National Liberation Army) was ferociously suppressed with the aid of British (later US) military force and a quasi-fascist royal cabal installed in Athens.

Elsewhere in newly-liberated Europe, both East and West, the local communists were induced to share office with non-communists in what were termed 'popular front' administrations to undertake the work of postwar reconstruction and renewal. In the Western states, the Anglo-US sphere according to the Yalta and other wartime agreements, they were very definitely subordinated, even where, as in France and Italy, they possessed a larger electorate than any other party. In fact local communists helped to discipline the labour forces in these countries and induce them to sacrifice their economic demands for the sake of national recovery. Their leaders were virtually instructed by Stalin to behave in this matter and to discipline any recalcitrant elements or leaders, such as André Marty or Charles Tillon in France, who pressed for more revolutionary responses.

In the Eastern states the CPs dominated the popular front administrations to a greater or lesser degree, but so long as they shared office, albeit unequally, with genuinely independent partners,[41] there was no question of transforming these states into miniature reproductions of the Soviet regime. Instead the new governments addressed the outstanding agendas of land reform and dismantling the remnants of pre-war feudal structures as well as reconstructing wartime damage and initiating industrial development.[42] If industry was universally transferred to state ownership and centralised economic planning adopted, this was a genuinely popular move and appeared simply to anticipate the wave of the future, West as well as East.

There is every reason to believe that Stalin in the aftermath of the war preferred to continue along similar lines and had no initial intention of sovietising his newly-acquired *cordon sanitaire*. This was most likely the case even in Poland, where the sensitivity of the country's location (its plains were the invariable invasion route from the west) required Moscow, whatever the domestic composition of the Polish government or circumstances elsewhere, to retain virtually total control over its foreign relations. The non-communist political forces in Poland were also vehemently anti-communist and anti-Soviet so, in a mirror image of the Greek drama, the weaker Polish communists were assisted by the Red Army to overwhelm their domestic enemies. Popular front government in that country was never more than an unconvincing formality, abruptly terminated by the onset of the Cold War.

Yet Stalin had very good reasons for wanting to avoid the Eastern European ring coming under the undisguised sole authority of local communists, no matter how tight the cords which bound the latter to Moscow. In the first place, being Stalin, he had no inclination to raise up a platoon of mini-Stalins, who would have to be accorded the formalities due to a ruling communist leader, of which he had hitherto been the sole example. Even more alarming, their status as sovereign national leaders might, despite every precaution, evoke in them or the parties they led, unacceptably independent habits and desires. As the dictator knew only too well, even the Soviet monolith, run by his cowed and frightened subordinates, was never completely secure. Creating a Soviet bloc would multiply immeasurably the risks of fission, and to expand 'socialism in one country' into 'socialism in a bloc' contradicted the basic strategy which had been followed ever since Stalin had established himself as the supreme boss. Considerations from the diplomatic angle pointed in a similar direction. An unvarnished Soviet hegemony over these states, exercised through a communist monopoly of their governments, their proclamation as workers' republics and – most significantly – the export of the Stalin revolution beyond the USSR's borders, would be intensely provocative to the Western partners whose alliance Moscow wanted to carry into the postwar years: the general deterioration in relations after April 1945 and the anger and dismay expressed by London and Washington over events in Poland were evidence enough of that.

In a sometimes bizarre fashion the social moderation of the new polities was at first advertised. In Romania for example the monarchy was maintained, despite a government led by the Romanian CP. More significant still was the determined effort made by Stalin to induce Tito's communist partisans, who had the country under their control by the end of hostilities, to enter into the same kind of arrangement with the Yugoslav royal pretender and to share power with the domestic forces they had defeated at the same time as the Germans, or at least to put together some form of face-saving popular front administration. Tito's refusal and insistence on complete takeover was the first defiance from a communist that Stalin had encountered since the 1920s – a token popular front was set up in Yugoslavia, but with scarcely even the pretence that it had any meaning. For the sake of public relations Stalin was in the meantime obliged to swallow his resentment and present Tito as a model communist and loyal Stalinist.

Meanwhile in Asia the anti-colonial tempest foreseen by Lenin had begun to rise. The Chinese communists, isolated during most of the 1930s with their partisan army in their remote Yenan stronghold, had emerged immeasurably strengthened from the anti-Japanese war. When the USSR had entered the Pacific war in its closing weeks, they had appropriated much captured Japanese military equipment, but Stalin wanted them to use their strength not to conquer power but to reach an accommodation with the spectacularly corrupt regime of the US-backed Chiang Kai-Shek. He feared reasonably perhaps an exhausting civil war in which the communists might waste their strength and any advantage the USSR derived from it, but there cannot be any doubt that he feared even more a speedy and outright victory by Mao's armies. A communist regime in Peking might be friendly and deferential, but it would be altogether outside his control, leading the most populous country on earth and establishing a second communist power centre. Even worse, he was well aware what the reaction of the US would be to a communist takeover of the gigantic market for which its elites hungered and which they confidently expected to exploit. It would destroy for the foreseeable future any prospects of detente or friendly relations with the Americans and create an enormous liability if the Soviet Union was ever obliged to come to its defence. Mao was pressed right up to the last to make a deal and refrain from pressing his military victories to a political conclusion. When he ignored the advice and drove the Kuomintang from the Chinese mainland in late 1949, Stalin was once more obliged to grit his teeth, applaud the revolution and sign a treaty of political, economic and military co-operation.

But well before this had taken place the Soviet bloc had been established in Europe and Stalin's nightmares regarding its likely consequences had been realised. In the end the maintenance of mixed governments and a degree of social flexibility *a la* Finland had come to seem incompatible with the USSR's own security. The Cold War had intervened and Moscow viewed it as imperative to allow its enemies no potential political, social or cultural foothold in these states. The US government (for reasons good or bad) was not prepared to reach an accommodation on Stalin's terms and had proclaimed its hostility and ill-will (along with a claim to US global hegemony) in the Truman Doctrine of March 1947. Hobsbawm remarks that the Kremlin would have been even more concerned had it known that the US Joint Chiefs of Staff had a plan to atom bomb the 20 principal Soviet cities within ten weeks of the war's end. The communist partners in the popular front governments of Western Europe were promptly expelled as potential fifth columnists and saboteurs – and the same or worse happened to their non-communist counterparts in the East.[43] The former wartime allies assumed stances of uncompromising hostility towards each other, developing to the threat of outright warfare in the course of 1948 – a breakdown in relations which the Chinese revolution could only underline and intensify.

Even as the 'socialist bloc' was coming into existence it was threatening to fragment. Following the declaration of the Truman Doctrine Stalin's spokesperson Zhadanov propounded the rival doctrine of the 'two camps' – that of socialism, embracing the CP-rules states, the communist parties outside the bloc and various Soviet-orientated national liberation movements confronting the camp of US-led aggressive imperialism[44] – which included social democratic parties that had placed themselves under the American umbrella. It was not quite 'class against class' reborn, but there were distinctive similarities.

The family likeness was emphasised by the re-formation in 1947 of a quasi-Comintern, the Communist Information Bureau, normally referred to by its similar-sounding acronym of Cominform.[45] The very composition of this organisation however, was symptomatic of the strains and contradictions imposed upon the Soviet leaders by their postwar role. Not all communist parties were members. At first glance it appeared to be made up of the governing parties, but in fact it did not have the restricted logic of being confined to all ruling CPs and to them only. European parties alone were members, and the Chinese CP was not invited to join, even after it had achieved power in 1949. The ruling parties in Europe excluded the Albanian CP – probably under pressure from the Yugoslav government, which at that stage expected Albania to become the seventh republic in the Yugoslav federation. On the other hand, the French and Italian CPs were included and had the responsibility of liaising with the smaller non-member parties on Cominform business. Such a puzzling jigsaw can only be accounted for on the understanding that far from being a genuinely international revolutionary organisation of any sort, the Cominform was designed exclusively as a weapon in the Soviet arsenal for its confrontation with the US *in Europe*. The contrast with the early Comintern is too evident to need stressing.

The Cominform could however prove useful for other functions. In 1948 the major internal disadvantage, to set beside the diplomatic one, of a Soviet bloc of formally independent states, was sensationally

realised. The Yugoslav leaders refused to accept Soviet direction
in their internal affairs and used their state sovereignty, backed up
with a formidable military apparatus and opportunistically rendered
assistance from the West, to make good their defection from the
bloc. The Cominform then became the forum in which Tito and
his colleagues were branded as longstanding agents of US
imperialism who had not merely reversed the socialist revolution
in Yugoslavia but had gone so far as to install a fascist regime in
its place – this Cominform mechanism gave the appearance,
however implausibly, of a condemnation that was more than a purely
Kremlin pronouncement. The aftermath was what might have
been expected from Stalin's methods of dealing with dissidence or
the merest hint of independent thought or action.

Tito, the source of the embarrassment and humiliation, was
beyond Stalin's reach, but potential imitators or deviators elsewhere
in Eastern Europe were not, and Soviet control over the governments
of the other People's Democracies remained firm and unshaken.
From 1949 onwards, that control was used to institute a series of
purge trials, following the Soviet model of the 1930s, of anyone in
responsible positions who might be suspected of any trace of Titoist
sympathies – or who might be chosen randomly to provide a
salutary example.[46] Victims included no less a personage than the
General Secretary of the Czechoslovak CP, Rudolf Slansky, the
leader who had, ironically, moved the original Cominform resolution
condemning the Yugoslavs.[47]

These events were not exactly a triumph in the propaganda and
ideological battle with the West, and did much, coming upon the
back of the initial Cold War developments, to drain away the good
opinion which many of the Western parties had briefly enjoyed.
These were of course obliged to applaud and endorse both the
anathema against Tito and the subsequent bloodlettings. The
renewed purges certainly had the effect of riveting the iron framework
of Stalinist conformity more tightly upon the states of the bloc,
making them less capable of internal adaptation in the future and
leaving behind a legacy which could never really be transcended.

Colonial Revolution and 'Socialist Third'

Asian developments were by no means confined to the Chinese
Revolution: the war initiated a political and social earthquake
across the continent and generalised anti-colonial revolt spread
among its peoples. In this the existence, official history and official
principles of the Soviet state appeared as an inspiration and a
model even to many anti-colonialists who rejected formal
identification with it, such as the leaders of the Indian National

Congress. Millions however were ready to respond to the communist message and find in it the instrument of liberation both from colonial subjection and the stagnation of the traditional society that Marx once bitingly characterised as 'rural idiocy'. Communist parties with mass followings emerged in Japan and Korea, in the Philippines, in Indonesia, in Malaya, in Burma, Vietnam, Ceylon and India – some of them having been the core of resistance movements under the Japanese occupation. Further to the west communist movements in Iran, Iraq and Syria, semi-colonial states, began to attract significant support from the local populations.

Shortly after, or in some cases even before the end of the war, a number of these parties found themselves engaged in armed conflict with the returning colonial power and/or its local surrogates. This was the case in the Philipines, as the US military returned to impose American authority upon its one directly-controlled Asian colony. Such events were exactly paralleled in Malaya, where the British government, albeit now a Labour one, had no intention of surrendering control over the colony's production of rubber and tin.[48] Most notoriously, British forces (assisted by the surrendered Japanese military, who were rearmed for the purpose) intervened to restore French authority in the major cities of Vietnam, so initiating 30 years of war in that country that later came to occupy the centre of world attention as the symbol of anti-imperial conflict. Only the Korean communists however, bordering on China and the USSR, were able to come to power, and then only in half of the country.

And so from the womb of Cold War in Europe and social and national revolution in Asia the communist bloc of CP-ruled states was born[49] and the 'socialist sixth of the world' expanded into 'the socialist third of the world' – with its immediate circle of mass parties struggling politically or militarily for power, and an outer ring of minor parties exercising influence to greater or lesser degrees in the industrial and public life of the states in which they were located.[50] It was scarcely what the founders of the Comintern had envisaged. The Soviet claim to have accomplished socialism would have been treated by them as a cruel joke; they would have been no less flabbergasted to perceive that the 'socialist third' comprised a less economically developed portion of the globe and none of the most industrially and culturally advanced states – for they would certainly not have included the USSR among them.

The contrast with the concepts of socialism consolidated in the late nineteenth century – let alone those of Marx and Engels – could not have been more dramatic or painful, and the claims of continuity which were made in order to provide legitimisation were founded upon a falsehood.

Not even the communist leadership could pretend that any state within the bloc had a population made up in the main of industrial workers, but in principle all communist parties were ostensibly workers' parties and responsible for providing a Marxist-Leninist stiffening to organisations representing other classes which might be grouped together in a popular front.[51] In actual fact, scarcely any of the new ruling parties had a majority of workers in their composition – the Czechoslovak and the East German at most. In Eastern Europe the majority membership of most of the parties derived from a petty-bourgeois or peasant background, and in Asia this was overwhelmingly the case. These facts could not be concealed, but it could be pretended that the CPs nevertheless embodied the historic destinies of the working class. Therefore the working class, regardless of its size, was pronounced to be the leading political and social force in all of these states.

This deception was only part of the deviation from original Marxist conceptions. The membership of these communist parties, regardless of whether they were 'workers, peasants or progressive intellectuals' (to use one of the formulae of the time) were divested of any independent agency or autonomous initiative, all significant control was concentrated within their leaderships, and a narrow circle of the leadership at that. Every communist party, whether in government or in opposition, whether operating legally or underground, whether engaged in conventional politics or armed conflict, was a tight autocracy, backed, in the states of the bloc, by a fearsome police power. In other words, they were thoroughly Stalinised bureaucracies, the very negation of meaningful democracy – though except in underground conditions a pretence to the contrary was always maintained. The supposed workers' states imposed one or another variety of 'barrack socialism' – the very notion and possibility of which had evoked Marx's scorn and contempt – while in their internal regimes the non-ruling CPs faithfully reflected the same sort of practices.[52]

World Movement

Yet it would be fatuous to imagine that this could all have been done by terror and coercion even in the states of the bloc – let alone in the Western democracies where Stalin's writ did not run. As suggested above, what we know as Stalinism may have been in part derived from Russian traditions, the particular Russian struggle which ensued from that history; and the rise to authority of a ruling bureaucratic caste in Soviet Russia; but it also represented an economical way to mobilise, organise and discipline a movement which was a combination of ideological church and political army and, on account of its ideological drive and the complexity of its doctrinal foundations, inherently prone to fragmentation. Hence the strident emphasis on and relentless enforcement of absolute conformity. Success in that however depended upon the existence of a papally infallible court of final appeal in Moscow, its pre-eminence ensured by the icon of the Russian Revolution and Stalin's sacerdotal personality.

What proportion of CP members among the ruling parties were opportunists and careerists and what percentage were convinced and honest believers is impossible to determine, though not many of the former could have joined the wartime underground in the occupied countries. In the non-ruling CPs, subjects of official hostility whose patronage did not extend beyond appointments in their own apparatus and bodies such as trade unions and cultural fronts, the latter were overwhelmingly predominant – at least numerically. They supplied an intangible asset to the Soviet state, but a very important one in the superpower confrontation. It was not that they might, on Kremlin instructions, provoke industrial or social unrest – that was of negligible significance and likely to be counter-productive in any case – but that they permitted the Soviet state to speak not only on behalf of itself or even of the bloc countries, but as the leader of adherents in nearly every part of the globe – a world-embracing movement. In the 'battle of ideas', which was as significant a dimension of the Cold War as the military-political confrontation, that enormously amplified the Soviet voice, and enabled it to face the West European governments with a permanent focus of internal opposition to their conduct of the Cold War.[53] At the same time the oppositional CPs could only be effective insofar as they were large and influential, in other words so far as they were *more* than an extension of Soviet diplomacy, so far as they could mobilise support by fulfilling their original and avowed purpose of leading the fight of the workers and oppressed masses generally in their own countries.

The apparatus of the Comintern and Cominform was therefore of very secondary importance to the USSR so long as sentiments of ardent loyalty, whether or not reinforced by material incentives and deterrents, prevailed among the leaderships and memberships of the other parties and it remained the prime focus of their political loyalty.[54] From the point of view of its international opponents however, this state of affairs meant that the USSR was violating a primary rule of international statehood. It was understood and accepted that powerful states might overawe lesser ones; governments might practice covert subversion of each other's governmental apparatus or seduce each other's citizens by bribery and blackmail into treasonous espionage; but what was improper was for a state not only to try overthrow them all in the name of universal revolution, as the early Comintern had done, but also to make permanent claims – explicit or implicit – on the political loyalties of other states' citizens.[55] That rule, after all, had been laid in the foundations of the system of sovereign states evolved to end the religious wars of early modern Europe. Consequently the USSR, right down to the last, could never be treated and negotiated with as a state like any other, for even after any directing role had been explicitly renounced and foreign CPs no longer recognised any special authority emanating from the CPSU, the shadow of an international movement still persisted. Moscow continued to maintain a 'special relationship' with political parties both ruling and otherwise outside its own frontiers, and anti-imperialist movements still looked to it for encouragement and assistance. The contrast with China is instructive for after the 1960s the Beijing government did drop all pretensions to being the centre of an oppositional international movement so that before long it not only received the Western acceptance which the USSR could never win, but even became Washington's long-term ally.

By the early 1950s the blocs were consolidated and confronting each other in a permanent nuclear stand-off. Europe and Asia were divided up, apart from a very few still contested areas. Africa and Latin America were as yet hardly touched by the Cold War. The chief antagonists were actually engaged in military operations against each other in the Korean peninsula, but the definitive fact about that war from a geopolitical perspective is its containment and confinement to the Korean locality – both sides had too much to lose from allowing it to spread. For the Soviet bloc and the communist movement at large, commitment to international revolution had faded into no more than a distant abstraction, and any intention of deliberately promoting it had been explicitly renounced. The notion of 'peaceful co-existence' was in the air, although only the faintest whiffs were as yet detectable.[56] For communists the concept explicitly did not imply long-term political stagnation and the end of global transformation in a socialist direction. Rather it presumed that the bloc would continue to develop economically and productively and become a growing pole of attraction to populations under the hegemony of an imperialist bloc increasingly racked by economic and social contradictions as the 'general crisis' of capitalism took its course. Thus, at individual and unconnected tempos imperialist as well as subject states would undergo revolutions that would orientate them – with Soviet assistance if they wanted it – along a socialist pathway, leading eventually towards the Soviet model.[57]

It is possible to see in a scenario like that a faint echo of the passive confidence of the Second International that the historic process would infallibly produce the socialist revolution in its own good time – but at least the Stalinist movement of the early 1950s had 'examples' to demonstrate that its conceptions had been submitted to the test of practice and had triumphantly passed it, however partisan the claim might be. It was therefore a context capable of inspiring much confidence in its adherents, even if they should live in fear of being purged in the USSR or Eastern Europe, or their parties had been forced into political retreat, as in the Western democracies. At the time in question, the Stalinist CPs held a virtual monopoly on revolutionary socialist claims, and apart from the Yugoslav defection (which like Trotskyism was stigmatised as a fascist counter-revolutionary provocation) still comprised an impressively united world movement. Such rivals and competitors as existed lived and conducted their business in a marginal half-world, ignored by everybody except their own minuscule bodies of adherents.[58] At the time of Stalin's death the revolutionary left meant the communist movement. Not only had Stalinism successfully appropriated Lenin's heritage and twisted it into barely recognisable shape, but he had taken over the greater and apparently more dynamic part of what it meant to be on the left.

CHAPTER 3

'Actually Existing Socialism'

The phrase appears to have originated at some point in the 1970s, and the feelings which it exposes are interesting and revealing. It suggests a great measure of disillusionment at the distance between what socialism might be hoped to mean according to its conceptualisation, and the reality as embodied in the professedly socialist regimes. But it stops short of rejecting the latter, accepting them with a weary resignation as all that can be realistically expected in present conditions.[1]

Not very long after Stalin's death in March 1953 the regime he created got rid of its most frightful nightmare, but in doing so his heirs also tore open the bindings which had up to that point held their international movement together. The essential strategy of Stalin's method of government had been to establish a bureaucratic layer of apparatchiks which was later demolished by a blood purge before it had time to consolidate itself and form a counterweight to his personalised style of rule. There was every indication that a further purge was being prepared in early 1953 and that its victims would include his longest surviving colleagues. It was therefore to be expected that these, along with the entire apparatus of the Communist Party and the state, would wish for nothing so much as to see the cloud of terror under which they worked lifted from them and to enjoy security in their jobs and their lives. This was done immediately: even as Stalin's funeral praises were being hymned the imminent purge was cancelled and coded assurances issued that there would never be another.[2]

Over the next three years the signals multiplied. Emphasis on 'collective leadership' and disparagement of the 'cult of personality' made plain to all informed observers that the traditions established since 1929 were not to be regarded as appropriate for future Soviet society. A dividing line was crossed in 1955 when Khrushchev and Bulganin, the two leaders in party and state flew to Belgrade and effectively apologised to Tito for Soviet behaviour in 1948. It was a sensational development because it constituted an admission of fallibility on the part of the Kremlin leadership and the repudiation of a central element in Stalin's postwar policy.

Even that was small change however compared to the impact of the 'secret speech' delivered by Khrushchev at the CPSU's 20th Congress in February 1956 in which Stalin was denounced as a tyrant and mass murderer, and, though the term wasn't actually employed, a criminal. It was one of the cardinal turning points in the internal history of the communist movement, comparable only to the 'socialism in a single country' debate and the defeat of the last of the inner-party oppositions. It may well be asked why the semi-publication of facts notoriously well-known to all non-communists, and doubtless guessed at by quite a number of communists too, should have provoked such a cataclysm. The reason was a combination of the nature of the realities which were being admitted combined with the fact that this was the first acknowledged rupture in the continuity of the movement's self-presentation. Up to this point history had been suppressed, distorted, rewritten, stood on its head in a manner which would have done credit to the early Christian church, but always hitherto it had been displayed as a seamless web with the CPSU and its infallible leadership crushing deviations to right or left and advancing in Marxist-Leninist wisdom. Now it was conceded that at the least major errors and abuses had occurred and the implication was unavoidable – there was nothing to ensure they could not occur again in the present or future. Papal infallibility was gone. These consequences were instantly apparent to quite a number of unregenerate Stalinists both inside the CPSU and the foreign parties. Their last hope was that before developments went any further Khrushchev would be overthrown by his foes in the Politburo; he could then be denounced as a renegade who had been forestalled just in time by the guardians of orthodoxy, and the secret speech, never officially acknowledged in any case, repudiated.[3] The attempted coup proved abortive, and there was nothing for it but to make the best of what had occurred.

The Chinese CP leaders, despite having plenty of reason for bitter memories of Stalin,[4] strongly disapproved of the speech, though they refrained from criticising what had been done and noted some points of fallibility in the dead dictator. The other Asian parties tended to have their hands too full with immediate pressing emergencies for it to become a major internal issue, but for the left, who were affected in a radical manner, there were two possible and diametrically contrary interpretations of the events of the mid-1950s. The first was that the Stalinist chickens were now coming home to roost and that the revelations of the 20th Congress signified the opening of a battle within a ruling clique which had exhausted its credibility and would prove unable to keep its quarrel behind the doors of the Kremlin. Once it spilled into the public Soviet domain the masses, according to this interpretation, would move to settle accounts with Stalinism root and branch and re-establish the authentic thread of Bolshevik traditions broken in the 1920s. The transactions of the Congress were the initial shocks of a political earthquake which might sooner rather than later bring the entire regime crashing down but leave intact its foundations of socialised property. Something like this constituted the interpretation favoured by most of the groupings of then existing Trotskyists and had the appearance of being confirmed in the Polish and Hungarian revolts of October/November 1956, when the consequences of destalinisation certainly looked as though they might be running out of control.

The other interpretation was that the regime was reformable, whatever disagreement there might be over the extent of the reforms needed. The presumption behind this was that under Stalin's leadership something viable had been created – economically, socially and culturally – however hideous the bureaucratic and terroristic tumours that had become attached to the Soviet body politic. From this viewpoint acknowledgement of the criminal nature of Stalin's practices was the first step in a process through which the healthy elements in Soviet society and culture would gradually supersede and displace the degenerate ones without the need for revolutionary upheaval – and this might well be guided by a radically transformed communist party. It was in essence the perspective adopted by the more intelligent of the Western European communists trying to come to terms with the new era (others assumed that the necessary improvements had already taken place). It was also that of Isaac Deutscher, who had written in his biography of Stalin, published in 1948, that future generations would have to cleanse the legacy of Stalin as thoroughly as the nineteenth century had done that of Napoleon – in other words that the rejection would be selective rather than total. The title of Deutscher's last major work, *Russia, the Unfinished Revolution*, develops the theme and is indicative of the light in which he saw matters. For this alleged concession to Stalinism he was bitterly indicted by the followers of what had come to be established as orthodox Trotskyism.

Latter Days of Hope

For some years strong indications existed that this interpretation was the right one. The East European crisis simmered down, and though the Hungarian Rising was bloodily suppressed and followed by vindictive reprisals, the re-established 'People's Democracy' evolved rapidly into the most culturally liberal and consumer-orientated state in bloc, while in the USSR itself destalinisation appeared to release energies likely to make it a worthy example for other societies.[5] The success of the Sputnik satellite in 1957 demonstrated that the Soviet Union could challenge and outmatch the US in the most advanced of all forms of technology. Industrial and consumer growth continued impressively, as did cultural relaxation, and at the 22nd Party Congress in 1961 Khrushchev proclaimed the target of overtaking the US as a consumer society within 20 years. A yet more staggering technological triumph and propaganda coup at US expense was secured in the same year when the first human being was sent into orbit. It was all a far cry from the trumpets of world revolution sounding in Petrograd between 1917 and 1921, but peaceful co-existence did appear to pay extraordinary dividends. Other aspects of its theoretical basis also seemed in the process of vindication when an initially national and bourgeois revolution in Cuba at the beginning of 1959 developed so as to bring its new regime – a charismatic and highly attractive one – voluntarily within the bloc, so establishing a socialist state 90 miles from the US coastline, inflicting sensational defeat on an invasion by pro-US exiles in 1961 and sending massive reverberations throughout Latin America.

This dramatic and unexpected development was not without its problems and it is highly questionable whether Moscow really welcomed it, despite the humiliation it represented to its global rival and the advantages of having an ally so close to the US coast. The relentless US enmity towards Castro's regime created obstacles and embarrassments to the pursuit of peaceful co-existence. Even more dangerously, Castroism stood for a much more impetuous and impatient revolutionism than that favoured by Moscow.[6] The new rulers in Havana set about trying to ignite guerrilla-based insurrections similar to their own throughout the Latin American continent and thereby soon found themselves at odds with the cautious and constitutionalist communist parties of that region who were backed by Moscow. However the relationship between the USSR's existence as an orthodox state and its international role still persisted – it had to be seen to continue to support social revolution, and Castro could not be disowned. Fortunately from the Kremlin's point of view the general failure of Castroite revolutionary attempts on the mainland and the exigencies to which Cuba was subjected by the American blockade made it so dependent on Soviet material support that its policy could be controlled in general outline if not in detail.

If the promises of the 22nd Congress had been borne out it is impossible to doubt (assuming that Cold War had not turned into hot) that the situation of the left in the 1990s would have been very different. (Whether in principle these hopes could have been realised is discussed below.) The USSR would then have continued to serve as a pole of attraction for the greater part of the left, would have grown stronger in that role and would more and more have come to look like the wave of the future for the twenty-first century – provided it had been able to combine expanding and balanced

material welfare with the revolutionary credibility the regime, in
spite of everything, continued to possess in many eyes. If 'socialism
in one country' and then the Five-Year Plan had achieved satisfactory
reconciliations between domestic and international demands,
peaceful co-existence and a buoyant Soviet consumer economy
promised to do so with even greater effect.

But the first shadows on the bright picture were evident as early
as 1961, right on the tail of the 22nd Congress and the Cuban and
space triumphs, for in August that year the Berlin Wall went up,
underlining the degree to which coercion still formed the
unconcealed basis for relations between the bloc governments and
their peoples. In the international crisis which followed, the Soviets
exploded a 50-megaton nuclear bomb as a display of military
power: the fears of the Cold War at its height gave signs of returning.
Worse, indeed the very worst, was to come a year later, when by
placing nuclear missiles on Cuban soil in an attempted move on
the geopolitical chessboard, Moscow came close to touching off a
third world war. Even as this was happening the bloc was splitting
irreversibly, for in the autumn of 1962 China had become embroiled
with its neighbour India in a limited war over their joint Himalayan
frontier. The USSR gave tacit support to its diplomatic ally, India,
and not to its fellow communist regime. The leadership of the Indian
CP went even further, with vocal support for its own government
at the expense of a fraternal CP.

The Split

For the leadership in Beijing this came as the culmination of more
than a decade of being patronised, slighted, politically ignored and
overridden; all of which they had so far swallowed with only coded
complaint. The Soviet leaders had assumed the right to make
policy for the world movement without the tiresome necessity of
taking the views of other parties into account except where it suited
them to do so. The disparagement which Mao and his colleagues
had been prepared to accept, however resentfully, from Lenin's
world-historic heir they were in no sense willing to put up with from
his puny inheritors, although until the early 1960s civilities were
preserved. The Soviet government for its part viewed with mounting
annoyance the recommendations of its technical advisers in China
being set aside and the Chinese following their own path of
development, which, the advisers accurately pointed out, ignored
the material realities confronting the regime and was likely to end
horrendously – as it did.

More of an issue still, and probably the dispute which widened
the disagreement into an unbridgeable rift, was the refusal of the

Soviets to supply the Chinese with nuclear weapons technology. Khrushchev was developing a diplomatic and propaganda offensive around the concept of 'peaceful co-existence' among whose priorities was to take the momentum out of the arms race and most certainly to obstruct nuclear proliferation. Soviet assistance to China in becoming a nuclear power – quite apart from any future danger that might pose to the territory of the USSR itself – was unthinkable. For the Chinese the Soviet attitude not only constituted an outrageous breach of international solidarity but demonstrated once again that they were not presumed to stand on a basis of equality. Soviet support for India during the conflict of 1962 was the ultimate betrayal and the final straw. Already a rift had occurred between Moscow and the Albanian regime over the latter's opposition to the dethronement of Stalin and – more immediately – the Soviet-Yugoslav reconciliation, which was viewed as a capital threat to Albanian security. The Chinese now established an alliance with Tirana and the CPC propaganda agencies opened a strident offensive against 'revisionist' Yugoslavia, extending this in the next few months to the communist parties of Italy and France, which were accused of demonstrating revisionist tendencies and unctuously advised to mend their ways. Simultaneously, tendencies sympathetic to the Chinese position were cultivated among communist parties throughout the movement.

Before the close of 1963 the pretence of attacking stalking horses like the Albanian, French or Italian CPs was exhausted, and the quarrel was out in the open. As noted, the Chinese had plenty to complain about in the way they had been treated by the Soviet leaders, though in the late 1950s Mao and his colleagues had refrained from pressing the point, having their hands full with the internal crises of the attempted industrial 'Great Leap Forward' and the political pseudo-liberalisation of the 'Hundred Flowers' period. Their concrete grievances against the USSR and the CPSU however formed a very minor theme in the polemics which now exploded in the foreign language presses of the rival parties – principally the dispute was conducted on a theoretical plane and that of world communist perspectives.

The theoretical stance of the Chinese communists is indicated in Chapter 6, and it was propagated energetically. The volume of the Soviet response was a good deal lower than that of the indictment which was hurled against the CPSU, and certainly a lot less shrill. Whether sincere or not, there were pleas for an amicable resolution of differences and restoration of relations – though in the background material sanctions were being taken to put pressure on the Chinese by withdrawing technical assistance, thus leaving major projects half-completed, and curtailing trade links on which the Chinese depended and even hinting at military threat. Both sides, particularly the

Russians, undoubtedly hoped that factional struggle in the other's hierarchy would bring to the top elements friendlier to their own position. When it became apparent that the breach was irreparable, Soviet propaganda took to accusing their opponents of irresponsible ultra-leftism, possibly Trotskyism, occasioned by the predominance of petty-bourgeois elements in the CPC and its leadership. The Chinese communists, it was claimed, had an insufficient proletarian base, the peasantry was over-represented within their ranks and this had led to the dilution and distortion of Marxism-Leninism together with the ideological and practical errors which had flowed from that.[7]

The unity of the international movement, which had been preserved at least in appearance for 35 years, was now irreparably ruptured. The replacement of co-operation and harmony between the two giants with ferocious enmity – soon to escalate into armed clashes on their common frontier – was only the most dramatic expression of the crisis. All communist parties found themselves in the position of having to take sides and most likely having to endure splits in the process.[8] The Indonesian CP, the largest and apparently strongest Asian CP outside China, lined up with Beijing, though it was soon to be destroyed by a military coup and vanish as a factor in communist affairs. The next largest and best established, the Communist Party of India, split down the middle, with rival factions taking their lead from the main contenders. Among smaller non-governing parties, in Asia the New Zealand CP went over to the Chinese side and in Europe the greater part of the Belgian party – though elsewhere in Europe the established parties were solidly with Moscow. The same was true for their counterparts in the Americas, but as in Europe pro-Chinese fragments split off to form organisations claiming to be the true heirs to the communist legacy – though it was not till later, with the 'cultural revolution', that Maoism was to achieve a degree of broader popularity in the Western hemisphere.

The appearance of a rival world communist centre even provided space for a somewhat greater degree of manoeuvre among the East European states of the bloc, although only one was willing or able to take advantage of it. Under Nicolae Ceausescu the Romanian regime, while avoiding Maoist rhetoric and remaining a member of the Warsaw Pact as well as maintaining a rigidly Stalinist internal order, started to assume a greater freedom in external affairs and adopted a posture towards China that was warmer than Moscow would have liked.

The other members of the East European bloc group were affected in different ways by the post-Stalinist era and underwent an internal evolution which interacted with that occurring in their dominant neighbour. Economic and cultural, though not political, destalinisation was encouraged during the Khrushchev era, but not surprisingly met considerable resistance from the entrenched bureaucrats who formed the ruling elites of these states, whose political formation had been Stalinist and whose privileges were tied into the perpetuation of that style of rule. Ironically, it was in Hungary, where repression had been violent and thorough in 1956 and afterwards, that it was eventually easiest to secure internal changes.

In the USSR itself the bright hopes of the 1950s and early 1960s diminished rapidly with the end of Khrushchev's reign. That has to be kept in perspective. Throughout the lengthy 'era of stagnation' of Brezhnev's tenure, living standards measured in the broadest sense of advancing consumption did continue to improve, although so slowly as to mock Khrushchev's promises of 1961 and at the expense of recklessly stripped natural assets and horrendous environmental damage.[9] Nor were there any further technological triumphs. It was the Americans who first reached the moon in 1969. Moreover, almost at once tighter cultural norms were re-imposed, exemplified in 1966 by the trial of the dissident writers Daniel and Sinyavsky, and although the dethronement of Stalin was not reversed, criticism of his regime was toned down considerably and moves towards further rehabilitation of purge trial victims stopped. By the beginning of 1968, for the left outside the bloc, the partially restored credibility of the USSR as a model was again severely compromised, though not yet exhausted.

It retained some because the old image of the victor over fascism, a society exempt from economic crisis and antagonistic social division, steadily advancing despite unspeakable difficulties towards the society of abundance, still had resonance with some, although undoubtedly a decreasing number. Another mark in its favour was its association with the Cuban regime, still a source of real inspiration, especially after Che Guevara acquired the halo of martyrdom in 1967 and underwent a secular canonisation. Most of all however in the mid-1960s it was the Soviet Union's role as upholder of the Vietnamese national revolution fighting for its life against a criminally inspired invasion by the US and its acolytes, a conflict around which the left was passionately engaged, that induced many to give it the benefit of the doubt and treat it as a regime with a democratic and humanitarian potential that might still hope to be unlocked.

Aborted Spring

There were as well some encouraging signs elsewhere in the bloc, and these were centred upon Czechoslovakia. It was a state which had emerged from the war with a mass communist party among the most genuinely popular in Europe, one which had headed the

poll in open postwar elections and led a popular front government
not overshadowed by the presence of Soviet troops. Until the Cold
War closed down, its non-communist leaders had hoped that the
country might serve as a bridge between East and West and use
the national traditions to construct a genuinely popular socialism.
Such neutralism was unacceptable to Stalin in the wake of the
Truman Doctrine and the Marshall Plan which followed it – apart
from anything else Czechoslovakia's geographical shape gave it, if
it became a base for Western operations, the semblance of a dagger
stuck into the heart of the Eastern bloc. Early in 1948, acting
under Soviet guidance, the Czech communists provoked their
partners into breaking up the popular front government then used
this action as a pretext to mobilise their armed militias, seize
undivided power and institute a one-party state.[10] The experience
was particularly bitter given the Czechs' democratic traditions and
what had happened to them only ten years earlier. It was
compounded when the country was the scene of the last but worst
of Stalin's East European purges. Since destalinisation a limited
and unpublicised rehabilitation of many of the surviving victims
had occurred, and a minor degree of economic liberalisation, but
in 1967 Czechoslovakia continued to be run by otherwise unreconstructed Stalinists who had been personal beneficiaries of the
tyranny, and internationally was the most unquestioning and
subservient of bloc members.

By the late 1960s, after 15 years free from all-encompassing terror,
with a general if modest rise in living standards and with awareness
of the political turmoil taking place in Western Europe where
various shades of communist and non-communist Marxism were
engaged in exploring their pre-Stalinist roots, fresh life began to
flow in the country's suppressed democratic traditions – for the
Stalinist straitjacket could not abolish popular memory, and as
conditions 'normalised' in the 1960s they began to resurface.
Under the pressure of a new generation they found expression in
the Czechoslovak Communist Party, where, stimulated by a crisis
in the command economy of the early 1960s, demands began to
be raised for an accounting with the past; economic reconstruction;
cultural freedom and political liberalisation within the CP structures.
Unsurprisingly, the demands were principally voiced among and
by the white-collar strata of the population, those who stood most
immediately to benefit from such a programme, and who may at
first have been regarded with some suspicion by manual workers
concerned that greater reliance on market forces in the economy
could threaten job security. Once the new course acquired a
resonance of Czech national expression and the release of
subordinated national sentiment, the bulk of the workers moved
behind it as well.

The dominant party bosses were overthrown by Central Committee vote following an internal struggle in the party hierarchy which drew upon rank and file dissatisfaction, replaced with leaders embodying the new aspirations and a dramatically radical reform programme adopted to nearly universal popular acclaim. The partisans of the ousted regime, its unreconciled functionaries and its convinced supporters – if any such existed – were isolated and politically helpless. There was however no question of instituting a multi-party state, the socialist basis of economic and social relations was to be maintained and the new leaders were loud in proclaiming their Soviet loyalty, their adhesion to the international principles of the bloc and commitment to the Warsaw Pact.

The impact upon Western communists and beyond[11] was, for the few months the episode lasted, sensational. This was no counter-revolution, breakaway or secession, but might herald a general transformation. It really did seem that 'actually existing socialism' was in the process of renewing itself under the leadership of an actually existing communist party. Where Czechoslovakia had shown the lead others might follow, with the reform in due course spreading to the USSR itself, enabling the process broken off with Khrushchev's overthrow to be resumed.[12]

What the Western left in general hoped for was exactly what the ruling elites in the remainder of the bloc feared. Perhaps they really did believe that the process would prove uncontrollable and that the Czechoslovak party and any others which might follow it would be swamped by the release of political and social forces which, once the constraints of neo-Stalinism were gone, would with Western aid drag these states back into the capitalist orbit. If so, they had little confidence in the intrinsic strength of their own social system. At any rate, what they unquestionably did fear was the loss of their own power and privileges if called to account through an opening up of their political systems by the peoples they had abused for two decades. With Ulbricht of the GDR in the forefront, the leaders of the Eastern bloc urged the Soviet government to put a forcible end to the process. Probably they didn't need much urging. In August 1968 troops from all the Warsaw Pact states with the exception of Romania, having disguised their intentions under the pretext of military manoeuvres, invaded Czechoslovakia and arrested its reformist government and party leadership.

Thereafter the country was turned into something resembling a laboratory of 'actually existing socialism'. The arrested leaders were pressured in Moscow into promising to rescind the key changes, to accept the indefinite presence of the invasion force and above all to reimpose censorship. They were then returned to Prague and soon afterwards replaced by more compliant figures. The CPCz, the government institutions, cultural, media and academic facilities were all thoroughly purged by expulsions and dismissals. A heavy blanket of demoralised apathy and stifling conformity – larded with official rhetoric in which nobody believed – descended upon the country. The few individuals who persisted in publicly expressing dissent were subjected to constant harassment, loss of employment and even imprisonment in really stubborn cases.

At the same time it is significant to note that in this repression, unlike all previous ones, nobody was actually executed. In addition, although the system of centralised economic planning and full employment was maintained, some of the intended market-orientated reforms were quietly introduced and distinct efforts made to improve the supply of consumer goods. It was a deliberate strategy of mass depoliticisation aiming to divert political and national dissatisfaction with material welfare, destroy civic consciousness and leave governmental processes in the hands of a subservient elite without any justification for their role beyond the abstraction of 'international communism' – in reality loyal subordination to the Soviet regime.

Among most Western communists,[13] no longer inclined to accept without argument the Soviet definition of reality, the moral credit of that regime became seriously overdrawn – although none of the parties went so far as to sever relations. For all the increasing drift towards nationalist agendas on the part of CPs outside the Soviet orbit, the international dimension centred on the Soviet Union remained crucial to their identities, as is attested by the remark from a bitterly hostile source, 'Czechoslovakia [caused] a full scale crisis in such an apparently unlikely a place as the Venezuelan CP'.[14] The Cuban and Vietnamese regimes, too dependent upon Soviet aid to risk offending the donor, approved the Warsaw Pact action in a perfunctory or ambiguous manner. The Chinese leadership, embroiled in the most intense phase of the Cultural Revolution, condemned the invasion, though for wholly opportunist propaganda purposes, being adamantly opposed to everything the Prague Spring represented.

'Era of Stagnation'?

By the mid-1970s the internal evolution of the Soviet bloc had ceased to be an inspiration to anybody. No striking economic superiority over the Western alliance was apparent – the rate of growth of Soviet GNP fell from 5.7 per cent in the 1950s to 2 per cent in the early 1980s – and no political renewal was in prospect. It was the first time since 1917 that such a double reality had come to pass. Soviet citizens in the main, or their Eastern European counterparts, nevertheless enjoyed a basic economic security, but at a fairly minimal level, and especially so away from the major cities. They were provided with a range of welfare services covering health, housing, education and recreation, except for the elite, of a pretty spartan sort. Accession to that elite, the *nomenklatura*, though far from egalitarian, and automatic for persons with the right family connections, remained possible for ambitious outsiders willing to learn the formulae of Marxism-Leninism and to jump through the hoops of the party's rituals.

Compared with the fate endured by most Third World citizens these might have been regarded as near paradisial conditions, but they could scarcely begin to compete with the attraction and glitter of Western consumer society. Indeed the central weakness in the framework of the bloc was that the system of centralised planning, adequate enough for capital goods construction, winning wars or even engaging in military competition with the US, simply could not cope with the demands of an increasingly consumer-orientated populace. Therefore the planners were faced with the example of the spectacle in which masses of unsaleable trousers or shoes piled up unpurchased in the stores while Western tourists were virtually having their jeans and shoes pulled off them in the streets by designer-hungry citizens and no visitor could walk in the central streets of Moscow or Leningrad without encountering a petty currency speculator.

The would-be rival centre of international communism likewise ceased to be such by the mid-1970s. The Cultural Revolution had wreaked such social and cultural devastation[15] that by that point its adherents in the party's inner counsels had become isolated, feared and hated – the precariousness of their position emphasised by the mysterious death and disgrace of Mao's chief military protege. Only the prestige and personality of the Great Helmsman maintained the political rhetoric of the 1960s, and even that had been abandoned on the international field when, in 1972, fences were mended with the US although the Vietnam War continued to rage. Following Mao's long-anticipated death in 1976 and the overthrow of his ideological heirs, the 'Gang of Four', Maoism as a movement was as dead as its founder. The presentation of China as a society of pristine socialist purity and commitment vanished as well; for though relations between Moscow and Beijing did not improve in any measure, the latter's economic and social policies reverted back towards the Soviet model.

By this stage few took seriously the Soviet bloc's claim (or China's for that matter) to be a socialist society corresponding in any sort of manner to the original Marxian conception, or entertained for it in the immediate future any great hopes in that direction. Paradoxically however, as the friend of revolution elsewhere, its credibility was far from exhausted, whether for the revolutionaries immediately concerned or sympathisers abroad. Largely that was because these revolutions were directed against regimes underpinned by the enemy superpower and might involve some strategic advantage for the USSR, but that position too was connected to an international reality that the Kremlin rulers might well have privately preferred to abolish, but were powerless to do so because it was intrinsic to their political legitimacy – for that international role was also the bedrock of the state's domestic ideology.

The USSR's historic foundations were laid in internationalism, however greatly the superstructure had been distorted in reality. All the apparatus of education and media were attuned to this theme. Without it the USSR as distinct from Russia lost all plausible justification and openly took on the character of the prison of nationalities that had existed in Tsarist times. The conjuring trick was to present what constituted an essentially national agenda in internationalist garb – but to be sustained over the long-term that posture required a measure of true belief and could not serve purely as a cynical manoeuvre. If the Soviet state was no longer the promoter of international socialist revolution it must still stand forth as the socialist guardian and exemplar. Whether they liked it or not, its leaders were compelled to be the leading force in an international movement of communist parties – and states. If they were to drop that pretension and assume the purely nationalist colours that would have found favour with the West, they would also have to reject the 'internationalism' which legitimated their rule over Eastern Europe, and at a deeper level also the historical justification of the Soviet state and its superpower role, with all the ideological and cultural consequences that would have involved – moral disarmament in the face of their formidable and menacing enemy. Consequently embattled revolutionary movements and regimes looked for Soviet support and assistance. The 1970s saw numerous occasions upon which such opportunities arose, and overall the decade had the appearance of bringing about a marked weakening in the West's international grip, with the USSR appearing as the backer and guarantor of a new revolutionary surge.

As the decade opened a revolutionary administration with major communist participation came to power in Chile by constitutional election. Its overthrow three years later by a peculiarly brutal military coup doubtless safeguarded US strategic interests but was desperately bad public relations for Washington and correspondingly showed Moscow in a favourable light.[16] Moscow had been behind the Allende government and, along with Western communists, worked assiduously to keep the horrors of the Pinochet regime in international consciousness and to care for the flood of left-wing refugees pouring out of the stricken country.[17]

Even as the Chilean tragedy was unfolding, however, the US was being compelled by military failure, economic pressure, the internal rot of its expeditionary force and growing popular dissent in US cities to wind up its direct intervention in Vietnam and pull out its own forces, leaving the line to be held by its local surrogates, albeit with the aid of lavishly supplied equipment and advice. The following year a Chilean-style endeavour against the left-leaning government in Cyprus went dramatically wrong and resulted instead in the fall of the US's client military regime in Greece, accompanied by the re-emergence of a strong left-wing party (and even the suppressed communists) in the latter country.[18] As if that were not enough even more alarming developments were taking place in Portugal, where the overthrow of the US-allied fascistoid dictatorship once again permitted the eruption of left-wing currents, this time, most frighteningly from Washington's viewpoint, strongly entrenched in the Portuguese armed forces themselves. For a time it looked as though the Portugese CP, whose record of underground struggle under the dictatorship had brought it mass popular support, was going to lead a governing coalition in alliance with the left-wing soldiers and remove Portugal from the Western orbit. In the same year the West's principal bastion and listening post in tropical Africa collapsed with the fall of the Ethiopian monarchy and its replacement by a radical military regime which speedily realigned the country with the Soviet bloc. In the US itself, the diplomatic initiatives of the right-wing President Richard Nixon in pursing detente with China failed to save him from enforced resignation amid unprecedented domestic scandal.

If 1974 was something of an *annus mirabilis* for 'actually existing socialism' internationally, 1975 saw the sensational climax of its post-Cold War triumphs. In April crushing military victory by the National Liberation Front's army extinguished the US's Vietnamese clients and took Saigon, from which the US embassy staff were filmed fleeing ignominiously by helicopter. The superpower had not only lost control over the Southeast Asian seaboard, along with thousands of service personnel and masses of equipment, defeated in a military contest by a ridiculously inferior enemy, but far more important had suffered overwhelming humiliation and disgrace. Any observer might well have been forgiven for concluding that the West was on the defensive. In addition to this string of defeats in the international arena, the postwar economic boom had broken and the global capitalist economy was sliding into recession with consequent domestic strains and likely political upheaval. Finally, a somewhat symbolic diplomatic success was secured by Moscow with the Helsinki Agreements in which the Western powers effectively recognised indefinite Soviet hegemony over Eastern Europe.

Nor did it stop there. The second part of the decade gave every appearance of confirming the tendencies of the first half. The communists were repulsed from the strongholds of government in Portugal, but they remained a threatening domestic presence. The two large Portugese African colonies, Angola and Mozambique, now secured their independence under unambiguously left-wing governments, following the decades-long guerrilla wars which had undermined the Lisbon regime, and now presented potential additional menaces to the apartheid regime to their south. The ex-colony on the west, Angola, was in 1976 the scene of a full-blown war between the MPLA, the left-wing political movement, strongest in the capital, Luanda, which had led the guerrilla struggle, and two US and South African backed rivals, the UPA in the north of the country and UNITA in the south. South African forces invaded Angola to support its protege. International solidarity might be said to have been evidenced when Cuban detachments crossed the Atlantic to assist the MPLA in defeating the invasion and establishing its control over most of the country – though it was unable to expunge the UNITA presence from its southern border, which in due course became a matter of the grimmest consequence for the Angolan population.

The Western dominoes did not stop falling, for in 1979 three further sovereign states passed out of its orbit. One of them admittedly was of negligible international importance, the tiny Caribbean island of Grenada, a member of the British Commonwealth. Still, it represented yet another defeat in the most sensitive geographical area for the American power, and a welcome ally for Cuba. A more significant one appeared on the Central American mainland with the guerrilla victory of the Sandinistas over the unspeakably corrupt and brutal – but safely Washington-aligned – personal regime of the Somoza family.[19] The Sandinistas moreover represented more than a local embarrassment, for they generated a lot of international enthusiasm along the same lines as Cuba had done in the early 1960s. The third defector was of crucial importance. The overthrow of the Shah of Iran, not by palace coup but by mass popular insurrection, knocked away a central strategic pillar of Washington's position in the Middle East, as well as placing enormous oil resources under the control of an adamantly hostile regime which refused to play by the rules of international diplomacy. However, the political character of the revolutionary government, which came to power on the slogan of an 'Islamic republic' of undefined content, remained at first obscure.

Reversal

The total reversal, within a decade, of the relationship of advantage and disadvantage between East and West is one of the most astonishing political turnarounds in the historical record, and the only one to have occurred on a global scale. Nor was it the case that appearances in the middle of 1979 were altogether deceptive. The apparent strength of actually existing socialism was certainly hollow, as deeper analysis of its economic and social relationships might have revealed,[20] but the West, if intrinsically stronger where it mattered, was also in real trouble at that point of the twentieth century. The 'long boom' of the 1950s and 1960s had exhausted itself, its unmistakable end signalled by the dramatic oil price hike of 1973; returns on investment were dropping throughout the Western market economies. The immediate response was a move into financial speculation and unconstrained lending underpinned by a regime of low interest rates and inflationary expansion. The historic contract between capital and labour which had underpinned the economic growth and social stability of the postwar era was disrupted. Inflationary pressures provoked in the advanced economies a response of growing labour restlessness and social tension as workforces struggled to preserve the continuous advance in real incomes to which they had grown accustomed. Governments ran up accumulating deficits, provoking further inflationary spirals, in attempting to sustain welfare programmes that were the other foundation stones of the consensus era. In some major states, including Britain, established labour movements gave signs of swinging to the left.

It is interesting to speculate what might have happened had the trends of internal pressures combined with international retreat continued to run their course – but it goes without saying that trends hardly ever do. If in a previous era of much more severe and indeed apparently terminal crisis, following the First World War, capitalism had regrouped, found the means of adapting to permanent economic deflation and of mounting political counter-attack, it proved no less resourceful in the much less threatening conditions of inflation and international challenge in the 1970s. The ideological framework for liquidating the detente and compromise with labour which had prevailed during the postwar boom was provided by the analyses and prescriptions of the New Right.

The central concepts of this school and its think-tanks involved the resurrection of pre-Keynesian sound money doctrines and dogmas of laissez-faire scope for private capital and unregulated markets. A financial turn was made at the end of the decade with the imposition of tight monetary policies and high interest rates which had the immediate effect of precipitating a lurch into recession and

soaring unemployment; at the same time a combatative stance
was assumed vis-a-vis labour. It was the populations of the First
and Third Worlds who were to feel the weight of the economic
strategy (see Chapter 5) but these were associated with a combined
economic, political and military drive against actually existing
socialism as well. The Reagan presidency in the United States and
the Thatcher government in Britain stood forward as the leading
protagonists and mobilisers of the capitalist ethos for the combat.
On both internal and external fronts success was dramatic.
Throughout the Western bloc trade unions and labour political
movements went down to defeat, and also:

> The recentralisation of purchasing power within the United States
> achieved almost instantly what US military might acting alone
> could not. The devastating effect of restrictive US monetary
> policies high real interest rates, and deregulation on Third
> World states quickly brought them to their knees.[21]

The international offensive, which was closely linked with the
curbing of Western labour and carried through by the same
governments, came to be termed the Second Cold War. During
the interwar years the Soviet regime had lived in constant terror
that the imperialist powers would combine to attack it: in the late
1940s that nightmare had come true, even if the USSR was
immeasurably stronger and the attack had not taken the form of a
shooting war. By the beginning of the 1980s, in a ghostly echo of
the 1930s, capitalist crisis had eventuated in an assault upon the
Soviet bloc, with the additional bitter irony that the Chinese
People's Republic, which should have been its principal ally, was
now on the enemy side.

The strategic heart of the Western offensive was the opening of
fresh nuclear threats. These centred upon new weapons systems
– the neutron bomb (which destroyed life while leaving material
facilities intact), the Cruise missile (which could mount a nuclear
attack underneath the Warsaw Pact's radar defences) and, most
formidably, the Strategic Defense Initiative (immediately termed
the Star Wars project) – intended to create a network of laser-
operated weapons in orbit which in the event of a nuclear exchange
would destroy incoming Soviet missiles and so render US cities
secure from retaliation: an invulnerability which would effectively
cancel out the Soviet nuclear strike force.[22] It is most unlikely that
the Washington planners envisaged any of these systems ever being
used any more than existing ones had been; their purpose was to
present an enhanced level of threat, to render the Soviet bloc more
compliant upon the international scene and to increase the pressure
upon its resources by forcing it to engage in the construction of
matching weaponry.

In concert with the strategic nuclear pressure, armed attacks were commenced around the globe upon Soviet-aligned regimes which had not yet consolidated themselves and where internal oppositions could be financed, armed and trained to harass them with military operations. In one instance indeed, where speedy results could be guaranteed and there was no danger of retaliation, the US used its own armed might. In 1983 the minuscule Caribbean island state of Grenada was invaded, its leftist government overwhelmed and a more accommodating regime installed. There cannot be any doubt that the same procedure would have been used in Nicaragua were it not for the fact that American casualties would have been high and the US been involved in a guerrilla war thereafter. Nevertheless threatening air and sea manoeuvres were maintained constantly around the country's coasts to screw up the tension, while, together with an economic blockade, elements of the overthrown Somoza dictatorship were sponsored to carry out a campaign of atrocity and destruction within the country's borders, keeping the population in a state of fear and alarm, nullifying the Sandinista government's construction efforts and stretching its resources to the limits. Eventually the strategy succeeded. Although the Sandinistas were not overthrown militarily, the Nicaraguans' morale was finally worn down and their objectionable government voted out.[23]

Similar approaches were used in Africa with even more devastating consequences for the Africans. The regimes in Mozambique and Angola both found themselves vulnerable to systematic campaigns of massacre and destruction carried out by US surrogates sheltered, equipped and at times militarily supported by the South African government. The economic and transport infrastructure of both countries was thoroughly wrecked and, in Angola in particular, the civil population suffered the appalling consequences of mutilation, starvation and demographic dislocation. Neither UNITA in Angola nor Renamo in Mozambique was able to win outright, but eventually the governments, being forced to accept patched-up accommodations with their enemies, each inherited a prostrated and virtually ungovernable country.[24]

But the most telling of all Western victories in the Second Cold War occurred in Asia. In the course of the 1970s a leftist regime had come to power in Kabul. Its ability to rule was based upon factions of the Afghan army, in which the Afghan communist party, itself bitterly divided and faction-ridden, was strongly entrenched. The new government began to implement programmes of land, social and cultural reform, including ones aimed at the emancipation of Afghan women who where among the most oppressed in the continent. In doing so it incited armed resistance by all social elements who had anything to lose or who were

attached to the old practices – and this in a country ideal for
guerrilla operations and inhabited by mountaineers peculiarly
skilled in that art.

Towards the end of 1979 the Kabul government, through a
combination of its own political errors, divisive actions and military
failure, was on the point of defeat by its guerrilla opponents. It called
upon its Soviet ally for assistance. It appears that within the
Politburo there was hesitation over how to respond – the dangers
of intervention in Afghanistan, where more than one would-be
occupier had come to grief, were well appreciated. However the
arguments for action appeared the more convincing. It would be
invidious to abandon a loudly trumpeted Marxist-Leninist regime
to its fate when Soviet help was readily available. Moreover the fall
of the Kabul government would also constitute a serious diplomatic
defeat for it would bring US influence – already entrenched in
Pakistan, a US satellite from where the guerrillas were being
sponsored – right up to the Soviet borders. It was calculated also
that the Afghan communists, with a modicum of Soviet help, had
sufficient strength to win.

Accordingly, Soviet troops entered the country in force, where
they occupied Kabul. However, they did not appear simply as
backing for the existing communist-led government. Since Afghan
communist rulers were held to have been partially the authors of
their own misfortunes, measures were taken for its reconstruction.
These measures, all overseen by Soviet officials, included raising
to a position of dominance the hitherto excluded faction of the
Afghan CP, and also the execution of the Afghan president, who
had come to be regarded as a liability.

In retrospect it might well qualify as the single most disastrous
decision a Soviet government ever took. Instead of a swift surgical
political-military operation, Afghanistan became the USSR's
Vietnam. It has to be emphasised that the regime, in spite of
everything, did continue to retain considerable support among the
modernising forces in Afghan society, but particularistic sentiments
(they could scarcely be termed national) were yet further alienated
by the fact that it now appeared to be the puppet of the infidel
Russians. Despite increasing commitment of troops and resources,
accompanied by terrorising military operations against enemy
areas, the war could not be won. As time passed the balance of
advantage began to turn slowly against the regime and its Soviet
backers. Casualties among the Soviet forces were heavy and their
captured soldiers and airmen were routinely killed by torture. For
all the total control of the Soviet media exercised by the Kremlin,
these realities could not be indefinitely concealed at home, with
devastating impact upon the public consciousness. All this apart
from the enormous material expense of sustaining the war.

Needless to say, all the belligerent motivation and expertise of the Afghan guerrillas would not have prevailed against the Soviet military machine had they not been provided with safe havens in Pakistan and unlimited backing by its military rulers, shored up in turn by the US. For the New Right forces coming to the fore in the US during the waning months of the Carter presidency, the Afghan events were a godsend. They put the USSR entirely in the wrong, portrayed it as an incorrigible aggressor and enabled the State Department to mobilise international opinion against it, symbolised in the official boycott of the 1980 Moscow Olympics, a public relations disaster for the Soviet government. The trade sanctions which also followed were a more material one.

The use of cold and hot military pressures upon the Soviet bloc and its allies was supplemented vigorously in the new decade by economic ones. The bloc itself had provided some of the opportunities. When borrowing was easy during the 1970s its members, especially the regime in Poland, had embarked on a strategy of solving its industrial and infrastructural problems by using this facility to the utmost. The problems were massive, consisting of outworn technology and plant with consequent low labour productivity, and a hopelessly inefficient agriculture based upon peasant smallholdings.[25] The inefficiency derived less from the small size of the holdings – petty agricultural production can be extremely productive given the right conditions – as from the lack of incentive caused by prices of farm products kept artificially low to ensure cheap food to the urban workforce. The loans were ill-used or squandered and, as interest rates rose, servicing the debt turned into a crushing burden upon the state budget, provoking a cycle of further economic deterioration. Attempts to break the vicious circle by raising agricultural prices sparked worker unrest, and political crisis duly followed, culminating in December 1981 – after the struggle of the Solidarity union had brutally exposed the nature of the relationship between the workers and the 'workers' state' under actually existing socialism – with the first military takeover in a 'socialist' state. Martial law was declared, the workers' movement suppressed and the military commander assumed the premiership. The impetus for the denouement came from Moscow, once again concerned that matters in a bloc state were running out of control and that the rigidity of governmental structures was being upset by popular mobilisation. Had General Jaruselski not succeeded with his coup, the alternative, despite all its frightening implications, would probably have been a Soviet invasion.

Once again it amounted to wretched publicity. 1981 was the year when, according to Khrushchev's projections, the USSR should have overtaken the US in consumer facilities and been rapidly proceeding towards the Marxist utopia of the society of abundance, in which money would become redundant. Indeed gross social production had more than trebled over the period and industrial production quadrupled, raising average real incomes by 100 per cent. But for all that the USSR remained a poor country compared with North America or Western Europe and in 1981 the harvest was so deficient that the figures were simply suppressed. The days of Yuri Gagarin and the 22nd Congress were a long way in the past and the hopes of that era largely extinguished, politically as much as economically. It was in the month of the Polish coup that Brezhnev celebrated his 75th birthday, covered to some degree in seven out of *Pravda*'s eight pages. By this time the General Secretary and head of state had accumulated more orders and medals than Stalin and Khrushchev combined and more military honours than Zhukov. It was a popular joke that his distinctive eyebrows were 'Stalin's moustache at a higher level'.[26]

Upon Brezhnev's death a year later in November 1982 the fact that a creeping malignancy was eating away the body of the Soviet state and party received implicit admission with the appointment of Yuri Andropov as his successor. Andropov's credentials were those of an austere enemy of corruption and cautious reformer, and indeed his short period in office was identified with energetic anti-corruption campaigns, resulting in the exposure of serious malpractice among the highest in the *nomenklatura*, including relatives of the late leader. Recognition that these merely scratched the surface of the problem came with the elevation in 1985 of Mikhail Gorbachev, the youngest member of the Politburo and Andropov's protege, following the latter's death and that of his decrepit immediate successor, Chernenko.

Gorbachev's Experiment

Gorbachev's aims were ambitious, amounting to nothing less than a process of structural transformation – something that was certain to raise profound misgivings among apparatchiks with entrenched interests at every level of the state and party bureaucracy. His election to the supreme office in the knowledge that such a programme would be launched was therefore a sign of awareness at the top that a deep degree of crisis existed and that radical measures were going to be required to counteract it.

The programme was encapsulated in the terms *glasnost* and *perestroika*, translating roughly as 'openness' and 'reconstruction'. Soviet society had been reconstructed more than once, but the *glasnost* marked an intended break with all Soviet tradition and practice since the early 1920s, for it implied that issues would henceforth be discussed truthfully and realistically rather than passed through a compulsory filter of whatever interpretation of Marxism-Leninism happened to be the prevailing one. The intention no doubt was pragmatic as much as principled – it was expected that opening the valves of public dialogue would strengthen the regime rather than undermine it and that public truthfulness would release public energies that could be mobilised for reconstruction to overcome hitherto immovable blockages in the economy and reverse the advancing deterioration in civic morale expressed in such characteristics as incorrigible and worsening alcoholism and absenteeism: for, 'The more a social system is bureaucratically formalised, regulated, planned, and yet unable to fully satisfy social requirements, the more it tends to create informal mechanisms that escape the control of the system.'[27]

The sense of a new start was deliberately cultivated, and among the Soviet population at large undoubtedly well received. However, there were also plenty of neo-Stalinists who found the existing system well to their liking and remained violently opposed to any large-scale political, social or even cultural experimentation. They were to be found not only inside the USSR, but throughout the East European states of the bloc and in nearly every instance comprised the ruling elite of these countries' governing CPs.[28]

Traditionalist communists in the non-bloc parties, for whom neo-Stalinism represented not merely 'actually existing socialism' but socialism as it ought to be, adhered to similar viewpoints and waited impatiently for Gorbachev's demise; but by contrast the new programme captured the imaginations and aroused lively enthusiasm among the left in the non-bloc countries, who were all too aware of the regime's shortcomings but still longed to believe that its potential wasn't yet exhausted. If the Prague Spring was reawakening, this time in Moscow, then history might at last be taking the long-awaited turn that would give instituted socialism an unchallengeable moral advantage over capitalism and provide it with irresistible appeal throughout the globe.

The signs at first looked promising, particularly in the aspect of *glasnost*. Serious and honest examination of governmental and administrative shortcomings began to appear in the Soviet press; meaningful and sensitive probing into Soviet history and its hitherto untouchable horrors was begun. Judicial rehabilitation got underway of some of the Great Purge victims, particularly Bukharin. Although the CPSU's party monopoly continued to be formally upheld, it became possible for the first time since the early 1920s to establish legal opposition groupings in the form of political clubs and associations, and for voters to enjoy a real choice of candidates at elections. It was no doubt however indicative of the limitations of *glasnost* that the Politburo, the KGB and the military high command remained off-limits to criticism.

While *glasnost* had got off to a promising start, *perestroika* constituted a much more problematical and intractable area, not surprisingly, since it had at its heart the question of resource allocation, and beyond that a looming and portentous question of whether any economy of the size and geographical spread of the USSR could be co-ordinated by any plan whatsoever or by anything other than market-dominated relations. While that was a problem of principle, much more concrete ones were generated by the reality that plans might be drawn up at the centre but getting them implemented at the level of republics, regions, and above all at the level of individual enterprises was another matter altogether, particularly where there was real resistance to doing so if increased efficiency or dynamic innovation implied the possibility of downgrading, loss of privileges or even loss of employment.

At any rate, *perestroika* implied lessened security, and this, combined with the possibility of open criticism and oppositional activity, proved a potent mixture. Early indications were to be seen in the large-scale strikes which swept the Soviet coalfields as long-dammed frustrations and discontents exploded and were exacerbated by proposals which implied that mineworkers would have to bear the burdens of reconstruction in that part of the Soviet fuel industry. The explosion of the Chernobyl atomic reactor in April 1986 was not in any way due to the new policies, but it exposed in the most horrific manner imaginable the unspeakably shoddy and decrepit state of the USSR's supposedly most technically advanced industry, and the official obfuscation which followed concerning the scale of the disaster and its consequences showed the limits of the impact of *glasnost* upon the bureaucracy at that stage. Further environmental catastrophes, nuclear and otherwise, began to be reported.

There was another unforeseen negative consequence of Gorbachev's initiatives. While the new departures might have held out the ultimate hope of creating a Soviet Union which would be a light to the nations – combining the social decency and democratic values of Sweden with a non-capitalist economy and the capacity to support in various ways struggling peoples all around the world – in the immediate term the admission of the extent of its problems and internal concentration on tackling them put in question the state's self-proclaimed historic mission and threatened the roots of its legitimacy. If socialism, as it was now officially acknowledged, needed such a drastic overhaul, what became of the rhetoric of over five decades proclaiming its irresistible advance from triumph to triumph, with only such minor imperfections as were embodied in the 'cult of personality' and 'violations of socialist legality'? What validity did Marxism-Leninism possess, and what then were the qualifications of the Soviet state to proclaim itself to be the cutting edge of history? Corrosive questions of this nature were reinforced by the line of foreign policy that followed from the logic of *perestroika*. The West at the time was pushing a confrontationist stance against the Soviet bloc, but even if counter-confrontation had been thought desirable politically, the state, with its lumbering economic apparatus and relative technological backwardness, did not have the resources both to achieve a politically difficult remodelling of itself and at the same time meet aggressiveness with aggressiveness.

Gorbachev's foreign policy orientations were therefore conciliatory in the highest degree. The central priority was to renew the process of detente and to remove the crushing burden of keeping pace as far as possible with the development of NATO's new weapons systems and having to accept the diversion of resources that entailed. Access to computer technology, in which the bloc was particularly deficient and which the West made a point of withholding, was a further incentive. To the dismay of the military establishment therefore, partial disarmament proposals conceding advantage to NATO were advanced in the field of strategic nuclear armaments as well as proposals for reducing tension in Central Europe. The General Secretary made visits to foreign capitals to impress foreign statesmen with his affability and went as far as he dared in the way of concessions at summit meetings with President Reagan.

Similar principles were applied in the cases of the festering conflicts throughout the world in which the USSR had an historic involvement, though this was no easy task – longstanding allies could not simply be abandoned to their fates. Military and economic aid, although a further drain on scarce resources, continued to be supplied to regimes like the Cuban, the Ethiopian, the Angolan, the Vietnamese and above all the Afghan – but now Moscow always pressed the dependent regimes to make whatever accommodation they could with their US-sponsored internal enemies (and with the US itself if possible) and bring the conflict to a close. The general intransigence of these regimes, who felt they were being sold out, represented a major obstacle; however the Kabul government could not prevent the USSR from liquidating its direct military participation. Overall, even before the direction of subsequent events for these dependent regimes became apparent – overthrow or prostration – the withdrawal of the Soviet government from any forward role in the Third World signalled the final extinction of the last remnants of Lenin's world-revolutionary objectives.

Less than five years after Gorbachev's assumption of office it was made clear that the regimes of the Eastern bloc were to be written off as well. As the direction of policy and events in Moscow revealed themselves, long-stifled popular dissent in the East European countries was able to re-emerge. It found leadership in spontaneously forming democratic and civic forums (in Poland the outlawed but continuing Solidarity), either destroying the regime structures, as in Poland or Hungary, or challenging them with mass demonstrations in the GDR, Czechoslovakia and Romania. The Romanian dictatorship resisted violently and its GDR equivalent wanted to do so, but the former was overwhelmed once the army leadership changed sides and the latter crumpled when informed that it could expect no assistance from the USSR.

The Soviet Union itself was by then on the point of disintegration. As the ideological bindings which gave the state legitimacy loosened and then snapped, nationalist sentiment appeared as an integrative force embracing and separating the multifarious linguistic components of the dying colossus. This was given an institutional framework, ironically, by the purported national autonomy and representative structures that the Soviet constitution accorded to the individual republics of the union.[29] The trend was apparent first in the three Baltic Republics of Estonia, Latvia and Lithuania, where the demand for secession was heard most strongly in the first instance, where it was embraced by some of the local communist leaderships, and where demonstrations around the issue led to deaths as the Soviet military and KGB units attempted to suppress the increasingly confident separatist upsurge.[30] Meantime the economic crisis worsened, bringing in its train social unravelling, with escalating levels of corruption and criminality. The ideological coherence of the CPSU had been destroyed, with competing factions now openly contending against one another and a generally accepted recognition that the party must formally divide in the near future. The political machinery was running out of the control of the leadership. Democratising armies, as Hobsbawm remarks, does not improve their efficiency. Open elections had placed bitter rivals of Gorbachev in key positions of power, such as the Presidency of the Russian Federation, captured by Boris Yeltsin. Political relaxation had permitted the re-emergence not only of dissident communists, social democratic tendencies, proposals for undoing 70-odd years of history with complete restoration of market relations and political pluralism,[31] but even the most sinister elements of monarchism and anti-semitism – sponsored and protected for their own purposes by factions within the state apparatus. As the framework of Marxist-Leninist ideological legitimacy collapsed, nationalist sentiment was on the march at the centre as well as the periphery.

In August 1991 traditionalist elements within the CPSU leadership made a despairing effort to reverse the disintegration of their world by staging a coup (while Gorbachev was absent from Moscow) intended to establish a committee of national salvation with military and police backing that would bypass the increasingly confused constitutional structures of the state and use repression to reassert the endangered Soviet order and the country's role as an international superpower.

The most remarkable characteristic of this revolt of the living dead was its staggering ineptitude. The conspirators broke virtually every rule for successful putsches (such as seizing communications centres and arresting key opponents). Some were even reported to have been drunk at the time. They appear to have thought that merely making their pronouncements would suffice and that Gorbachev, once confronted with the reality, would join them as a figurehead.[32] Most instructively, the attempt was conducted entirely at the high levels of the state: in the most ironic contrast with 1917 imaginable, there wasn't even a pretence at mass mobilisation, to bring the working class – or anybody else – out into the streets in support of this proclaimed reassertion of socialist norms. A platonic call for supporting action in the workplaces was all but universally ignored. Such mobilisation as there was of that sort was carried out by the opponents of the coup, though the public outside Moscow, and most Muscovites as well, remained passive, waiting to see how events would turn out.

They soon turned out badly for the conspirators. Gorbachev refused to co-operate. Even more importantly, the military and KGB chiefs, though the plotters had made a particular appeal to them and their programme must have had some attractiveness, turned away, fearful of large-scale mutiny and the prospect of civil war. The enterprise speedily fell apart, with Yeltsin, who had stood in the limelight as public symbol of the new democracy, the principal gainer. When he (quite unconstitutionally) declared the CPSU to be outlawed, a surge of popular fury swept the party into oblivion (temporarily as it turned out), demolished its organisation, seized its property and defaced its symbols. No class-conscious masses rushed to its defence. Despite its pretensions to be the leading force in society, the guardian of the present and the future, the party had been incapable of any coherent response to the attempted coup or even finding a quorum for its central committee. It had become a parasitic excrescence on Soviet society, one which had debilitated the body almost to the point of death and itself died some time since of internal rot. In the end it collapsed almost as easily and comprehensively as the Tsarist regime in March 1917. The Soviet Union itself soon followed it into history, with the independence of the constituent republics being formally recognised (in their Union borders) and the USSR pronounced dead at the end of 1991.

'Actually Existing Socialism' in Perspective

That is what happened. As to why it happened, one of the best and most succinct summaries of the reasons for the overthrow are to be found in Eric Hobsbawm's *Age of Extremes* (pp. 480–95), where they are placed in the historic context of Soviet development. Hobsbawm's argument in essence is that in its industrialisation drive of the 1930s and the postwar reconstruction the Soviet Union created what was in effect a nineteenth-century economy of iron and smoke, organised by a massively inefficient central planning apparatus rather than the market, then proceeded to export the model to the other nations of the bloc. Nuclear power, military and space technology were later added to this, but did not alter the foundations of the system, and so far as electronics and computerisation were concerned, actually existing socialism persisted in the stone age. Such economies, he goes on to argue, retained viability so long as they remained insulated from the West by the rigours of the first Cold War and its 1960s aftermath, but once they started to open up in the 1970s, tempted by high oil prices and easy loans, their vulnerability was exposed. This combined with the suddenly imposed demands of the second Cold War – which strained even the prodigious resources of the US economy – to bring them down. The argument, which seems convincing, mirrors that of Trotsky and his followers, who predicted from the 1930s that the power of the world market would sooner or later overwhelm the project of socialism in a single country.

For a left trying to assess the meaning of the debacle for its own situation and future, the even more significant question is whether it need necessarily have happened – and beyond that how 'accidental' or otherwise was the the ascendancy of Stalinism and the course upon which this regime set the Soviet state and subsequently the bloc.

Could Stalinism itself have been avoided? When examined from a micro-historical viewpoint Stalin's emergence as the 'autocrat of all the Russias' following the revolution appears as a series of contingent accidents, some of them highly improbable and any of which might as readily have turned out otherwise. Without the unexpected death of the Central Committee Secretary, Yakov Sverdlov, in 1919 he would never have been appointed General Secretary in the first place; that office in itself would not have given him decisive political leverage in the Politburo had he not been co-opted by Zinoviev and Kamanev in furtherance of their rivalry with Trotsky, in which case Lenin's Testament would have ensured his demotion; for all his organisational power he would not have been able to defeat his former partners had he not been able to find a political ally in another renowned Old Bolshevik, Nikolai Bukharin.

All this is not to deny that Stalin, as well as being a brutal and machiavellian dissimulator, was a skilled and intelligent politician. His great enemy grievously underestimated him in pouring scorn on his theoretical capacity and stigmatising him as a 'grey blur'. Nevertheless Trotsky was undoubtedly correct in defining Stalin's role as that of representing a bureaucratic stratum which had coalesced in the party and state, rather than a *diabolus ex machina* who had arisen out of nowhere to pervert an otherwise pristine revolutionary regime.

Where Trotsky was wrong was in imagining that this stratum was only or largely the expression of the primitive socio-economic state of the country rendered more primitive by the searing traumas of war, revolution and civil war; or of the postponement of international revolution. In the circumstances of 1920s Soviet Russia, Weber or even Michels would have been better guides than Marx, even though their theoretical models of bureaucratisation had been built around very different societies. True, the utter economic prostration of 1921 had been tackled by the reinstitution of market relations – even the state-owned enterprises had to function according to market criteria – thereby paradoxically turning the industrial working class, such as it was, into the Cinderella of the Soviet household. Consequently the administrative apparatus, staffed or at least controlled down to its most basic units by party members, was enmeshed, and necessarily so, in production and exchange relations driven by market imperatives and the material accumulation which unavoidably accompanied them. Overwhelming temptation existed to take advantage of the opportunities, provided by relations with Nepmen (the petty traders) and kulaks, which the centre tried ineffectually to counter with regular 'purges'[33] but these in their turn only became occasions for further corruption.

Even prior to Lenin's incapacity the problem had become largely uncontrollable and probably would have been so even supposing every Soviet communist had been steeped in Marxism and started out with an impeccably principled character. But the opposite was the case in reality. Only five years beforehand the Bolsheviks had been a party of a few thousand revolutionaries concentrating on the destruction of the state. They had subsequently taken upon themselves the responsibility of running it in unimaginably difficult circumstances. The ranks of the party had swelled enormously between March and November 1917, further during the civil war, and most of all after victory. The inundation of new recruits inevitably diluted and modified the character of the organisation.[34] The mechanisms of party education and training could not cope and anyway there were more vitally urgent things to think about. Those who joined in 1917 did so for the most part because of the Bolsheviks' immediate slogans. While the issue of the civil war remained in doubt nobody was likely to become a member for careerist reasons, but sincerity of motivation did not give immediate access to political understanding nor administrative competence. After the Red victory however a party card became the passport to positions of authority and relative privilege.

In short, as an administrative machine – not always a very efficient one – the Communist Party was fulfilling a function totally different from the one it had been created for. That it was able to do so with even a minimal degree of success says a great deal for the determination and historic confidence of its leaders. But it was unquestionably a negation of democracy, Soviet or any other sort. Only the iron harness provided by the CPSU could hold together a state compounded of the twentieth century and the Middle Ages, under perpetual threat of external attack and internal disintegration. No doubt some of the characteristics Lenin had tried to instil into the party in its early days (with indifferent success) fitted it for the role. In principle if not initially in practice the structure of the Bolshevik organisation was intensely hierarchical and authoritarian: once it was in power and facing emergency conditions these Jacobin principles came into their own and found full expression.

Although every one of the principal Bolshevik leaders (and most of the second-rank ones) was of middle-class extraction the party adhered to the naive assumption that politically or socially reprehensible acts were directly linked to the contamination of its body by alien classes and their inherently anti-socialist ideologies. Consequently in the early years of its power the party persisted in blaming its internal problems upon an excess of middle-class elements in the membership and corresponding deficiency in working-class recruits. Indeed most of the original working-class cadre had been lost in the course of the civil war, on the battlefield, through the collapse of industry or by absorption into the administrative apparatus.

Setting workers to supervise state bureaucrats and drafting more of them into the party was assumed to be the starting point of a solution to the proliferating bureaucratic jungle which was rooting itself on the soil of the workers' state, together with the petty authoritarianism and corruption which accompanied it. Such measures only served to exacerbate the problems. The Workers' and Peasants' Inspectorate (Rabkrin) – under Stalin's tutelage – merely added a yet further layer of uncontrollable bureaucratic inefficiency, and changing the social composition of the party in the absence of any oppositional political space made no discernible difference.

If the institutions of Soviet state and society, from soviets to trade unions, had become hollowed out in the sense of losing all autonomy and degenerating into tools for the party's enforcement of its will, the same thing had effectively happened to the party in that its rank and file had been divested of all independent initiative and its lower organs become nothing other than transmission belts for decisions taken at the centre. By Lenin's death even the Central Committee itself had been turned into not much more than a rubber stamp for whatever the Politburo, in theory a subordinate committee, chose to decree. Even elections to positions of responsibility had become largely meaningless, with outcomes decided in advance, and at the lower levels often superseded by appointment from the centre.

In the circumstances it would have been more than a miracle if the state had not passed from being the dictatorship of the proletariat, if it ever was, to being and remaining the dictatorship of the party centre. While Russia persisted in impoverished isolation the only alternatives lay between reversion to market relations in their entirety, with corresponding political institutions, and the forcible and coercive prolongation of the party-state by methods which represented the negation of democratic norms in both state and party. The one development which might have transformed the situation would have been the realisation of the revolution's original hopes – its expansion westward and the creation of alternative centres of revolutionary power. The adoption of 'socialism in a single country' underscored the effective though naturally not the rhetorical abandonment of such expectations.

Was 'socialism in a single country' the original sin which ultimately ensured the damnation of all the hopes, labour and blood invested in achieving it? Or could it, under a more civilised and enlightened political direction, free from the pressures of invasion and the Cold War, have been made to work and evolved by slow stages from authoritarian to democratic forms? In historical perspective it appears clear that the answer to the latter question is that it almost certainly could not. For a start, quite apart from the arms race, the targets and objectives, the norms at which this socialism aimed, were set by the industrialised West. The intrinsic direction of these economies, driven by the inbuilt imperatives of capital and regardless of all the detours imposed by war and slump, was towards high mass consumption, a trend evident from at least the last quarter of the nineteenth century, and one with which the centrally planned economy could not hope to compete. It was a contest into which the Soviet Union was irresistibly pulled by 'peaceful co-existence' and 'peaceful competition', for which Khrushchev's 1961 speech raised the banner.

The point was recognised in a perverse way by the communist regimes which denounced individualist mass consumption as a desirable objective and asserted the virtues of collectivist poverty and the superiority of moral-political incentives against material ones. The first of these was the Chinese, and accusations around such points featured prominently in their tirades at the time of the rupture; but a similar approach applied with variations to the Cubans and the North Koreans. The Cuban economy was severely retarded by the US blockade and the other two lagged far behind the USSR industrially, in each case it could be that all three were making a virtue out of necessity, but their political instinct also told them, correctly, that the USSR and European regimes were embarking on a race that they could never win.

The race was not simply in the production of material goods. To win it the Soviet state and bloc would have been obliged to uproot all the traditions established since 1928 that had become taken for granted elements of its existence. These involved the suppression of civil society, in the sense that every institution and even voluntary association beyond the elementary family unit, from the educational system through the periodical press to sports clubs were directly linked to the party-state, accountable to it and obliged to reflect its values as part of a compulsory ongoing historical project. From this followed the sheer *intrusiveness* of the state, virtually annihilating private space, and meaning that in every sphere of public communication, from breakfast to supper and from creche to geriatric hospital, the citizen was bombarded with a propagandist message (often at odds with experienced reality) which was more likely to turn off its recipients than to imbue them with the desired consciousness.[35] It amounted to a form of enforced permanent political mobilisation for all the population, the only comparable examples outside the bloc coming from states faced with overwhelming emergencies such as total war and postwar reconstruction, as in the UK between 1940 and 1948. The lesson from that was that voluntary mobilisation of that sort could only be sustained for a limited number of years before the public was infected with alienation and cynicism – certainly not as a permanent state of being.[36] The socialist bloc was unique in that its regimes tried to make its populations live politics in a relentless and permanent fashion. There have been many worse tyrannies, both in the twentieth century and in previous eras, than the regimes of post-Stalinist 'actually existing socialism', but these, like the ones of representative democracy, tended to partition off politics into a separate realm[37] and only to intervene in the sphere of civil society when actively threatened by developments taking place there.

The alternative to 'goulash communism'[38] therefore was not a regime of consciously understood and accepted limitations on excessive consumption and resource depletion, underpinned by harmoniously balanced and environmentally-aware production, but 'barrack socialism' dependent on authoritarian coercion and cultural repression, reaching its grisly endpoint under the Khmer

Rouge in Cambodia between 1975 and 1979. In any case, the passion for politically pure poverty in China did not last very long and within less than two decades of the cultural revolution individual enrichment became not merely permissible but the governing strategy – although no less authoritarian than the Maoist regime had been. North Korea and Cuba, though still professing adherence to the former principles have clearly reached the end of their tethers and are unlikely to be able to sustain them very much longer (see Chapter 4). Within a global economy which had developed, for better or worse, into one dominated by mass consumption of the products of advanced technology (agricultural as well as industrial), socialism in one country or one bloc never stood a chance. The notion that it could generate from its own resources, in competition with the West, something approximating to the 'society of abundance' never amounted to more than a utopian mirage. But for the binding pressures of wartime emergency followed by permanent external threat it would probably have fallen even sooner than it did, as Hobsbawm surmises.

We can conclude that the decision of the mid-1920s to embark on this course was a fatal one. Had its original conception of the NEP as 'market socialism' been continued, instead of being violently wrenched by Stalin in a changed direction, it is overwhelmingly likely, all authorities agree, that the pressure of the mass of peasant producers and private distribution networks would have dislodged or else defined out of recognition the communists' political rule and brought the Soviet experiment to a conclusion. The USSR would have anticipated the fate that the Chinese Revolution is currently undergoing. What would have occurred thereafter would have depended on whether or not the Nazis succeeded in seizing power in Germany, and whether the world slump had come to an end. That the latter would have happened is a reasonably safe prediction – in long perspective the First World War and the slump can be seen to have marked not the bankruptcy of capitalism but exceptionally violent adjustments in its global evolution. In reality it was restored by the Second World War, eventuating in subsequent US hegemony, but was headed for that destination anyway, and would almost certainly have got there by some other route, although probably over a longer timespan, if war had not acted as an accelerator.[39]

We can push the argument back still further. If the international revolution was not on the agenda in 1917–21 – and all the evidence indicated overwhelmingly that it was not – then the Bolsheviks' initial conviction that their own undertaking was certainly doomed in the long or short term can be seen to have been well-founded. Admittedly Lenin himself, even while the new state was fighting for its life, had shifted somewhat in his opinion and introduced a new term into

his political equations.[40] Even if the Western proletariats failed to
follow rapidly in the footsteps of the Russians, he considered that
imperialism could be decisively undermined and brought to
destruction by the (so it was thought) rapidly maturing colonial
revolution. When this erupted the main economic prop of state
monopoly capitalism would be destroyed and revolutionary advance
would then become irresistible if it had not previously done so. But
in any case the colonial revolution was not nearly so far matured
as Lenin hoped; it was delayed for another three decades and
would almost certainly have been delayed further but for the impact
of the Second World War. Furthermore, the imperial powers, as
it proved, were perfectly capable of getting along without exercising
direct political authority over their dependencies. It was useful to
them, but so long as the economies of what would become known
as the Third World remained tied into the global market system,
not vitally necessary.

The Bolshevik revolution – or rather their continued grip on power,
for in principle they could have ended Russian participation in the
war, distributed the land and then bowed out – made sense *only*
on the presumption that international revolution was imminent or
a decade away at most. A state founded as a stronghold for and
inspirer of such revolution did not have the potential for long-term
survival, either as an accepted member in the (capitalist) community
of nations, nor internally, because of the permanent state of
mobilisation its international role obliged it to impose upon its
citizens. Up to 1928 it could have – hypothetically – survived in
name by formally renouncing all revolutionary intentions, embracing
nationalist ideology and turning over to the market the state-
controlled sectors of its economy – as the Chinese state is doing
now. Once collectivisation and the industrialisation drive were
underway however, there was no turning back; the allegedly socialist
and revolutionary identity had to be asserted unreservedly and indeed
provided the justification for the suffering and privations which the
population was made to endure.

The assumption that the essential problems would have been
solved by international proletarian revolution occurring before
Stalin's emergence is however wholly misplaced, for it evades the
question of how the political power of the international working
class could actually have been translated into the management of
the international economy. A 'United Socialist States of Europe'
(or of Europe and America) would rapidly have run into the same
problem as manifested itself in the USSR and its bloc partners despite
(or even because of) the international economy's enormously
higher level – namely, how to co-ordinate without a market the
infinitude of specific producing and consuming decisions. Not

even the most elementary necessities of such an undertaking had begun to be considered.

We can only regret though that the international working class was never given the opportunity to try. Whatever the outcome, it could scarcely have been worse than what the remainder of the twentieth century was actually to bring. Historically, however different it may once have looked, the balance of social and political forces was such that the socialist revolution was never on the cards in the states of advanced economy. That being so, 'actually existing socialism' represented the reality of socialism in action as the lesser segment of a divided world. It must be concluded furthermore, that providing it survived the military assaults levelled at it, the bloc would in all probability, even supposing external circumstances to have been different from what they actually were, have evolved towards an endpoint of Brezhnevite stagnation and subsequent breakdown as soon as it became fully exposed to the disintegrative forces of the world market, in commodities, capital – and ideas.

CHAPTER 4

The Fragments

Statistical relationships can be extremely misleading. It has been observed that whereas prior to 1989–91 the number of people living under ostensibly Marxist-Leninist regimes amounted to approximately 1.7 billion, the figure following the upheavals worked out at around 1.4 billion – a warning perhaps not to be too Eurocentric in reaching conclusions. To superficial observation it might even appear that the figure was in the process of creeping upwards again, for in several of the Eastern bloc states, the former CPs, under changed titles, have topped the polls in democratic elections and formed or participated in the formation of governments. The Russian case has been on the face of things even more sensational. The CP, which was outlawed in 1991, and, even after the ban was lifted, then plunged into an advanced state of disintegration, with parts breaking off to form contending successor parties, not only re-consolidated itself but topped the poll in the parliamentary election of 1995 – without even having to drop its communist title.[1]

Appearances however could not be more misleading. The events of 1991 marked not only the end of the Soviet regime and the Soviet Union, but the end of the communist global-historic project which had been sustained, in however attenuated a form, since 1917. Almost all the surviving or successor parties in the communist or former communist states, and likewise the existing CPs, which have never been in power, pursue wholly local agendas. Moreover they do so under the acceptance that there is no viable alternative to global capitalism: the most that is attainable is a strong placement in the world market and some mitigation by government policy of the social costs. Their stances, particularly of those in power, have therefore moved increasingly in nationalist directions and have already become, or will soon be, indistinguishable from a nationalist position resting on market foundations. The regimes in China and Vietnam have both consciously committed themselves to developing options along those lines. Large-scale privatisation of publicly-owned assets is as yet ruled out, more on grounds of technical difficulty than of principle, but marketisation is proceeding with speed and private entrepreneurship being encouraged wherever possible. Privitisation, if some way down the line, would appear inevitable in the long term.

The Unreconciled

It will be best to begin with the two regimes which have refused to follow this path and maintain postures of defiant commitment to the principles of an earlier era. They differ enormously in character, to the degree that it makes little sense to place them in the same classification for any other reason than that they both had their origins in the spreading postwar reach of international communism.

The North Korean regime emerged at the end of the Second World War out of a popular resistance movement against Japanese occupation on the Korean peninsula. Its establishment in the North was therefore indigenous although assisted by Soviet forces, in the same manner as its frustration in the South was determined by US intervention. The guerrilla leader, Kim Il Sung, though sponsored as leader of the new state by the Soviet and Chinese communists, appears nevertheless to have been a popular and widely-respected figure; the land reforms which were implemented in the North satisfied long-cherished peasant aspirations.[2] The unspeakably destructive war from 1950 to 1953 against the US and its allies demonstrated no absence of popular support and no sign of eagerness to collaborate with the occupying forces during the period when most of the state was overrun. It has been remarked that between the 1940s and 1989 North Korea was the only Marxist-Leninist country to experience 'liberation', but that no lessons regarding political or social reconstruction appear to have been drawn from the episode by Western Cold War academics or policy institutes.

In short, North Korea, in the years following the war, with rapid and successful reconstruction, appeared, despite the regime's unyielding authoritarianism, to hold every advantage over the squalid US-client dictatorship in the south of the peninsula. The subsequent transformation has been both startling and horrific. North Korea in the 1990s has the appearance of having been planned by someone who read *Nineteen Eighty-Four* and thought it a good idea. As the centrally controlled economic base deteriorated, so demands were intensified upon the country's major resource, its peasantry, reducing them in general to conditions of absolute destitution and privation, enforced by an implacable and pervasive police and party apparatus. The political leadership and its central figure in particular became a textbook illustration of Lord Acton's dictum on the corruptions of power. Kim Il Sung grew into a magnified version of Big Brother. Everything that was achieved in North Korea, real or imagined, was attributed to him personally. Culture was virtually abolished in the country to pander to his cult of personality: The Great Leader – his official title – was even designated the author of every new text of the few published in the country. 'Autonomy has been sucked upwards in an irresistible vortex from the citizens to the leader and his retinue.'[3] The longest-surviving dictator of the second half of the century, Kim's eventual interment in a mausoleum dwarfing Lenin's was followed by the succession of his son, the officially titled Dear Leader – the first example of the hereditary principle being applied in a Marxist-Leninist state.

The most well-informed commentators confess themselves at a loss to account for the horrific scale of the deterioration or the nature of the political culture which allowed the megalomania of a single individual to devour an entire society in a manner far surpassing the Pharaohs, the Caesars or even Stalin, but any tentative explanation would focus on three elements. In the first place this 'relic of the most intense arena of the Cold War'[4] continued to be threatened as no other member of the communist bloc by renewed invasion or nuclear annihilation at any moment and with an implacable enemy entrenched not many miles from its capital, it existed on a constant emergency footing. Secondly, taking advantage of these circumstances 'Kim Il Sung built a centralised party of iron discipline and gradually purged one after another of the factions other than his own until he was in unquestioned control and absolute loyalty to him the touchstone of political purity'[5] – the parallels with Stalin are striking. Thirdly, the regime drew upon a pre-existing Confucian culture equating power with virtue and transmogrified it into the untranslatable concept of 'Juche', which incorporates both the notion of independence vis-a-vis the outside world and the utter dependence of the culture upon the leader. The relationship of both concept and regime to Marxism is purely nominal and at the time of writing the country is reported to be threatened with famine and hoping for relief from the South. It would appear unlikely that the regime can hope to last a great deal longer, but in any event it is certainly not going to provide a beacon of inspiration for anybody.[6]

Very different considerations apply to the other example, Cuba, now the only regime left to which unreconciled communists of the Soviet bloc era can still accord unqualified approval. Material conditions are straitened in the extreme, more on account of the US blockade than the government's economic failures, though the latter are undoubtedly present. In addition, the state of siege in which the country has been placed since the early 1960s, together with armed assistance to friendly regimes in Africa, had produced an enormously inflated military establishment. Circumstances were harsh even at the time when the USSR and Eastern Europe supplied large-scale aid; now that has disappeared they have become desperate – and yet the regime's rationing mechanisms and welfare facilities still give the island a higher overall standard of living than any other

Latin American country. Extremes of wealth and poverty are not a feature of its cities.

Authoritarian and repressive though Castro's government is – which it can claim to justify by the ever-present menace of Yankee imperialism 150 miles across the water and the gangster-run Miami exiles waiting the hour of their revenge – it is not a terror regime, and some aura of its romantic beginnings still adheres to it. Its leaders defiantly proclaim their continuing attachment to the principles of international Marxist revolution and there is little doubt that they would strive to re-ignite it on the Latin American continent if they were in a position to do so. However it must be reckoned that there is probably little positive enthusiasm left for the regime among the population at large. The generation which had direct personal experience of the Batista tyranny and benefited immediately from the revolution is ageing, while their successors have known only consumer shortages, confinement to the island, restricted culture and endless mobilising exhortations. Experience shows that nations will accept such sacrifices and respond to such appeals for a period of time when they believe them to be justified by worthy purposes, but not for ever. Castro is in the position of a lone survivor, abandoned by history, and if socialism in one country, when that country covered half a continent, proved impossible, it is all the more impossible in one small island.[7] It is hardly to be doubted that the regime, like the North Korean, is doomed, though unlike the latter, many will regret its passing. The only thing that could conceivably save it would be a renewed upsurge of left-wing revolution throughout the world, and that appears very much less than likely.

Vietnam and China

The ruling communist parties of China and Vietnam (with its protectorate, Laos),[8] whatever their problems, are in an entirely different league. Both govern large strong economies, more than viable in the long-term, and in the case of China, a potential titan. It is clear that here every effort is being made to secure integration into the world market economy, as is testified to not least by the commercial disputes China engages in from time to time with the United States. The fact that the state has evolved outside US hegemony and that its legal system is not integrated into the international order enforced by the US is of positive advantage, for example in the area of computer software, where it has proved impossible to prevent the piracy of American designs. China remains a coherent and well-ordered society, resting on its ancient foundations and with resilient civil structures well equipped to take advantage of commercial opportunity, while possessing a regime resting on the foundations of its Stalinist past and no less well equipped to control and suppress the tensions and discontents generated by the new course.

Two particularly pertinent questions are why the collapse of world communism affected China so differently from its Soviet counterpart[9] and whether – admittedly now of only abstract interest – the Soviet regime might have survived on the same basis as the Chinese one succeeded in doing. It is clear that striking similarities existed between the economic policies pursued under Deng and the *perestroika* programme initiated by Gorbachev.[10] There was however no counterpart in China to *glasnost*, and popular demand for extended liberties was mercilessly suppressed regardless of international condemnation. The established Chinese leaders therefore, unlike those in the Kremlin, were able to retain control of the situation: it could be claimed that they had a better strategic perspective and were indifferent to outside approval or otherwise in pursuing it. The possibility cannot be excluded altogether that a more forceful display of will on the part of the Soviet authorities might have produced a very different outcome, although that would have been very difficult to carry through in the context of the second Cold War and the need to retain as much credibility as possible with the Western publics.

However there was a far more weighty structural differentiation between the two situations. The USSR was a much more urbanised society, with a large part of its workforce concentrated in giant industrial complexes – and its agriculture was collectivised so that the rural workforce was also gathered in huge centrally organised enterprises, all operating in a non-market economy. The individual members of the workforce were (and are) to an extraordinary extent dependent not only for employment and wages but for social and cultural services upon their particular enterprise and plant. When the central plan which co-ordinated everything stalled the system began to unravel. Hyperinflation took off as money was created and borrowed recklessly to keep these enterprises functioning; a form of industrial feudalism emerged. If capitalism, in classic Marxist terminology, operates through an anarchy of production the anarchy was compounded and extended beyond measure in the chaotic post-Soviet economy.

The Chinese economy, in embarking upon its transition to the market had the advantage of greater dispersal, a less centralised planning system, and above all an agricultural base where collectivisation had not followed the Soviet model of agrarian factories and where it could be rapidly reversed, as it was in the late 1970s, to general peasant acclaim. It was therefore possible to allow peasant entrepreneurship to flourish and float the still state-owned industrial enterprises upon the sea of a market in primary agricultural products generated by the peasantry. The costs of this success were not negligible. It resulted inevitably in rapid social differentiation in the countryside and the disintegration of the commune structure, with the peasants best placed to take advantage of the new conditions prospering and extending their control over village resources while their less fortunate neighbours found themselves pushed towards the status of an agricultural semi-proletariat even more immersed in poverty.

The future development of China is evidently going to hold immense implications for the character of the twenty-first century, but it is manifestly clear that whether its regime evolves without major disruptions or whether a sharp break of some kind occurs, the ideologies of the rulers will be domestically driven, will make no pretence of interest in revolutionary developments elsewhere in the world, and their concern with external relations will be purely great-power ones. Evolving towards a powerful authoritarian national capitalism and with the communist inheritance of the Chinese revolution fading increasingly into the background, there is no prospect that the Chinese state of the future could ever fulfil the role for the left internationally that the Soviet one used to occupy.[11]

The Soviet Bloc

According to one report the destitute in St Petersburg, including children and war veterans, are dying by the score of cold and starvation.[12] This may be exaggerated, but what is unquestionable is that for the population of the Russian Federation the end of the USSR has proved to be one of the great calamities suffered by them in the course of the present century. The most positive thing that can be said about it is that it has not produced a generalised bloodbath nor mass famine. Both of these are negative virtues and neither can be confidently predicted as continuing certainties. The matter has been summed up in the comment that Russia is rapidly being returned to the status of a Third World nation and experiencing the 'political economy of disintegration'. If the gibe about Upper Volta with rockets was true before 1991 it is all the more emphatically justified today.

Economically, politically and ideologically the right has won out all along the line: the left as an organised force in Russia at present has to all intents and purposes ceased to exist. It was evident that, in the two years or so prior to the final catastrophe, the CPSU was far gone in decay and that disparate and incompatible political tendencies which had been forced together under the umbrella of a single monolithic party were setting out their own agendas and manoeuvring for position. The introduction of open elections to state assemblies accelerated the process. At the time a strong and convincing intellectual tendency represented by individuals such as Roy Medvedev and Boris Kagarlitsky appeared to hold out the promise of a genuine Marxist left being recreated within Soviet culture, either in a social democratic or new indigenous guise, probably in the form of a splitting-off from the CPSU.[13] The popular response was missing however. What had been 90 years earlier a doctrine of hope and future promise was in terminal exhaustion following its prolonged cohabitation with Stalin and Brezhnev and the attempted coup in its name of August 1991 finished it off. Not surprisingly, the right, in two contrasting forms, proved formidably stronger.

At first the most successful, and sweeping everything before them, were the imported doctrines of laissez-faire theology. This tendency found its political expression in Boris Yeltsin, who soon pushed aside the unfortunate Gorbachev and acquired temporarily impregnable authority as a result of his performance during the coup. His administrations were formed from the Western-advised ideologues of 'shock therapy', who dreamed of turning Russia into a fully-fledged market economy in the space of a few years or even months. They constituted the more 'international' and sophisticated wing of the former Soviet political class, the people with the technique to handle Russia's insertion into the new world order, implacable 'Westernisers', now bent on establishing themselves as the new ruling stratum of politicians, administrators, financiers and bankers – the top layer of a capitalist class in formation. Some openly hankered for the appearance of a Russian Pinochet who would hold Russia down while the economic surgeons of the Chicago School performed shock therapy (without anaesthetic) upon its body.

Their impatience derived from the reluctance of Russia and the Russian peoples to conform to their prescriptions. A competent and experienced entrepreneurial class failed to spring out of the ground. Instead what emerged was an entrepreneurship of a different sort, a pervasive criminality in the shape of the Russian mafias, parasitic enterprise in the economies of protection rackets, drug peddling, prostitution, political corruption – terrorising honest citizens and indulging in uninhibited gang warfare, reaching such a level of dominance in the consumer economy that prices come to be established by mafias rather than markets, particularly in the consumer street markets.[14] The industrial economy, as we have seen, retreated into its fortified enterprises, operating an economy of what amounted virtually to inter-plant barter. Output and living standards declined catastrophically; the former fell 60 per cent between 1992 and 1996; 30 per cent of the population are estimated to be below the *officially prescribed* poverty line; according to the Moscow police, there are between 250,000 and 300,000 homeless persons in that city.[15] Since shock therapy had involved primarily the abolition of central planning and cuts in real expenditure on social welfare the worst sufferers were citizens dependent directly upon state benefits – the most vulnerable groups in society. These were paid in worthless roubles when only foreign currency was negotiable in the market. The neo-liberal theologians, surveying the results of their endeavours and noting that matters had not turned out quite as expected, prescribed yet larger doses of shock therapy.

The social wasteland created by the free marketeers destroyed their figurehead, Yeltsin, politically, morally and physically. Such conditions, it might be thought, would have been tailor-made for a left revival, but utter rejection of Marxist rhetoric left the victimised populace without theoretical tools to analyse their situation, and older traditions were nearer to hand. The culture of Great-Russian chauvinism and its shadow, anti-semitism, had never really died during the Soviet years, and Stalin in his day had more than toyed with it. *Glasnost*, by a bitter irony, had provided the first opportunity for its open emergence, along with Tsarist nostalgia,[16] in the shape of the organisation *Pamyat* (Memory) founded ostensibly to encourage the preservation of war and other memorials. With growing confidence that it would not be proceeded against, *Pamyat's* anti-semitism grew more vociferous. It set up a paramilitary squad and instigated a violent pogrom in the Writers' Union. The reason for the confidence was that *Pamyat* had contacts and sympathisers in the highest levels of the state and party apparatus.

It was a foretaste of things to come. Those segments of the *nomenklatura* which had not succeeded in climbing aboard the westernising gravy train first of all consolidated themselves around an amalgam of Soviet and nationalist, Russian exclusivist traditions in varying proportions and then, as public disillusionment with the marketisation economic programme developed, broadened out their appeal to the embittered publics of the Federation. They were substantially assisted in this course by the actions of the demagogue Zhirinovsky. His role was to articulate first in brutal and immoderate terms the fears and resentments filling the consciousness of ordinary Russians; his ludicrously named Liberal Democratic Party became an overnight wonder and a source of Western alarm due to its overtly fascist overtones. Zhirinovsky was too much of a clown and lacked the political sensitivity to imitate Hitler, but he created the electoral space which smoother-edged politicians are now making haste to fill. Among those are the individuals who now run the core of the old CPSU, having got rid of its liberalising, social democratic or authentically Marxist elements. The manifesto of this party for the Duma elections of December 1995 or Presidential elections of

1996 had absolutely nothing to say regarding social or economic programmes – what it promised was the vigorous promotion of nationalist agendas, including threats to border states considered to be persecuting Russian minorities and the recreation of a surrogate USSR, together with action to restore law and order. It proclaimed itself 'the party of Gagarin' – not of Lenin. Apart from the name its posture was indistinguishable from that of its overtly nationalist rivals, even if Hillel Ticktin's assertion that the closest British comparison would be the National Front is a pardonable exaggeration.[17]

Most clearly this party has nothing whatsoever to do with socialism or the left and any ideas that its comparative electoral success in 1995 represents a revival of socialist sentiment in Russia could not be more misplaced. The very prevalence of the term 'red-brown coalition' (the alliance, termed the 'Fatherland Front' between the Communist Party of the Russian Federation and the fascistoid nationalists) is an index of how far the former CPSU has moved from being the party of Lenin or even that of his successors, and of how politically and ideologically degenerate it has become. In the former 'heartland and fortress of socialism' the left as a meaningful force has been annihilated, the prostration of its remnants (a few individuals and groupuscules) never been greater – and all without any carnival of blood or sweeping scale of arrests.

Eastern Europe

The dialectic of laissez-faire economics and virulent nationalism has followed a similar yet different course in the former 'people's democracies' from that in the ex-USSR. The most marked difference is that the successors of the ruling communist parties, having been identified in the days of their power with subordination to Moscow, are now not in a position – with the peculiar exception of Slovakia – to appear in ultra-nationalist colours. This has been on the whole to their benefit if not to their advantage, and they have tended to adopt the postures of social democracy – sometimes actually using that name – resigning themselves to the dominance of the market with the hope of controlling its workings at the margin and alleviating some of its more implacable social consequences.

The fall of the party-state regimes in 1989 was brought about by overwhelming popular rejection, able to to express itself once the USSR had withdrawn military protection from its client governments.[18] The actual centres of mobilisation, the groupings who orchestrated the demonstrations, and pushed the revolutionary process forward, were mostly the civic and democratic forums made up of democratically-minded intellectual dissidents, frequently including oppositional elements from within the ruling parties themselves. In terms of the traditional right–left spectrum their political status may be considered ambiguous but it is clear that they never dreamt of dismantling the systems of full employment and basic but comprehensive welfare provision established under the old regimes. Perhaps they can be thought of as the last flicker of 'socialism with a human face'.[19] Their ascendancy however, political or ideological, was short-lived in the extreme, amateurs that they were, and in no time they had been pushed aside by the professionals, hard-faced men who had done well out of the liberation. In some cases, for example Slovakia, these were the old leaders, who had opportunely changed their colours.[20] In the GDR it was the West German Christian Democrats, who moved in to exploit the new opportunities, in others individuals from the professional classes and state executive positions who had not been members of the communist parties.[21]

The new regimes[22] were barely in place before they were subjected to a double assault, economic and ideological. Opening up their economies and currencies to the world market, which their governments hastened to do, proved catastrophic, not surprisingly, for their industrial bases, which were far in arrears of Western standards of productivity and technology,[23] even in the most developed example, namely Hungary. Enterprises shut down *en masse* and unemployment rocketed. The strategic priority of East European governments came to be to gain admission to the EC and its economic support mechanisms, but the existing EC members enjoying the benefits of that club were understandably in no hurry to open the door to these importunate paupers.[24]

The trends imposed by the market were reinforced as the political intelligentsia, even many who had previously been involved in the civic or democratic forum movements, hurried to the enthusiastic embrace of the laissez-faire ideologies associated with Hayek and Freidman.[25] Western conservative ideologues hastened eastwards to advance the process.[26] Socialism with a human face or social democracy or some balance between private and public ownership, between state and market, was superseded by a vision dominated by images of absolute good and evil in which all the woes of the past were attributed to 'collectivism' and the unconstrained market prescribed as the sovereign remedy for every ill of politics or society. The neatness of the juxtaposition and opposition looked convincing. The theory of neo-classical economics possesses a powerful and compelling logic. According to Hayek, 'If it were the result of deliberate human design [the market] would have been acclaimed as one of the great triumphs of the human mind.'[27] Its central premise, that state planning could not cope with an advanced consumer economy, had been amply demonstrated in the economic sphere and its forcible imposition had been associated with decades of dictatorship, misery and national humiliation. That neo-classicism's other premises were absurd abstractions, deriving from the presumption that unconstrained market relations result in the optimum allocation of resources, was not something that was immediately obvious, and anyone who drew attention to that fact could be stigmatised as a crypto-communist. The most distant theoretical association was sufficient to imply guilt. Eric Hobsbawm has commented that when state control and market individualism come to be perceived as polar opposites the assumption takes hold that conditions at each pole must also be polar opposites – in the same way that the climate is radically different at the North and South Poles ... .

Balanced state budgets became the holy grail and that, in conjunction with the free market ideology, soon spelt the end of systems of social protection. As is regularly the case in economies governed by such principles, women are expected to pick up the pieces and to serve (in both senses of the term) as the privatised social welfare system. Consequently attempts were put in hand to abolish the state-supported facilities relating to maternity and child care that were intended to give some meaning to prescriptions of legal sexual equality. These too could be condemned by association with the discredited past. In Poland this threat has been especially pressing due to the political and ideological influence of the Catholic Church, which made it a priority objective to criminalise abortion. These developments have been resisted, but to what effect remains unclear.

It is also in Poland that 'shock therapy' has been most systematically applied,[28] although cushioned in some degree by an unusually high inflow of foreign investment compared with other East European countries. The impact of the marketisation programmes has been to reduce living standards across the entire region, even in Romania and Albania where they were already about as low as could be imagined under their neo-Stalinist regimes. It has naturally provoked social and political tensions, with one result being the breakup of Czechoslovakia.

The Czech lands were, since the formation of the state, the most developed and dynamic half of the federation[29] and indeed, leaving aside the special case of the GDR, the part of the bloc best placed to take advantage of the new conditions. There marketisation and privatisation were systematically applied, and the pale alternative offered by the former communist parties in other states is absent because of the total discrediting of the CPCz due to its role after 1968. Although a Czech communist party still exists under that name and receives a respectable vote it is, unlike the reformed CPs elsewhere in Eastern Europe, isolated and marginalised. A thoroughgoing witchhunt, focused on the academic world and the media, has been pursued against anyone associated in any way with left-wing principles – and this has included former communist dissidents from the era of the Prague Spring. The fact that they had communist connections is held to damn them regardless of their commitment to socialism with a human face and also regardless of their persecution by the previous authorities. Many inspirers of the witchhunt held administrative positions under the old regime, but they excuse themselves by drawing an impassable line between the *party* and the *state*. Bad faith is evident, the expression of guilty consciousness, but in more practical terms the attack is designed to marginalise and intimidate potential intellectual articulators of popular grievance. The new rulers have certainly experienced some success in turning the Czech Republic into a Western-style economy, with industries newly implanted – the most flourishing of those being tourism, drug trafficking and prostitution.[30] The programme however provoked a social and national reaction in the other less developed part of the federation, under demands for the protection of Slovak economy and culture. In this climate the Slovak former party bosses in new political garb, being the most immediately available people with political know-how, were able to present themselves as the people's defenders against the economic devastation emanating from Prague and to retain office on a nationalist platform. The prevalent sentiment in the Czech lands was that the Slovaks constituted an economic, political, and cultural deadweight and nuisance, and so the federation was sundered, with ill will accompanied by relief on both sides.

Throughout the region a similar pattern has been repeated with local variations. As with Russia, hasty and unconsidered adoption of free market models pushed by academic economists from the West, Reaganites and Thatcherites hostile in principle to collective or state-guided solutions, has brought about a response that grows out of chauvinist nationalism; the ethnic community appearing to provide the only stable point of reference in a quicksand of social disintegration. Such nationalism is aggressive, exclusivist, scapegoating and predatory when the opportunity offers. It bases itself upon the simple and brutal proposition that if resources are scarce you try to take them from somebody else, and has no scruples about advancing an impossible programme of national economic self-sufficiency as a block to the pitiless global market. It easily topples over into one or another version of neo-fascism. There is no shortage of traditions and history in Eastern Europe for such growths to feed upon, as the reconstitution of the interwar Iron Guard in Romania shows only too clearly. Less blatant revivals have occurred in all the states of the region.[31] The logical end of the road is exemplified in former Yugoslavia, where a smooth progression of the former Serbian and Croatian communist elites into ferocious nationalist demagogues[32] of mutually hostile stripes was made easy by their previous roles as upholders of Yugoslav independence against the Soviet bloc.

However, the region as a whole has – so far – avoided taking this route. The events in Yugoslavia were not predetermined, they were the outcome of specific decisions made by particular political leaders who chose to yield to chauvinist pressures rather than mobilise the best aspects of Titoism to resist them. A factor present in most East European states (including the Baltic Republics) but not in Russia is a currently viable social democracy, either constructed out of the ruins of the former communist parties or a revived indigenous tradition. Its ambitions are modest, its aims limited, its posture towards global capitalism one of deference, and it has no international resonance. It is also a fragile plant, dependent for survival on socio-economic conditions not deteriorating too much further, but at the same time the only alternative available to demented market individualism or rampant nationalism. For the moment it appears to be in the ascendant electorally – how long that can continue is another question.

Two Anomalies

There exist also two communist parties whose situations to all appearances have been scarcely affected by the debacle of the international movement. Both are powerful organisations with extensive popular support. Neither governs a sovereign state, and so both have been exempted from the fate which has overtaken every communist regime, collapsed or surviving, but both are much more than merely strong oppositions within capitalist social formations. They are also very different in character.

These are the communist parties of West Bengal and of South Africa. The former in fact is part of the Communist Party of India (Marxist), but West Bengal is the only area in which it has taken root as a mass reality, with a membership of around 200,000. Following the establishment of the Comintern the desperate conditions of the Indian peasantry and emergent industrial working class enabled the CPI, despite intense persecution, to become strongly established on the subcontinent by 1939. These political assets were largely squandered first by the party's refusal to support the independence struggle while Britain was allied to the USSR and subsequently by adventurist attempts to seize power at the time of Independence. The CPI was not destroyed or even marginalised but it lost any hope it might have had of superseding the Congress movement. However in West Bengal the fusion of a specific culture with the implantation of communist politics among sections of the rural poor in an area where the evolution of agrarian class relations had assumed distinctive forms under a British administration stretching back to 1757, enabled a very well organised and disciplined regional party to recover from the disaster. As the principal component of a Left Front, this party has actually led the local state government of West Bengal since 1977. It has established deep penetration into local popular organisations, more in the countryside than the capital Calcutta, although the latter also is saturated with its symbols. The fact that no electoral rival can displace it, despite embarrassments in recent years over corrupt practices and electoral violence, is evidence enough of its mass standing, its ability to satisfy the expectations of its constituency – 'The land reform programme has been the most ambitious and successful in India'[33] – and to avoid alienating the support which it enjoys, expressed through a system of elected village councils which have 'given the rural poor a political voice for the first time'.[34]

What it cannot do however is to transform the circumstances of those same masses. Without sovereign power it cannot decree the expropriation of wealth or capital (supposing it wished to do so) and even less can it control the currency, external trade or decree a centrally-planned industrial revolution.[35] Perhaps its lack of sovereign authority serves it well in this respect, for it excuses it from having to undertake these things and handle the turmoil that would ensue. On the other hand, its constitutional situation (the central government could close it down at any time) drastically limits its options and it can only alleviate in the most minimal degree the indescribable poverty and wretchedness of the Bengali masses. Calcutta is also the city of Mother Theresa. Nor is there the slightest reason to expect that the example of West Bengal is going to spread to other regions of India. It remains and will remain a purely local phenomenon – a polity under permanent siege and doubtless not impregnable.

The situation of the South African Communist Party at the end of apartheid rule was in some senses reminiscent of that of the French or Italian CPs at the time of the liberation. Its standing was high, earned in decades of underground struggle, and its relations with the mass organisation of African emancipation, the African National Congress, were better than amicable. On the formation of the ANC-led coalition government its leaders for the most part assumed responsible positions in the state. Their role was such as to lead to accusations that the CPSA was the real power behind the government and was responsible for guiding and directing the ANC strategy – in effect that the CP was the brains of the new regime.[36]

There is probably at least an element of truth in these allegations, and it may well be that some ANC ministers are unacknowledged members of the party. The irony is that it would make very little difference whether the claims were true or not, for any South African government would be compelled by circumstances to pursue much the same course as the current one is doing – except that the influence of politically sophisticated communists might enable them to do it more easily. The postwar French and Italian CPs were absolved from having to take life-and-death decisions on their own account – Stalin did it on their behalf. Their South African successors are forced to rely upon their own judgment and are confronted with a double paradox. The first is that they are compelled, whatever their exact role may be, to participate in trying to guide the new South Africa towards a regime of stable capitalism with not too dramatically enhanced rights for labour – one which capital is pleased to welcome as a bargain price for political stability and international acceptance. Equal political rights is to be regarded as the only revolutionary discontinuity and thereafter social and economic advance is to be slow and cumulative, never tolerating a hint of instability.[37] The rhetoric is readily to hand – how could anybody risk endangering by irresponsible demands or actions the stupendous achievement of liberation? The CPSA therefore finds itself out of its own experience doing much the same kind of thing that its French and Italian counterparts did at Stalin's command. Without a doubt this is the sensible line to pursue, but it has no international revolutionary implications. The other paradox is that the party feels obliged to operate in the background lest its name, the reality notwithstanding, should frighten the international community. This of course fuels suspicions of backstairs intrigue and secret agendas when almost certainly none are present.

The CPSA is the prisoner of its local conditions as much as the CP in West Bengal. A fanciful hope might imagine that if a revolutionary or even radical left were to be revived throughout the world the communist parties of South Africa and West Bengal could form nuclei around which such formations would be able to coalesce. The reality shows on the contrary that they have relevance only to Bengali and South African circumstances.

The Others

Communist parties all around the world experienced the collapse of the bloc and the USSR at a time when they themselves were almost universally in retreat from the general crisis of the movement's self-belief, refracted through particular national circumstances. Response has been varied, and generally speaking much has depended on the individual party's size and standing – a minuscule organisation, to an extent, has greater room for flexibility than one which has acquired an extensive institutional base and has responsibilities for great accumulations of property and large numbers of personnel.

One response has been to soldier on, even to the extent of retaining the communist name, but this means now doing so without any meaningful strategic objective or long-term perspective. Such has been the option followed by the large CPs of France[38] and Portugal. Not accidentally perhaps, these were the parties traditionally renowned as the most Stalinist in Western Europe. The same course has been followed by the insignificant CP of the US[39] which possesses, as Eric Hobsbawm puts it, as much influence in that state as Buddhism does in the Irish Republic. At the other end of the scale some small ones, like the British or Dutch, have embraced the logic of events to the extent of dissolving themselves, with or without successor organisations which are no longer political parties. In between exists, in a number of variants, the option of a name change, a regroupment and the search for an altered role in the political structures of individual states.

The majority Italian communists are the largest and weightiest of the former CPs to pursue such a strategy. The Party of the Democratic Left (PDS), as the successor organisation, has filled the space into which the Italian Communist Party (PCI) had in any case been moving for some time, that of social democratic parliamentary, local government and cultural practice. The collapse and disintegration of formally recognised social democracy, represented by the Italian Socialist Party (PSI), along with most of the Italian political system, has made the transition easier. Whether the PCI's traditions of incorruptibility and abstention from clientage politics, based on the principle of votes in return for favours to representitives of particular groups, can survive for long the removal of the communist framework is another matter. Other parties to have followed equivalent routes are the former East German communists, as well as the CPs of the Scandinavian and Benelux nations, in whose case the transition was occurring even before the debacle. Since in all of these cases, unlike Italy, the social democratic ground was already well occupied, such parties have made their pitch as an independent left – in the form of red-green combinations in Scandinavia.[40]

Finally, for some communists, although their parties have read the signs, it has proved impossible to recognise that a historical mountain has slid into the sea and that the landscape surveyed by the left has altered out of recognition. They continue to try to maintain the pretence of a communist life after death. Only one such attempt can be regarded as being in any sense serious. This again is to be found in Italy, in the shape of Communist Refoundation, which has a comparatively big membership and some electoral strength as well as an element of intellectual adherence. Although frequently dismissed as a Stalinist hangover, that is too simplistic a verdict in this particular case. Its counterparts elsewhere however are pathetic, doomed and futile enterprises, either overtly Stalinist groupuscules or a few individuals warming themselves over the embers of nostalgia. Britain for instance has no less than three splinters of the old CPGB using the communist name.

These parties which remain in suspended animation or which have continued while discarding their communist identity constitute, however, the biggest part of the former communist movement outside the bloc. But whether Stalinoid like the Portuguese, social democratic like the Italian or responding to other national peculiarity, they all have one feature in common. They operate in no international framework of fraternal parties with a global mission and they have no historical perspective which shows them the meaning of what the communist and socialist movement has struggled for over the last century and what the long-term objective of their present struggles can be. All that vanished when the Soviet regime foundered. The role which such parties now fulfil is that of serving as political representatives for particular constituencies within individual states. That is by no means an insignificant or ignoble remit, for these constituencies contain often enough some of the most immiserated, wretched and defenceless of human beings: but it is a long way from the visionary hopes of the early Comintern of transcending capitalism on an international scale or of engineering the transition from the realm of necessity to the realm of freedom.

CHAPTER 5

Social Democracy

The Great War and the revolutions of 1917–19 transformed the character of the left as it had existed up to that point, irreparably split the loosely unified socialist movement of the Second International and turned what had been, up to 1914, divergent trends within a quarrelsome but basically allied family into mortal enemies who were prepared to and sometimes actually did kill each other. The rupture left the old name of social democracy to be inherited by the political formations of organised labour which during the war had backed their national governments in its prosecution. For the remainder of what Eric Hobsbawm has termed the 'short twentieth century' (1914–91) – while Leninism evolved into Stalinism, through the course of the Cold War, 'actually existing socialism' and colonial liberation – social democracy stood as the alternative to and enemy of communism, critical of but in essence allied to international capital.

It is important of course not to oversimplify. Generally the parties and political forces who initially came under this rubric contained a great diversity of trends and tendencies. Some of these were unquestionably left-wing, some even regarded themselves as revolutionary and differed from the communists only in objecting to the latter's centralising authoritarianism and subordination to the Comintern and Moscow. Such left-leaning tendencies were themselves in a state of permanent subordination to those by whom the identity of social democracy was to be defined; namely the 'labour lieutenants of capital' (in Lenin's phrase) whose commitment was absolute to both the structures of the existing state and the political culture whose norms were founded by the traditional establishment.

In fact the wartime experience and the communist-social democratic split clarified, defined and institutionalised what had for decades been the dominant tendency of the labour movements of Western and Central Europe (and the US) to adapt to and integrate with the societies in which their members were the basic producers[1] and to bargain or hope to bargain over the distribution of the social surplus. The integration had been disguised and overlaid by revolutionary rhetoric on one hand and the social fear and hatred of labour felt by the elites on the other, but even before 1914 there were spokespersons on both sides of the line who were clear enough about the way events were turning and argued for open recognition.[2]

The labour leaders might be more or less ambitious over the terms of the bargain they hoped to strike. Its fundamental aspect was the rate of wages paid and the level of earnings which resulted, but might include what in a later epoch would be termed the 'social wage' – welfare benefits of various sorts and the manner of their distribution. What was clear was that political as well as industrial muscle was invaluable in securing a favourable bargain – both the Australian and British Labour parties were established by trade union movements opening a political front to supplement the industrial. In other words what was sought was leverage within the machinery of the state, issuing in legislation which protected labour's position,[3] but there was no real intention, rhetoric on the part of Marxist social democrats notwithstanding, of trying forcibly to seize control of the state and doing so by violence if the opportunity presented itself. Indeed why should there be? However wretched the conditions of most of the workforce, gambling their lives and their families' on the uncertain prospects of a revolutionary overturn was scarcely a very rational choice, even supposing that Marxist conviction had disposed them to sympathise with the idea. It was even less rational in conditions where discernible, albeit modest, gains were to be had through much less risky varieties of struggle, gains which once secured created a further premium on not recklessly imperilling them. However much the ruling class might be hated in principle by a class-conscious worker, the course of political and social reform generated a hidden interaction, supplemented by all the weight of education, propaganda and culture sounding on the themes of patriotic nationhood.

Lenin was undoubtedly correct in one respect.[4] Trade union struggle in itself would produce only a trade union consciousness, not revealing to its participants the necessities of revolution and socialism other than for minorities attracted by the unreal and self-defeating fantasies of syndicalism. It was supposed to be the duty of the workers' party, informed by Marxism, to infuse that scientific understanding into the proletarian masses and to prepare them for the revolutionary opportunity. Until 1914 he assumed the German Social Democratic Party (SPD) to be a model party of that sort,[5] but in fact the expectation was wholly unrealistic. By the twentieth century the party had in reality an enormous material and moral investment in the continuing stability of German society as the goose which laid gilt-plated eggs for its constituents – and given time and growing SPD influence might begin to lay genuine golden ones in the shape of the eight-hour day, unemployment insurance and compulsory union recognition. The situation was no different with all the socialist and labour parties west of the Russian Empire and the Balkans.

Evidently enough in these circumstances the labour movements throughout Europe dreaded the prospect of war, and the endeavours of their leaders to exhort and threaten the states of the rival power blocs with a working-class refusal were perfectly genuine. Once war had erupted, however, in spite of their efforts, and faced with the choice between the dangers for themselves and their organisations of adopting an oppositional posture and the attractions of social gains and recognition from contributing to the war effort, there could be little doubt about the way the decision would go – the more so when it was clear that the workers were gripped by patriotic frenzy no less than any other social class.[6]

After four years of unprecedented cataclysm and slaughter that consensus was still only partially shaken in the warring states of Germany, France and the UK.[7] The resilience of their respective regimes was truly astonishing and would have been entirely unpredictable in 1914 when the war was expected to be short and limited in casualties. In the light of what the belligerent states had done to a generation of their youth any rational observer would surely have presumed confidently that their governments would be swept away amid popular fury and loathing. The Bolsheviks certainly did so.

In Britain and France there was not even an outside possibility that such a thing would happen, in spite of the fears of both governments, although the formation of communist parties in both countries intensified social conflict and dramatic but isolated outbreaks of industrial strife. Nor was the potential in the defeated *Kaiserreich* anywhere near sufficient to produce a Soviet regime. The leaders of the International, as noted above, mistakenly convinced themselves that the failure of events in Germany to follow the expected path was to be attributed to the absence there of a political party equivalent to the Bolsheviks, 'tried and tested' by years of struggle against opportunism, reformism and vacillation.

Where the communist analysis was not mistaken however was in indicting German Social Democracy and its leaders for the way in which matters subsequently turned out. Beneath the cloak of democratic and parliamentary forms the most intransigently regressive forces in German society remained entrenched within its institutions and culture – the military, civil service, judiciary, universities, not to speak of business – awaiting the hour of their restored supremacy. The SPD leaders conciliated and deferred to them at every turn, commencing with their employment of ultra-reactionary military chiefs and Freikorps units to crush the Berlin insurrection attempted by the Spartacists and left-wing workers in January 1919 in protest at the government's capitulation to the forces of reaction. This class treason was compounded by government failure to punish Liebknecht's and Luxemburg's murderers and continued with a commitment, during the brief period when the SPD dominated the parliamentary majority, to preserve unchanged the traditional structures of the state apparatus and especially the army's status of exemption from civilian control.[8] It was a particularly extreme and brutal example, but emblematic of the future relationship that postwar social democracy, outside Russia the dominant branch of the old International, was to maintain with the capitalist establishment.

Other options would have been available to them. In the turbulent months following the Armistice the SPD government allowed the shaken military leadership to reconsolidate itself when, even in terms of the Social Democrats' own perspectives, there was no necessity to do so.[9] Ludendorf and Hindenburg were in a blind panic and had wholly lost control of events; the former had fled the country in disguise and the latter could have been arrested, or at least deposed, to popular acclaim. The unhappy and unwilling SPD Chancellor Ebert and his colleagues chose to let the military leaders off the hook. Even accepting its firm opposition to continuing the revolution, the respectable Council of People's Commissars might have defended itself against the left insurgents easily enough with its own paramilitaries or radicalised military units outside the control of the high command but loyal to the new government. Or they could have called the bluff of the nationalist right by threatening the resumption of a war which the latter refused to accept had been genuinely lost. They did none of those things but instead, 'thoroughly compromised by the armed and resurgent right',[10] allowed the military and the Freikorps to appear as saviours of the bourgeois republic they loathed and despised. If that were not sufficient, on two further occasions when the ultra-right was put on the defensive – following the unsuccessful Kapp putsch of 1920 and the murder of the foreign minister Rathenau in 1992 – the SPD declined to seize the initiative which was there for the taking to evict the enemies of democracy from their strongholds in the state apparatus.

The SPD leaders were mostly elderly men, cautious, socially conservative, loyal to institutions rather than ideas and in their own fashion hardly less nationalistic than their right-wing opponents. On top of that, they were called to take command in the storm of defeat and revolution and subsequently to steer their party through seas of social disintegration, political violence and economic collapse. During the lifespan of the Weimar Republic the SPD retained the electoral loyalty of the majority of the German working class[11] and entered into temporary and tactical alliances with the less irreconcilable elements of the anti-republican spectrum to keep the republic in being, preserve the modest gains of the semi-revolution and resist by parliamentary manoeuvre the encroaching ultra-right tide. When the final crisis of the Weimar Republic arrived, the main responsibility on the part of the left for the Nazi catastrophe lay undoubtedly with the KPD (Communist Party) and the lunatic directions from the Comintern which made it regard the social democrats as its main enemy, but the SPD was far from guiltless. Its leaders refused to contemplate anything but a policy of principled legality against an enemy which openly boasted of its contempt for legality as anything more than a tactic on the route to unconstrained power. When there was at least a possibility of saving the situation and the republic by calling a general strike and drawing its supporters and paramilitary units[12] out onto the streets it resolutely declined to do so.

It was however more than merely a question of the personal characteristics of the party leaders, who by being unwilling to risk anything ended with losing everything; or even of the rigid structures of an organisation which prevented more dynamic elements from taking control and altering political direction when the emergency desperately required such a move. The SPD, unlike its communist rival, was not bound by the discipline of the Comintern: its autonomy might have provided scope for a more responsive leadership to emerge, but that did not occur. The party had a left wing as well as a right, but all along the right remained in invulnerable and virtually unchallenged control of its affairs. In fact the trajectory of the SPD between 1918 and 1933 symbolised what social democracy had become and what it was to be. The SPD had been the glory of the old Socialist International, the archetypal Marxian socialist party. What happened in 1918 confirmed what had been revealed in 1914 – that the party had repudiated, in reality though not yet in words, its heritage of revolutionary Marxism. For a mass party operating in a constitutional state that may or may not have been inescapable – the SPD's major tragedy was that it failed to replace its abandoned Marxist perspectives with a dynamic and inspiring alternative.

The revolution of 1918 erupted from below and took the parliamentary and trade union leaders by surprise. By a twisted irony of history a situation envisaged by the prewar SPD theorists actually came to pass – the bourgeoisie found itself incapable of continuing to rule and voluntarily handed over the reigns of power to the socialists. But of course it did so not in order to liquidate bourgeois hegemony but to preserve it – the bourgeois politicians knew their men. Ebert and his colleagues assumed governmental office with the utmost reluctance and accepted only because of patriotic conviction that this sacrifice on their part was necessary to preserve order and forestall anarchy.

> There might be something of exaltation in waking up famous
> like Byron ... but it was less pleasant to find oneself in the
> morning the Supreme Commander of the Revolution after
> going to bed as a member of the respectable middle class.[13]

Power frightened them and they lost no time in handing it back to
where it was properly seen to belong – the traditional sources of
authority minus, in Germany's case, the monarchy, which Ebert
in any case would have preferred to retain.

The SPD's actions brought it closer to the British Labour Party,
which was contemporaneously shifting in a marginally more leftward
direction though no less terrified of leading a challenge to the
powers that be.[14] The generic term social democracy, spurned by
the communists, came to define the political formation that based
itself upon the organised workforce and took collectivist reformism
as its guiding principle. Its central feature was historical subordination
in that, as a movement representing an ethic in contradiction to
the ruling principles of existing society, it was dependent upon the
uninterrupted and effective functioning of that same social order
to attain its central objective of a favourable wage bargain. It could
posit an alternative order – as its left-wing did – only abstractly,
envisaging a process of cumulative legislative encroachment upon
the strongholds of private capital in the context of that same private
capital continuing to fulfil its function meantime, until the national
economy or its commanding heights had been socialised. But its
dominant tendencies resisted such speculation, fixing attention
instead upon the project of tidying up and humanising the existing
order as a more than sufficient historic responsibility – undoubtedly
this was a lot more realistic. That did not exclude the possibility
of the project being forwarded amid war and crisis – as the events
in Britain between 1940 and 1950 were to show – only so long as
the capitalist national economy kept on functioning. Indeed, such
emergency situations might actually prove quite favourable, since
they greatly enhanced the bargaining power of the workforce and
its party and compelled capital to accept state-enforced discipline.

Historical Trajectory

It is a fairly safe presumption that even without the intervention
of world wars, revolution and dictatorship, social democracy of the
pre-1914 sort would have developed in roughly the same manner.
There existed an intrinsic and unremitting internal pressure upon
any labour movement developing within a constitutional political
framework as it accumulated assets, acquired institutional stability
and saw its members depending upon it to represent their day-to-
day grievances, to bend in this direction and abandon revolutionary
visions either implicitly or explicitly.

'The journey is everything: the goal is nothing!' The revisionist debate at the turn of the century foreshadowed all that was to come. Bernstein drew attention to several respects in which the course of economic and social development in Germany and Europe was contradicting the projections that Marx and Engels had advanced in the expectation that maturing crises within the capitalist economies would bring intensified social polarisation, together with decisive revolutionary confrontations. At the same time as he questioned the theoretical soundness of classic Marxist interpretations, Bernstein was simultaneously making a plea for the SPD to stop disguising its practice behind the cloak of revolutionary rhetoric and bring its formal positions into line with what it was actually doing – a proposition which offended the right-wing as much as the left, since the former found the ambiguity too convenient to be discarded and preferred simply to exclude the matter from discussion.

The revisionists had recognised an important truth: namely that the notion was a myth of intensifying social polarisation in which the middle class decayed until its greater part became absorbed into a proletariat which, schooled by its perpetual struggle with capital, grew in class consciousness and self-confidence until capitalist breakdown catapulted it into power. But in identifying and dismissing one myth the revisionists, and the reformists who inspired them, were happy to embrace another no less unreal – namely that of confidence in the long-term economic stability of capitalism and in the ethical purposes of the bourgeois state. These illusions led them even into according endorsement to imperialism and the European empires of the era on the argument that there were or could be reciprocal benefits to be obtained by the working classes of the metropolitan powers and the indigenous inhabitants of the colonised territories. Lenin's absolutely correct insight by contrast, derived from experience of the Tsarist power but appropriately extended to all contemporary states, was that utter immorality constituted the inner essence of class rule (however disguised or whatever concessions might be extorted from it) and that its undeviating structural objective remained at all times the safeguarding and perpetuation of exploitation in its multitudinous shapes. His own expression of the relationship was that all capitalist polities, including the most formally democratic, were to be regarded as one or another form of the dictatorship of the bourgeoisie.

How to Proceed?

The interwar years exposed all too depressingly the inability of social democracy to uphold a viable alternative to communism on the one part and capitalism (usually embodied in conservatism or dictatorship) on the other.

The fact, frequently admitted by social democratic politicians, was that they did not know how to proceed to the realisation of their programme. The choice of industries which were to be nationalised, methods of financing, techniques of management, and the mutual relations among the sectors turned out to be technical problems for which the social democrats were unprepared. Hence they formed study commissions and waited.[15]

In Germany, Austria,[16] Italy and Spain social democracy was annihilated, in France and the UK it went down to comprehensive political defeat. In one part of Europe nevertheless, the reality appeared to be otherwise. The exception was Scandinavia, excluding Finland.[17] In Norway, Sweden and Denmark there appeared to be achieved what the Italian communists of another era were to term a 'historic compromise' – a standoff between capital and labour with the numerous small farmers joining labour in a social coalition and the social democratic parties emerging as the leading actors within the countries' political framework. Under this dispensation capital permitted itself to be regulated in return for self-restraint on the part of labour in exploiting its potential strength on the wage bargaining front. The compromise was overseen by social democrat dominated governments who also employed techniques of demand management and deficit financing to generate the economic growth required to render the policy viable.[18]

That such a corporatist compromise could work successfully during an era of world slump and within the Europe of the dictators appears at first sight all the more remarkable. In fact under the particular circumstances of Scandinavian history the slump, by depleting the strength of local capital in a small region without imperial possessions or prospects, made it more rather than less accommodating. Moreover, the two countries where the development was carried furthest, Norway and Sweden, enjoyed comparatively small populations amidst enormous natural resources, two of which, timber and iron ore, could find available European markets even under depression conditions – especially once German rearmament got under way.[19]

What was put together with some success in interwar Scandinavia was also attempted elsewhere. At the other end of the world labour parties based on the British model enjoyed considerably happier times during those years than did their parent. Prior to the war Australia and New Zealand had been in the forefront both of extended electoral rights and welfare programmes. By the 1930s both, but especially New Zealand, were embryonic welfare societies. Their social democratic movements failed to achieve a hegemonic electoral strength equivalent to that of the Scandinavian counterparts, but the favourable developments were a response to their pressures. Once again however the exceptional wealth of these societies[20] and, from the 1930s, their protected agricultural markets in the UK have to be taken into account.

The most significant of these interwar developments however, pointing the direction for the future following the second international conflict, occurred in the US in the shape of the Roosevelt New Deal programme. Its relationship to social democracy was paradoxical. In one sense it had nothing at all to do with that political formation, for in point of fact social democracy in the US had been destroyed by the war and its aftermath. What had been before 1914 a significant and growing movement able to mount a respectable electoral challenge in Presidential contests was not invited by government, unlike its European counterparts, to embed itself in the state apparatus by co-operating in the mobilisation of the workforce for the war effort. By the early 1920s it was wholly ineffectual and carried to the political margins by the reactionary tide which swept the country in the aftermath of the Russian Revolution.

It can and has been argued that the tradition implanted by Roosevelt in the US Democratic Party made it into a surrogate version of social democracy 'in a pro-capitalist, anti-socialist guise'.[21] In essence I believe this argument to be valid, in that the politics of the New Deal represented the same broad historical current of state intervention to secure social improvement as did social democracy in Europe. But the relationship between the US labour movement and even the populist left of the Democratic Party was a detached one. The New Deal did not take its inspiration from the labour movement and was not organisationally related to it, but was the outcome of that older populist tradition, mobilised by Roosevelt in a broad Democratic Party coalition around himself and integrating the industrial organisations of unionised workers in a subordinate role.

In actual reality the New Deal was not particularly successful – its impact on the depression was fairly marginal in terms of the numbers returned to work by state and public action, or in enhancing living standards or entrenching the rights of labour. Its scale was restricted in any case by comparison with the extent of the problems to be addressed and much even of that was sabotaged by reactionary obstruction.[22] A modest market upturn during the second half of the 1930s contributed rather more than the New Deal programme to such economic alleviation as did occur. Nevertheless its *political* impact was far-reaching, for in this case the presentation was a lot more important than the reality. It made generally acceptable, far more than the Scandinavian experiment ever could, the notion that

governments *could* exercise macroeconomic controls and moreover
that they had the responsibility to do so.

The New Deal can be viewed as a pragmatic, *ad hoc*, untheorised
application of the economic strategies for the salvation of capitalism
which were being currently developed by John Maynard Keynes
(who was a Liberal in politics) and which were even in the 1930s
growing in acceptability among the more open-minded and
innovative elements at the British Treasury.[23] Keynesian theory was
to provide social democracy with the instrument it had previously
lacked – a credible means of macroeconomic management within
a continuing market framework.

> And this was not all: Keynsianism was not only a theory that
> justified socialist participation in government but, even more
> fortuitously from the social democratic point of view, it was a
> theory which suddenly granted universalistic status to the
> interests of workers ... in the logic of Keynes theory higher
> wages ... meant an increase of aggregate demand, which implied
> increased expectations of profit, increased investment and hence
> economic stimulation.[24]

There was a measure of initial resistance. Mainstream continental
social democracy – or what was left of it in the 1930s – still regarded
itself as springing from a Marxian tradition, to which Keynes was
explicitly hostile. Even the resolutely anti-Marxist leaders of the
British Labour Party distrusted the lack of concern with *ownership*
– private as against social – which characterised Keynes's outlook.
Social ownership and economic planning were intrinsic to social
democracy's ideology, but no real consideration had been given to
how those could be operated in a culture of political democracy
with a large or even majority private sector continuing in being.
The only model existing up to that point which combined the two
features was the wholly unacceptable – for social democrats –
party-state authoritarian version currently being practised in
the USSR.

It was therefore as inevitable as anything could historically be
that Keynesianism should be taken over by any social democracy
that aspired to govern the state, and indeed that the theory should
come to constitute its defining centre, pushing the emphasis on social
ownership and centrality of workforce interests into a subordinate
relationship. It promised a tool to produce uninterrupted and
substantial economic growth out of which could be financed far-
reaching improvements in earnings along with an unprecedented
expansion in welfare – without at the same time infringing too far
upon the rights of wealth and property and thereby generating
uncontrollable political antagonism. But the central fact was that
in adopting one or another version of Keynesianism as its guiding

compass, social democracy was drawing its central principles from the capitalist order which it had come into being to oppose, and thereby posed itself as a secondary social vision, with primacy being conceded to its ancient enemy. For Keynesian principles could as easily be applied by enlightened liberal administrations and were in fact intended to be so – though a defender might have responded that it scarcely mattered so long as a decent and just society emerged as a result.

Cold War and Golden Age

It is clear that the mere existence of Keynesian theory in itself would not have been sufficient to transform the prospects of social democracy from their nadir in the 1930s. It was not necessarily electorally attractive, even to electorates caught in the grip of the slump. Policy proposals based upon its essential principles had served as the foundation of the Liberal Party manifesto in the British general election of 1929 and disaster had followed at the polls – not so much because the proposals were seen as abhorrent as because the voters exercised their franchise on other grounds, namely the social and class identities which the parties were believed to reflect.

The turn of the historical wheel which transformed social democracy's fortunes, and for a lengthy period made its guiding principles the common sense of the non-communist world's most important states, was the Second World War and the Cold War which followed, inaugurating what Eric Hobsbawm has termed 'the golden age'. The years of the conflict between 1940 and 1945 constituted a demonstration of what government control, planning and deficit financing could do in mobilising and directing resources for a life-and-death struggle, as well as, in the British case, improving average living standards and welfare amidst the rigours of rationing and extreme shortages. The social character of the esteemed Soviet ally was also, for a time, an asset to the credibility of planned economies and social ownership. It was not only the social democratic ideology which was raised to heights of acceptability and popularity: in the sphere of political movements and organisations the German SPD was rescued from likely extinction by the efforts of the British Labour Party and later the British government in keeping its exile organisation alive for reimplantation in a liberated Germany. As the war drew towards its close and the likely features of postwar European politics started to take shape, the possibility of using of a revived SPD to act as a counterweight to the expected expansion of communist influence in Germany and elsewhere, began to preoccupy the Foreign Office.[25]

Even so, the integration of social democratic principles into the political universe of postwar Europe[26] and their populist equivalent in the US, might well have been cut short but for the onset of the Cold War. The scale of material devastation, accompanied in 1946–7 by exceptionally unfavourable weather conditions[27] meant that in the first two years following the allied victory the economies of the former European belligerents were barely holding their own and some of the worst affected, particularly Germany, were in a state of utter prostration. The crisis, threatening to turn into catastrophe, had implications for the United States as well, both economically and politically. An economically ruined Europe made a poor trading partner and threatened the continuation of its own wartime boom – with the nightmare of returning depression in the background. Politically it might tip the balance in Western Europe towards the assertive and self-confident communist parties which had emerged from war and resistance – with domestic implications for the US, particularly among its Italian immigrant community.

Keynes had died in 1946 leaving behind a heritage that was about to come into its own. His influence was exercised not only in the sphere of economic policy but institutionally as well. The International Monetary Fund (IMF), the World Bank and the General Agreement on Tariffs and Trade (GATT) were his brainchildren, designed to iron out so far as possible seizures and blockages in world trade flows caused by liquidity shortages or by unbridled protectionism. They fitted in well with the basic US strategy for a global open door to sustain its own level of exported products and capital. They presupposed, however, that the principal centres of world production and exchange were functioning with at least a semblance of normality, and by the spring of 1947 it looked as though that could no longer be taken for granted as far as Western Europe was concerned.

The US administration was acutely aware of the problem, and its response was the European Recovery Programme (ERP), better known as Marshall Aid. The ERP was closely tied in with the deteriorating state of superpower relations, and indeed its announcement in March 1947 is generally recognised as marking the declaration of the Cold War. That perception is accurate, but it was not so much a case of the ERP being designed as the economic accompaniment to diplomatic and military aid for resisting communist aggression, as communism being inflated into a European menace in order to get the appropriations for funding the ERP past a Congress proverbially suspicious of foreign commitments. The initial draft of the declaration did in fact place its main emphasis on Europe's desperate state and its arguments for the funding were principally economic ones. General Marshall, Truman's Secretary of State, convinced him that rewriting it in a fire-breathing anti-communist fashion to stress the Soviet threat to all and sundry, but especially in the Eastern Mediterranean, would greatly improve its chances of getting through.[28]

The technique of using government intervention to redress the inadequacies of market relations but of yoking the measures with anti-communist rhetoric and action as a means of conciliating the right was observed in US domestic politics as well as foreign ones. In terms of economic management it was Truman more than Roosevelt who really implemented the New Deal. Welfare provision during the immediate postwar years was more lavish than anything the US had previously witnessed, some of the bite of the measures' violation of traditional American values being taken out by the fact that they were directed especially at veterans. Federal funding too was used extensively in various guises to support individual enterprises, and the official trade union movement in the shape of the AFL-CIO recognised as a partner, if a junior one, in the project of economic growth, stability and rising incomes.

It all went ahead however to the accompaniment of a ferocious persecution of the American left in general and the CPUSA in particular, chiefly embodied in the witch-hunt associated with the name of Senator Joe McCarthy, the foundations for which were laid with the establishment of the Soviet bloc in Europe, the revolutionary successes of communism in Asia and the nuclear accomplishments of Soviet science, all of which, in an atmosphere of escalating hysteria, had the effect of deligitimising the left in the US as a political actor. The dual strategy of demonising communism and everything political or cultural that could be associated with it, while taking over parts of reformist and redistributive programmes, took on a particular virulence in the United States, where there were no longer social democratic organisations of any note, and where anything genuinely left-wing was held guilty by association. In essence however it was the same strategy as was followed, if less aggressively, by the ruling elites in Britain and in liberated Western Europe.

The political climate of the industrialised countries in the postwar years was suffused with social democratic values, yet by the 1950s social democratic administrations outside Scandinavia were nowhere firmly in power.[29] In Western Germany the revived party was the second political force in what was virtually a two-party system, yet had never been in government and seemed destined for permanent opposition. In Britain, following a decade of epic achievements in coalition and in government, the Labour Party had lost office on an electoral quirk, but thereafter appeared to be set on a declining political curve. In France the official name, the French Section of the Workers' International, was a mockery of the reality – a subordinate partner in the ever-changing governments of the

Fourth Republic, implicated in colonial repression and imperialist war. The situation in Italy was unusually complicated. Following the liberation, the position of the Communist Party (PCI) was so hegemonic that overwhelmingly the left gravitated towards it. The Socialist Party (PSI), while maintaining its organisational independence, worked until the 1950s in close political collaboration with the communists and therefore rendered itself obnoxious in the eyes of respectable political society. The threat of a PCI-PSI coalition coming to power in Italy by electoral means was regarded as so alarming that the US had trained a secret underground armed right-wing force to commence operations in such an eventuality. The danger was abated by the use of CIA funding to encourage the defection in 1947 of a part of the PSI to form a safely anti-communist Social Democratic Party, which was immediately accorded political respectability. In the end the PSI proceeded along a similar path.[30]

I have argued elsewhere that the Conservative governments of Britain in the 1950s implemented what were in fact labourist policies and governed the country in a labourist manner, probably more effectively than the then Labour Party could have done. That decade, rather than the 1940s, represents on this argument the high tide of labourism. An equivalent argument can be advanced for the Western world as a whole – the leading states of the bipolar world which succeeded the height of the Cold War confrontation, though governed in the main by conservatives, ordered their affairs according to the tenets of social democracy. The consensus was real, and it was the social democratic side which was hegemonic. The Cold War was as much a confrontation between social democracy and actually existing socialism as between capitalism and communism.

Future of Socialism?

In the mid-1950s the frontiers of the blocs had stabilised in Europe – and even to a lesser degree in Asia; Stalin's demise and the end of the Korean War had resulted in a degree of abatement to inter-bloc tensions and the fury of the US witch-hunt, and the leading social democratic parties were out of office but seeing the essence of their programmes being implemented by their ostensible political opponents. Significantly, it was then, when the long boom had become firmly embedded in the global economy and the glories of consumer society had started to reveal themselves, that Tony Crosland was to publish the volume that came to be regarded as the most articulate statement, indeed the bible, of social democratic revisionism.

The Future of Socialism was a product of optimism and self-confidence. It is more striking and remarkable for the assumptions and presuppositions which informed it than for its specific vision of socialism's future. For Crosland, capitalism had been transformed out of recognition (which indeed, in a sense it had). What had occurred since 1945 was interpreted as a historically irreversible shift, so that never again could the predatory capitalism of the nineteenth and early twentieth centuries dominate economy and society. The countervailing powers of organised labour and popularly elected governments would ensure that concentrations of wealth and ownership were not permitted to abuse their economic and social advantages; with its wings clipped and its claws trimmed, capitalism remained the most dynamic and effective force for economic growth.

> Capitalism has been reformed almost out of recognition. Despite occasional minor recessions and balance of payments crises, full employment and at least a tolerable degree of stability are likely to be maintained.[31]

Crosland's thesis exemplified how deeply Keynesian presumptions had sunk into the ideological framework of social democracy. The work betrayed limitless confidence in the potential of Keynesian tools in government hands:

> Acting mainly through the Budget, though with the aid of other instruments, government can exert any influence it likes on income distribution, and can also determine within broad limits the division of total output between consumption, investment, exports and social expenditure.[32]

In other words the author was interpreting the unquestionably novel but specific and historically contingent circumstances of the 1950s as a tectonic shift within capitalism's structures. At root he was afflicted with the same misperception as had been his ideological forebears in Bernstein's camp over half a century before – that ruling classes could be educated, by government, countervailing powers or whatever, into a permanent condition of benign motivation. Marxists of the time, whatever their other shortcomings, were able to point out that however much capitalism in 1956 might look like a tame pussy-cat, when the chips were down it would revert rapidly to its tigerish disposition and workforce, pensioners, and all other vulnerable social groups would soon be sacrificed to the maintenance of profit levels. Perhaps Crosland imagined that the chips never would be down, although his career, as well as *The Future of Socialism* itself suggests that he was sincerely convinced that capitalism had been changed intrinsically rather than merely sedated. To be fair, an individual writing at the time the volume was published could hardly foresee that the day would come when governments would be able deliberately to generate mass unemployment and yet continue to win elections.

Crosland's volume focused on specifically British conditions though he made it clear that his general conceptions related to the industrialised West as a whole and that he regarded the US, at that time governed by a Republican president (with Richard Nixon as his vice-president) as adhering to Keynesian and in effect social democratic principles – though he did not of course use the term in such a connection. He was one of the new thinkers – the leading one in fact – grouped around the British Labour Party leader Hugh Gaitskell, who, using Crosland as their text, embarked upon a project of persuading the party to discard the ideological baggage of class struggle and rapacious bosses inherited from the past and to embrace the new perspectives of social harmony made possible by a structurally reformed capitalism. The project was only partially successful, on account of the labourist reflexes embedded in the consciousness of the party's grassroots and its trade union hierarchies: the elimination from the party's constitution of the socialist icon, Clause IV, with its commitments to public ownership of the 'means of production, distribution and exchange', which would have symbolised the intended transformation, was blocked and Gaitskell's unexpected death enabled the issue to be evaded.

What British social democracy was unable or unwilling to undertake was accomplished by the other major party within the tradition, the German SPD. Suffering like its British counterpart a series of discouraging electoral defeats in the course of the 1950s, it formally disowned its Marxist heritage at the Bad Godesberg congress of 1959 and attired itself in reformist garb to a degree that exceeded even the British pioneer of reformism. According to *The Times*:

> Democratic Socialism, the preamble states, is rooted in Christian ethics, humanism and classical philosophy ...[a critique of capitalism embodied in the preamble of the initial draft of the programme had been dropped]
>
> If this is not enough to make its distinguished former member Karl Marx turn in his grave the draft goes on to condemn Communism and proposes the creation of a property-owning democracy not too unlike that visualised by Professor Erhard [a Christian Democrat leader].
>
> A centrally controlled economy destroys freedom; the party therefore approves a free economy ... Freedom ... of business initiative [is] essential, and free competition is an important element in a free economy ... [11 September 1959]

The development was a momentous one. Notwithstanding significant left-wings still existing and arguing in all such parties, European social democracy had now committed itself unequivocally to reconciliation with what it conceived to be a reformed and benevolent capitalism, with its own role, as its unreconciled critics expressed it, confined to 'managing capitalism better than the capitalists' while promoting cultural and social improvement at the margin.

Advances

In the decade following European social democracy appeared to reap a gratifying electoral harvest from the seeds of pragmatism it had sown during the 1950s, and was imitated in a ghostly fashion across the Atlantic where social democracy in a formal sense had no resonance. Apart from social democrat parties' continuing hegemonic grip on Scandinavian politics, a Labour government was elected to office in Britain in 1964 and remained in power for the remainder of the decade. The SPD entered into a Grand Coalition with the governing Christian Democrats following the elections of 1966, though much to the indignation of the party's left-wing and an expanding extra-parliamentary opposition. New elections in 1969 however, enabled it to form a government (with the minority Liberal Democrats) for the first time in the postwar era. In France the SFIO was reorganised under the direction of Francois Mitterand as the Socialist Party (PS) and although it did not break the Gaullist hold upon government, began to overtake its communist rival as the foremost party of opposition. In Italy the formation of 'centre-left' administrations (still designed to exclude the PCI) allowed the now safely social democratic PSI[33] to enter coalitions and its leaders to aspire to the highest offices including the premiership. Even further afield in Greece, in the context of what remained a highly authoritarian and still only semi-democratic political system following the defeat of the communists in the civil war of the late 1940s, a social democratic formation began to make impressive headway.

In the US the populist tradition was continued and even intensified, expanding to embrace the black minority. Institutionalised racism in the southern states was overthrown by grassroots revolt, initially with reluctant and minimal Federal support. Following J. F. Kennedy's assassination in 1963, his vice-presidential successor Lyndon Johnson moved to inaugurate what can reasonably be interpreted as the last kick of the New Deal, as well as its most ambitious extension. The Great Society project actually was intended, within the framework of US corporate capitalism, to alleviate the worst features of impoverishment and multiple deprivation, particularly concentrated among the country's ethnic minorities, above all blacks. In the presidential election of 1964 the promise and the expectations generated rewarded the Democrats with a landslide majority and buried the ultra-right contender Barry Goldwater in contempt and ridicule.[34]

At the same time, as in the late 1940s, this programme of welfare and improvement was run in tandem with a foreign policy of unreconstructed anti-communism and accelerating militarisation. The nuclear arms race proceeded apace.[35] The commitment of Johnson's government to crushing the peasant revolt in Vietnam at all costs in the name of anti-communism expanded until it began sending US troops to die in spectacular numbers and blotted out every other aspect of the administration's record. The initial steps towards the Indochina quagmire had been taken under Kennedy, and the foreign policy of his short administration had been dominated by the vendetta with another weak Third World socialist regime, Cuba – victimised by threat, blockade and attempted surrogate invasion though no conceivable threat to the US other than that it might set a bad example to other Latin American populations. Johnson continued to maintain and tighten the stranglehold. As the process of decolonisation accelerated in Africa US secret services increasingly turned their attention to ensuring that the successor regimes would be capital-friendly and strenuously anti-communist. It was done, above all, in the former Belgian Congo (Zaire) regardless of the cost in blood and the excruciating misery which the Western-backed tyrants proceeded to inflict upon their luckless peoples.

At home too, for all its welfare pretensions the Johnson administration did not scruple to attack the revolutionary elements which appeared on the scene by means of rigged trials and police assassination, a technique employed most notably against the Black Panthers.[36] In all of these instances at home and abroad the European social democratic governments of the Western Alliance unflinchingly refused to criticise the US actions in domestic or foreign forums and/or expressed their diplomatic support and maintained that stance even in the face of outraged revolt among their grassroots and youth movements. The integration of their leaderships into a framework of US-dominated, violent and militarised global capitalism had become total. It was a denouement which would have horrified Bernstein, but these politicians did not view it as betrayal – to them it represented the necessary if unfortunate accompaniment to a process of secular global improvement in which the US was necessarily the leading element and communism a hindrance and a menace to be suppressed by whichever means were appropriate in the circumstances – isolation in the advanced countries: death and devastation in the Third World.[37]

The 1970s saw apparent striking advances for a communist bloc that had in reality entered a state of terminal decay. Social democracy, with its fate and its future firmly pinned to its interaction with managed transnational capitalism, was also in the same decade to register a number of apparent triumphs. The SPD administration in the Federal Republic set in motion a process of detente with the Soviet bloc in general and its communist German neighbour, the GDR in particular – moves which led to what looked on the face of things for a few years, a general European diplomatic settlement. The British Labour Party, having lost office in 1970 returned in 1974. The French socialists remained out of office, but had become the senior partner in a left coalition which by the end of the decade had the Gaullists visibly on the ropes.

The most striking advances were registered however following the collapse of the remaining fascistoid European regimes, two of them survivors from the 1930s. All were located in the Mediterranean region and the three countries involved were Portugal, Spain and Greece. They fell for different reasons. The dictatorship of the Greek colonels, imposed in 1967 specifically to avert possible left-wing government, collapsed because it over-reached itself and, by trying to bring the republic of Cyprus within its orbit, provoked a Turkish invasion of the island. The Salazer regime in Portugal outlived its founder only by a few years before going down to a military revolt. The Francoist state in Spain expired with the dictator in 1975. In each case, after periods of greater or less turmoil, social democratic parties proved to be the political inheritors of the polities left behind by discredited right-wing autocracy.

In Greece and Spain the social democratic triumph developed naturally out of the pre-existing conditions. Both states under their respective dictatorships continued to have strong and functioning underground communist parties[38] as expressions of popular resistance, but repression had naturally taken its toll and both countries also possessed a viable social democratic alternative. In Spain the PSOE was part of a surviving historic tradition going back to the interwar years and the Civil War as well as being under the leadership of a particularly charismatic individual, Felipe Gonzalez. By contrast the Greek PASOK was a new formation of the 1960s which had gathered together the strands of non-communist political and social opposition to the authoritarian conservatism imposed upon Greece since 1944 and had been heading for office when the colonels' coup intervened. By social democratic standards it maintained an unusually left-wing rhetoric and incorporated a strain of fervent nationalism in reaction to Greece's economic, political and military subordination to the Atlantic alliance. Like its Spanish counterpart PASOK too was fronted by a politician of exceptional charisma, Andreas Papendreou.

Both these parties rapidly emerged from illegality and both were well placed to profit electorally from the surge of popular radical sentiment released in Greece and Spain by the restoration of democracy. Their communist rivals continued to be tainted by memories and bitterness inherited from the past of these countries' civil wars.[39] Their electorates were also doubtless conscious of the difficulties which would be created with NATO, the US and their own military establishments should communists be elected to run the government: the lesson of what had occurred in Chile as recently as 1973 was not one to be overlooked.

The case of Portugal was very different although the outcome varied little in the long run. The dictatorships in Greece and Spain had disappeared in a civil collapse – the former rulers had departed peacefully once their rule had become unsustainable and in Spain had even handled the transition under the cloak of a restored monarchy. In Portugal by contrast they were expelled by armed (though bloodless) revolution. The guns were held, not by an insurgent populace, but by the military. This was no standard military coup, however, designed to either suppress or pre-empt popular uprising. Instead it released the flood of popular anger and aspiration suppressed for five decades and part of which was a radicalised military.

It was in these emergency circumstances that the Portuguese Socialist Party was virtually created out of nowhere to act as a political counterweight to a communist party threatening to take control of the state in circumstances where there was no possibility of imposing a right-wing military solution along Chilean lines – though naturally the intelligence services of the Western powers worked energetically to divide the military and win over whichever elements they could among its leaders. In the left-wing climate of the times all anti-communist sentiment rallied around the only credible alternative to the communists, a party with a socialist title.[40] Mario Soares's party benefited additionally by generous financial subsidies and organisational assistance from the British Labour Party and the German SPD acting both independently and through the Socialist International. The strategy proved successful. The radical military rulers were successfully split and the communists politically outmanoeuvred. The subsequent general election, with the left in disarray, returned the expected Socialist victory and commenced the long process of instituting orthodox norms of finance and government and reversing the radical social reforms of the revolutionary phase. The threat of a communist regime on the Atlantic seaboard was averted, thanks to social democracy.

In 1981 the long Gaullist domination of French politics came to an end at last when the Socialist Party won both presidential and parliamentary elections. Francois Mitterrand was installed in the Elysee Palace and a socialist-led administration was formed. The administration included two communist ministers (though in minor capacities), for the victory had been won by a united left coalition achieved after a decade of breakdowns and reconciliations.

By the early part of the decade therefore most of the major and medium states of Western Europe were governed by socialist administrations of one sort or another: Spain, France, Germany, Portugal, Greece, the Scandinavian countries: or, like Italy, Belgium and the Netherlands had socialist parties as virtually permanent partners in their coalition administrations. The major exception was Britain, but even there in 1981 it looked very much as though the unprecedentedly unpopular Thatcher government was doomed and sure to be succeeded at the next election by a Labour administration of dramatically left-wing temper.

It represented an historically unique situation and did seem to suggest that the West European future – at least – belonged to social democracy and that the potential for harmonious economic management and controlled social improvement according to social democratic prescription had never been better. At the fag-end of the Brezhnev era traditional Marxism-Leninism had lost any authentic appeal that it might ever have possessed and the Eurocommunist alternative of the 1970s (see below) had also shot its bolt. Of the large surviving CPs the Spanish one was in advanced disintegration and there was no longer any reason to fear that either the Eurocommunist PCI nor the Stalinist Portuguese CP, let alone the now definitely subordinated French PCF, might succeed in leading a government. It might appear that social democracy was now on the point of inheriting politically what had been established in Europe since 1945 in regimes of managed economy, full employment and extensive welfare provision.

Recessional

Within a few years all these hopes were profoundly blighted, for the ground on which these parties and social democracy as a whole stood was already disintergrating. The recession which commenced in 1973 turned out to be not another cyclical blip such as had occurred throughout the lifetime of the secular long boom. It was the first intimation that the structure of global prosperity founded on cheap energy and the strong dollar was starting to cave in[41] and in the 1980s and 1990s, the industrial working class, which had up to that point been growing in global terms, began to contract.

The viability of social democratic programmes, as repeatedly emphasised, depended upon the health and vitality of the capitalist economies to which they were addressed – to provide the economic growth out of which social welfare in the most general sense (including full employment) might be financed, while permitting the accumulation of capital to proceed and thereby make bearable for propertied elites the historic compromise which these programmes represented. Keen observers were becoming aware as early as the late 1960s[42] that in Britain, the country where the compromise was being practised amidst a ramshackle industrial base and commitment to a world financial role, it was already played out. The strength of labour in what remained a full-employment economy was causing wages to gain over profits to the extent that the overall rate of profit was declining towards zero – an evidently unsustainable state of affairs which Labour and Conservative governments repeatedly failed to rectify by futile attempts to impose wages policies. Consequently the crisis of the historic compromise struck earliest in Britain, where at first the power of labour prevailed, overthrowing an unsympathetic government in 1974 and replacing it with one which undertook not merely to maintain but to improve upon the terms of the postwar social consensus.

It was in vain. In the straitened financial circumstances which had descended upon Britain and the world the Wilson-Callaghan governments could not deliver on their promises without serious infringements on the power and freedom of capital – an evidently unthinkable departure. They were forced to capitulate, to the IMF in the first instance, and impose a programme of austerity – for the workforce and low-income groups. The new programme stipulated continued wage controls, allowed unemployment to rise to previously unimaginable levels and provoked an industrial struggle, complicated by internal nationalisms which the social democratic leaders could neither comprehend nor handle and which finally destroyed their government.

The British experience proved to be a foreshadowing of what was to happen with variations throughout social democratic Europe in the course of the 1980s. The parties in office in Spain, France and Greece discovered that attempting to implement what they had undertaken threatened economic breakdown, runaway inflation and the risk of provoking a strike on the part of capital. They retreated. The left coalition in France broke up, probably to the relief of both partners. One observer concluded that: 'Socialism in its original inspirational meaning, as a working-class movement to change society, is quite simply being liquidated in France.' Even the SPD administration in Germany, less committed by ambitious promises and in charge of a much stronger economy, was forced to retreat from its decidedly more modest projects before losing office. Its counterparts in southern Europe held on to office in whole or in part, but lost any distinctive orientation, any political identity beyond their names which separated them from the opposing parties of economic liberalism and social conservatism.

Even the Scandinavian stronghold fell at last. The governments found themselves compelled to implement austerity programmes, as the social coalitions which had hitherto sustained them started to break apart. The Danish Social Democrats lost office in 1982 and began to move rightwards, the Norwegian Labour Party in 1981, returning only as a minority administration with a free-market orientation. Swedish capital, long thought to be the most tamed variety of the species anywhere in the world, had by the mid-1980s broken out of its cage and was vociferously demanding removal of controls and the effective dismantling of the Swedish welfare state. The social democrat government was compelled to bow, but tried to balance its austerity measures with a scheme to extend industrial ownership through the institutions of the Swedish labour movement. The idea was looked upon without enthusiasm by the workforce itself but met with passionate opposition from capital and the privately-owned media. It also provoked a middle-class backlash with street demonstrations and in due course led to conservative electoral victory.

It all amounted to a dramatic and dramatically fast reversal of the trend of development which had dominated European politics in one fashion or another for nearly four decades. Social democracy had been holed below the waterline, principally but not only by the long-term economic downturn: two additional and interlinked developments compounded its woes. In the long-run phase of global capitalism, which supervened with the ending of the long boom, concentration shifted from manufacture to the movement of liquid capital and paper claims. Investment banking increasingly came to overshadow industry, but the investments were made to a growing extent not for the purpose of production but to finance institutional loans, insurance, buy-outs and takeovers: financial institutions such as stock exchanges were reorganised to accommodate the trend.[43] As the process accelerated the transnational features of global capitalism, remarked upon from the 1960s, grew steadily more prominent. Its corporate structures transcended national boundaries, it moved as and where it pleased, settling and taking off according to the profitability of the location and began shifting manufacturing industry increasingly towards the low-wage economies of the Pacific Rim. Global capitalism's movements became in practice uncontrollable by national governments[44] whereas the principles and programmes of social democracy were premised on the management by governments of *national* economies.

The second and associated trend which made these developments possible and pushed them along was a technological one – the revolution in information technology which effectively turned the whole world into a virtual stock exchange and bank wherever cable networks existed and an office could be equipped with personal computers. It transformed the media as well, both print and airwaves, and in association with satellite broadcasting concentrated yet more resources and influence into the hands of right-wing moguls like Rupert Murdoch as well as accelerating the 'privatisation of the soul' and reducing the scope of public debate.

Social democracy's great asset (whether or not embodied in specifically social democratic parties), the secret weapon which had enabled it to defeat the communist challenge time after time in the developed countries of Europe, even in circumstances of political cataclysm and economic breakdown, was its offer to bring about far-reaching improvements and to satisfy a rising gradient of expectations *without* occasioning significant disruption in the lives of ordinary people. For more than a generation it had appeared able to pull off this miracle, but in the prophetic words of Tony Crosland at the time of the 1976 sterling crisis, unconsciously repudiating in a single phrase all that he had written in *The Future of Socialism*, 'The party's over'. Its symbiotic attachment to managed capitalism now spelt its doom, for capitalism could no longer be managed, and there were plenty of right-wing ideologues, the free-market theologians, ready to take advantage of the times and proclaim that it should not be. Their political triumph followed in due course, in Britain, the United States and finally Europe as well.[45]

All this is not to deny that the social democratic objections to the practices of communist regimes were well-founded, or that their attachment to political democracy, pluralism and the rule of law was valid, even when proceeding from false consciousness or bad faith. These institutions were all conquests of the great bourgeois revolutions and are indeed intrinsic to any fully human version of civic relationships. The tragedy of social democracy, specifically the social democracy of the Western labour movements, arose from treating them on the same basis as did its political and social enemies – namely as metaphysical absolutes rather than as historically limited and conditioned processes which lost half their efficacy so long as the societies in which they were established were governed at the bottom line not by an educated and knowledgeable popular will but by massive concentrations of property.

There followed from this circumstance what among all the historic ironies of the cruel twentieth century might well qualify as the greatest irony of all – the fact that social democracy (except insofar as parties bearing that name sprang up on the ruins of the fallen East European CPs) failed to gain any advantage whatever from the demise of its longstanding rival on the left.[46] Popular rejection of socialism even in its most timorous varieties (and again, of its American cognate, New Deal liberalism[47]) accompanied the intellectual discredit which overtook it among opinion formers in academia and the media. The collapse of the Eastern bloc regimes was not seen as clearing the ground in a manner which would enable 'socialism with a human face' to flourish but as damning the alternative versions as well through guilt by association, as all springing from the same intellectual error of 'collectivism' and therefore naturally driving the public along 'the road to serfdom', in Hayek's phrase. No doubt in all of this there was a degree of conscious calculation on the part of the right, which now saw an unprecedentedly favourable historic opportunity, but it could not have succeeded without an already existing and far-reaching popular disillusionment.

In Germany the SPD suffered electoral defeat and the Christian Democratic Union entrenched itself as the natural party of government, going on to preside over the reunification of the country following the liquidation of the GDR and reaping the electoral benefit despite mounting economic difficulties. In France the PSF, having been forced to renege on its election pledges of the early 1980s and therefore failing to effect any social or economic transformation, was driven from office by stages, amid growing corruption and scandal. The devastation of Britain's industrial base by Thatcher's governments and the endeavours they made to shatter the foundations of the welfare state did not prevent them from winning two general elections by overwhelming margins and her successor to win yet again, albeit more narrowly. The Scandinavian governing parties were thrown out – in Sweden losing by a landslide – and although they subsequently returned they did so no longer committed to the unique Scandinavian version of welfare-centred economic management. In Portugal Soares', social democrats, who termed themselves the Socialist Party, lost office to a further right party misleadingly called the Social Democrats, who pursued policies of orthodox economic liberalism and brought the country into the European Economic Community. Communists and conservatives combined to turn out the PASOK government, which had broken its promises of withdrawing from NATO and refusing EEC membership though it subsequently regained office despite the ill health and bizarre personal life of its leader, Andreas Papendreou. Perhaps it was the memory of the 1930s and the dictatorship which made Spanish conservatism electorally obnoxious even in its democratic guise: Gonzales's PSOE survived easily at the polls, but only after abandoning any pretensions to a recognisably socialist project, joining NATO in the face of massive popular objection and adopting economic strategies which permitted unemployment in Spain to attain a figure approaching 20 per cent.[48] It too lost office in 1996 – although by a much narrower margin than expected.

The Italian experience was entirely different in form but illustrated in essence a similar correlation of political forces. The long-term recession of the 1970s had made Italy the most unstable of the Western states outside the Iberian peninsula. The country was distracted by ultra-left terrorism directed at the political, police and judicial systems and by putschist plotting on the part of ultra-right elements within the state and 'security' apparatus[49] (the two may not have been unconnected) as well as overt and indiscriminate fascist[50] terrorism pursuing a strategy aimed at provoking the putsch. The political machinery revolved around the Christian Democrat (DC) party, the permanent party of government in coalition administrations since 1945 with all the others apart from the communists (and fascists) attached as satellites. With the passage of time all the governing parties had become deeply mired in financial and other forms of corruption[51] and the DC deeply implicated with the south Italian and Sicilian criminal enterprises, the Camora and Mafia: votes and money being exchanged for favours in the shape of government protection and contracts.

Since 1947 the political structure had been designed to exclude the communists, both during the Cold War era and even when the PCI pioneers of Eurocommunism had dropped their radically oppositional stance and sought to negotiate a 'historic compromise' – a term which they invented. The Communist Party remained untainted by corruption apart from a few minor and unauthorised breaches by low-level functionaries. In 1992–3 this political edifice imploded in spectacular fashion, its collapse occasioned by popular revulsion following revelation of the extent of corrupt dealing, and Mafia assassinations of investigative judges. The Christian Democrats[52] and the Socialist Party went down as dramatically as the CPSU, suffering membership collapse and an impending electoral wipe-out.[53] The separatist and ambiguously right-wing Northern League (originally the Lombard League) found its progress stalled as popular sentiment regrouped around the PCI and reforming fragments seceding from the discredited parties. It appeared that the hour of the Italian left had arrived at last.

What happened next demonstrated both the capacity of the late twentieth-century media to channel popular political sentiment and no less the power of certain deeply impressed fears and prejudices to influence an electorate when skilfully and continuously evoked. There stepped onto the stage Silvio Berlusconi, a media tycoon in the tradition of Alfred Hugenberg from the 1920s or Rupert Murdoch from the 1970s, to put his wealth and media influence to work for the purpose of rallying a demoralised right. Using the structures of his business empire he erected virtually overnight a political party, to which he gave the name of the Italian football team's slogan, Forza Italia and compelled his business employees to function as his political agents. He devised an electoral pact with the two right-wing forces uninvolved in corruption and which could therefore safely denounce it – the neo-fascist MSI (which changed its name to Allianza Italia for the occasion) and the Northern League. The new formation, with enormous propaganda resources at its disposal, presented itself both as the hammer of corruption and the shield against a revived red menace. It registered complete electoral success. Berlusconi did not survive long as prime minister, but he had fulfilled his function – and even if the new centre-left, pivoted on the PDS, should in the near future form a government it is clear that it would be compelled to pursue policies of financial orthodoxy no less than the PSOE in Spain.[54]

A long-term trend is evident. From being parties (whether Marxist or not) that regarded themselves as the heralds of an historically guaranteed new society and based firmly upon the industrial working class as their primary and central constituency, social democracy throughout the continent has evolved through stages towards a position of being liberalism with (more or less of) a social conscience. Just as the British Labour Party in the early years of the century foreshadowed the road which the ensemble of such parties was to take, so at the end of the century that party has moved furthest in the direction of abandoning all the features which formerly distinguished it from the Liberal Party which it replaced. The symbolic and platonic commitment to public ownership of productive resources has gone, as has the perspective of income redistribution or the use of Keynesian models of economic management. Indeed, the British Liberal Democrats themselves are undoubtedly further to the left on this score. All that remains is the trade union link, steadily growing weaker and likely soon to be no more of a consideration than the similar links of the Gladstonian Liberal Party a century ago.

Third World

Not unnaturally, social democracy's principal strength has been manifested in advanced industrial societies – ones where the largest social surplus has been available for distribution, sufficient to keep capital (relatively) happy and still sustain reasonable standards of existence for the bulk of the workforce. Its has achieved political success primarily in Western Europe, Australasia, and (in a different formulation) North America. However it has not been absent from parts of the world where the potential for long-term social stability has been less propitious. Parties of a social democratic complexion, whether or not affiliated to the Socialist International have appeared extensively in the Caribbean, Latin America, Asia[55] and Africa. In general they have represented social layers which like their 'Western' counterparts, were orientated towards policies of gradualist social alleviation but no profound restructuring of property relations or break with the international market. Julius Braunthal, in the third volume of his massive history of the Internationals, devotes a great deal of space to them[56] – not omitting the Nepali Congress, which actually led a successful anti-feudal revolution in 1950–1.

The most significant by far was the Congress Party of India, though not a member of the International and, like the Democratic Party in the US, maintaining in equilibrium (prior to its fragmentation) a bloc of interests, many elements of which were conservative or even reactionary. There were, however, some exceptions to the general rule of non-radicalism among Third World social democrats. The Jamaican People's National Party (confusingly, its right-wing opponent was called the Labour Party) incurred the wrath of Washington and was forced out of office for trying to institute genuinely redistributive policies. The New Jewel movement of Grenada, damned as 'communist' and overthrown by US invasion in 1983, was actually affiliated to the Socialist International.

The future for social democratic parties – formal or informal – in the Third World can scarcely be regarded as promising. It is certainly possible that political forces of this type, whether or not they use the name or affiliate to the International, will emerge in the 'tiger economies' of the Pacific Rim as industrialisation proceeds, along with the firm establishment of a large and concentrated industrial workforce – and if political repression is eased. On the other side of the world, Brazil in recent years has seen the emergence of the first entirely new mass working-class party for nearly a century – the Workers' Party (PT), described as an amalgam of workerism and liberalism[57] rejecting the politics of clientelism and state control. Nonetheless, if social democracy in First World countries, with enormous per capita resources and incomes, is under severe siege and in the process of dismantling its social programmes, it is hard to imagine how its much weaker equivalents in the impoverished quarters of the globe can pose much of an effective challenge to the powers of rampant transnational capital.

Conclusion

As much as the fall of the Soviet bloc and the marketisation of the main surviving 'Marxist-Leninist' regimes, the fate of social democracy reflects the ascendancy of the global market, the laissez-faire configuration that it has assumed and the values associated with such a development. In the almost two-century-long contest between socialism and capitalism, socialism had suffered comprehensive defeat. Its parties were prostrated or in capitulation, its social bases in hopeless disarray and their organisations broken, the ideologies which had sustained it discredited and derided. No aspect of the present could give any cause for optimism regarding the future.

PART II

ALTERNATIVES

CHAPTER 6

Trotskyism, Maoism, Eurocommunism

Until the 1980s both 'actually existing socialism' and social democracy continued to appear as well established formations likely to enjoy lengthy futures, although few outside their own apparatus were wholly satisfied with the forms which they had assumed. At the same time, it had been clear for decades, and demonstrated spectacularly in 1968, that the former was deeply degenerate, while equally the latter had long lost any real will to achieve the ambition enunciated in the Socialist International declaration of 1951 – 'Socialists strive to build a new society in freedom and by democratic means'. In consequence, on various occasions since the 1930s, groups and individual actors upon the left – disillusioned defectors or new entrants into its culture – had endeavoured to repair what they regarded as broken and perverted traditions or to establish new and better ones. This chapter will consider the three major attempts deriving from the Leninist tradition, the following one the multiple dimensions of the 'new left'.

On the face of things Trotskyism, Maoism and Eurocommunism appear to have little in common other than the fact of their springing from a Leninist source of origin. In principles and ideological outlook they differed as much from each other as social democracy did from Marxist-Leninist orthodoxy. On the other hand, they did have a negative feature in common in spite of the vast separation of their politics: that they came to be posed – even if they were not strictly conceived as – alternatives to the Marxist-Leninist orthodoxy promulgated from Moscow. All three of these strands were indeed symptoms of the gaps and absences in the official ideology, the unanswered question of history, current politics and future vision, as well the practical shortcomings of the Soviet state and the political culture of official communism.

Trotskyism

Leon Trotsky is the great tragic figure of the twentieth century. The tragedy does not lie primarily in the fact that he was driven from high office in the young Soviet state, carried into exile, saw his children murdered by Stalin's terror apparatus and was finally killed himself – though that summary biography is wrenching enough. His personal story has all the elements of a mighty and sombre drama to which only an exceptional author could give adequate expression – but it occurred in real life. But the tragedy lies rather in the depth of the abyss between the nature of the hopes and aspirations he embodied with spectacular seeming initial success and the ultimate total defeat: a tragedy compounded by a growing failure of political judgment in his later years. The latter was a failure which foreshadowed the wretchedness of the movement founded in his name; a movement which has been a story of endlessly repeated doomed futility, in spite of providing on occasion a political home to some individuals of exceptional historical insight.[1]

Trotsky, along with Rosa Luxemburg, has been described as a revolutionary steeped in the Marxist values of the Second International, who took the movement's historic revolutionary mission seriously rather than a cloak for opportunist and reformist politics. The aspiration was to world revolution, with the proletariat as the revolutionary actor and the purpose of world revolution the entry into what Marx had termed the 'realm of freedom', which would enable individual intellectual and creative powers to be unshackled by collective control over the forces of production and their direction towards human ends. From this standpoint, shared with all his colleagues at the time of the Russian Revolution and the establishment of the Communist International, revolution was global or it was nothing.

Any sober estimate of the subsequent disputes and faction fights within the governing bodies of the USSR can only conclude that it was Trotsky and his supporters, rather than Stalin, Bukharin[2] and theirs, who represented the original Bolshevik aims and aspirations and that Lenin, had he lived, would have been in the same camp. That does not necessarily prescribe which faction possessed the more realistic appreciation of Soviet actuality and of what was in fact possible given the circumstances of the Soviet republic in the mid-1920s. How Trotsky, supposing he had won the struggle, would have coped with entrenched peasant backwardness and commitment to petty capitalism and small-scale uneconomic production is an interesting historical speculation. What we can be certain of is that the situation would not have been transformed by the spread of revolution westward, for the supposedly missed opportunities in Germany in 1923, Britain in 1926 or Spain a decade later, were not revolutionary opportunities in the sense in which Trotskyists have come to understand them – as potentially world-transforming insurgencies whose potential was blighted by Stalin or Zinoviev. It was not simply that the world was drawing away from the 'hopes of October' – though that was certainly happening – it was that these hopes, however convincing they appeared around 1919, and however understandable it might have been that Lenin and his co-thinkers should have adhered to them, were never realistic in the first place. The First World War did not herald the final uncontrollable crisis of capitalism or imperialism: the structures of bourgeois society may have been shaken, but not so shaken that they were upon the point of collapse; that society had plenty in reserve, both economically and politically. The crisis of the war and interwar years signalled the shift of global capital into a new cycle of accumulation centred on the United States, and not its imminent demise.

The characteristic temper of Trotsky's political outlook was that he anticipated world revolution with total seriousness and hence likewise the meaning and work of the Comintern. His evaluation of Russian affairs was in relation to world revolution, not the other way around, whereas for the political leaders who came to the forefront following Lenin's death, or at least after Zinoviev and Kamanev were sidelined, international revolution was something to be downplayed, put on the back burner or brushed up as necessary, depending on the exigencies of Soviet politics. The concept of 'permanent revolution', in its formulation of the mid-1920s, which became the touchstone of Trotskyist orthodoxy, was a theoretical attempt to reconcile the world-revolutionary expectations which the Soviet government had inherited from the October Revolution with the realities of politics in the developed countries, where the revolution looked likely to kick its heels for a long time into the future.

In his perception that the delay in the spread of the revolution westwards was connected with the growing bureaucratisation of Soviet, state, society and the CPSU, Trotsky was quite accurate. He had personally made more than a minimal contribution to reducing the soviets to mere instruments of the party and to undemocratic practices and structures within the party and in the workplace – and even advocated the militarisation of labour. He was naturally no adherent of bourgeois democracy or the political pluralism which accompanied it and happily defended the party's monopoly role. There is however no reason to believe that he was anything but sincere in wanting genuine democracy for the working class and its communist party, and that the restrictions he accepted and advocated were regarded as temporary measures for backward Russia alone, justified by emergency conditions.

Trotsky struggled to devise a theoretical analysis for a state of affairs never remotely envisaged in classical Marxism – an ostensibly workers' state aspiring to be the torchbearer of international revolution but left isolated and besieged within the international community, reduced to the extreme depths of pauperisation, its technological infrastructure wrecked, its industrial workforce annihilated or dispersed, its principles of workers' democracy turned into the opposite and replaced with iron but hopelessly inefficient centralisation. When there is a superfluity of consumer goods, he noted, people buy at will: when there is a shortage (assuming price control) queues have to be formed, and when the queues grow inordinately long coercive measures have to be applied to keep them in order. Such, Trotsky reasoned, is the starting-point of bureaucracy or at any rate of the sort of bureaucracy that came to prevail in the USSR. Bureaucratic frameworks of any type also provide career ladders, and one of this particular kind supplied ladders which elevated people into positions of arbitrary authority removed from public accountability. The tallest and firmest of these ladders was of course the Soviet Communist Party itself.

Hence the Soviet state, party and society entered into a phase of bureaucratic degeneration. The experiences of civil war, hunger, economic disruption and isolation had destroyed, physically or organisationally, large segments of the revolutionary working class and demoralised the remainder, swamped in any case by a peasant mass attached to individualism, petty production and social and cultural stagnation. The energy and aspiration of 1917 was gone five years later, and Trotsky's own pronouncements and warnings sounded increasingly hollow in the deepening political void forming around him.

That would have remained true even if the multiplying plague of bureaucrats within the body of Soviet society had been composed entirely of honest and principled individuals (as indeed many of them were). But inevitably careerists, place hunters, authoritarians by temperament and straightforward corruptionists out to accumulate privilege, power and status, emerged from the woodwork to exploit the opportunities offered by an autocratic party-state which took upon itself an immensely greater range of responsibilities than its Tsarist predecessor – in its own day a byword for repressive bureaucracy – had ever done. The ascendancy of Stalin, a negligible personality in Trotsky's view, a 'grey blur',[3] was attributed to this individual's role as the representative and spokesperson for that parasitic layer. 'His strength lies in the fact that he expresses the instinct of self-preservation of the ruling caste more firmly, more decisively and more pitilessly than anyone else.'[4]

In the renewed upswing of the revolution, which Trotsky to the end of his days confidently expected to occur in the not too distant future both in Europe and in the Soviet Union itself, resided his hopes for the overthrow of the leaders and the counter-revolutionary functionaries who had expropriated the political and social victories of 1917. He remained however adamantly opposed to any interpretation which designated the bureaucracy as a social class which had returned the state to a form of class rule, let alone the extreme version of that thesis, which defined the regime as one of 'state capitalism' with the bureaucracy as the new capitalists extracting a surplus from the producers through the mechanisms of central planning rather than the market. On the contrary, he insisted that socialised property relations had been preserved (and extended, in however grisly a fashion, by collectivisation and the five-year plans) because of popular commitment to social ownership and that therefore what was needed now was not a social revolution but a political one to remove the parasitic bureaucratic nightmare and allow the real potential of social property and planned production to develop. Unless that happened, he predicted, the world market combined with the greater productivity of labour in the developed world would infallibly undermine and ultimately destroy the foundations of 'socialism in a single country'.

Until the Comintern-directed behaviour of the Communist Party of Germany (KPD) helped to open the way for Hitler's accession to power, Trotsky did not despair of the Third International and of hopes that it might break with Stalinism. He encouraged his sympathisers, of whom there were many, to continue to work within it, i.e. within the official communist parties, and to avoid expulsion if they could. On the eve of the blood purges in the USSR he was to claim that the international opposition which he inspired had its strongest and most widespread element located within that country.

The purges appeared to Trotsky the final proof that official communism had reached such a stage of utter degeneracy that nothing more was to be expected of it. In 1938 his followers established the Fourth International as an intended independent revolutionary force to lead the still confidently expected global proletarian advance. It was asserted that the Stalinist-dominated movement had become irredeemably counter-revolutionary and that nothing further could be hoped from it. The programme of the new international opened with the declaration that its positions would soon be adopted by millions of proletarians around the world. Unhappily, Marx's comment about the first time as a tragedy, the second time as a farce, comes irresistibly to mind. The Fourth International was a gesture of desperation, not a serious political departure, and in every way unworthy of its founder. Trotsky's following had been reduced since the beginning of the decade, by persecution and defection, to isolated individuals and groupuscules without significant support in the working class or anywhere else.

The founding meeting in Paris in 1938, attended by 21 individuals, was an ill-prepared, hurried and clandestine affair and was penetrated by a Stalinist spy. From Trotsky's own perspectives, those of the original Comintern and from Marxist judgment generally it was a tragic blunder.[5] Such an initiative should have been taken on a rising tide of proletarian advance, to clarify and focus emerging revolutionary possibilities, not at a point when the labour movement all over Europe and elsewhere was in precipitate retreat and disorganisation and Trotskyism reduced to the status of a persecuted sect. The Fourth International made no impact whatsoever on world affairs, and worse, was detrimental to Trotskyism by putting in place a structure to which its organisations, such as they were, were compelled to relate but without any capacity to support or guide them – it was a certain recipe for fragmentation and infighting among theoretically-minded and highly contentious individuals divorced from the reality of mass political organisations.

Prophet Outcast

In 1940 the Fourth International's founder died at the hands of a Stalinist assassin, but his creation continued to live on – after a fashion. Two features strike the observer regarding Trotskyism since 1940 and in particular since the end of the Second World War. One is the persistent political weakness of all movements politically active in Trotsky's name or even within a broader tradition partly embodying his outlook. It has survived as a collection of bitterly divided and mutually anathematising sects which have only very occasionally, untypically and without permanent effect, succeeded in mobilising a mass following. In a half-century of revolutions this revolutionary movement has found itself singularly impotent. In every political confrontation of those years, whether revolutionary, quasi-revolutionary or played out in a bourgeois-democratic arena; whether in Europe, Asia, Africa or the Americas, the representatives of this tradition have always lost. But the other feature is that it *has* nevertheless persisted in spite of its perpetually defeated and frequently absurd character. In some form or another Trotskyism unquestionably answers to a political and intellectual need, albeit one felt by very restricted minorities.

As has turned out to be the case with Marxism itself, Trotskyism's strongest and most fruitful entrenchment has been within the academy; whether that of formal academic institutions or the universe of left-wing intellectual journals and publishing. In other words it has been as a guide to historical interpretation – casting an ironic and paradoxical light on Marx's maxim about the point being to change the world rather than interpret it. Leaving aside his exposure of the purges, which would doubtless have been undertaken sooner or later by other hands, any serious examination of any aspect of the USSR during the 1920s and 1930s has to take into account if not to begin from Trotsky's critique of Stalinist politics and social management. The central concept of a bureaucratic layer imposing itself upon a shattered social order, acting in the name of Leninism but drastically perverting it, may not be the complete story, but it is certainly a large part of it. Leaving aside his incontestably appropriate recommendations for what the German labour parties should have done to block Hitler's path to the chancellorship, Trotsky was also in part responsible for a conceptual model of fascism as a species of Bonapartism. This model has its weaknesses, but it is suggestive and points in the right direction.

Above all in terms of his intellectual attainment, Trotsky was the earliest and as yet the best historian of the Russian Revolution. Even if the state which he helped to found has perished irretrievably, his account of the climactic moment of its foundation will survive as a historiographical classic of the first order. It is also highly inspirational, and here we encounter the secret of Trotskyism's ability to reproduce itself down the years and find fresh levies of adherents, regardless of their limited numbers, relentless internal disputes and mutual vituperation. He combined what is, strictly speaking, a utopian vision in its longing for a transformed order of things to be accomplished quickly, with – for a brief space of time – the apparent actual accomplishment; and along with those the ability to express both the vision and the manner of its attainment with matchless eloquence.

These strengths were also the sources of Trotsky and Trotskyism's intrinsic weakness and the fatal misjudgments which followed from it. As Isaac Deutscher notes in his biography, for all the masterly deployment of analysis and narrative in the *History*, there is a problem with it. As an orthodox Marxist (and whatever his theoretical innovations Trotsky was certainly that) he could not admit that the presence or absence of a single individual could profoundly affect or turn the direction of titanic historical forces. But as a central participant he knew very well that if he and/or Lenin had been absent from Petrograd the Bolshevik revolution would never have happened. This realisation, at odds with the Marxian ideology out of which the author is writing, creates an unresolved tension running throughout the *History* (which is none the worse for it). But in fact the October Revolution was accomplished against the historical odds and indeed against the grain of history. It was not for nothing that Gramsci termed it 'the revolution against *Capital*' (rather than against capital) and that orthodox Marxists like Plekhanov were horrified at what had been done. A unique and unrepeatable historical conjuncture, compounded of the condition of Tsarist Russia and the urban workforce it produced, the defeats suffered in the war and the thorough incapacity of the Provisional government permitted a group of Marxists with unusually revolutionary and voluntarist dispositions to, as they thought, open the locks to the supposedly incipient world revolution beating on the door.[6] Not surprisingly, the events of November 1917 in Petrograd and the major Russian cities were not recognised as exceptional but as the model which might be expected to be followed as soon as the proletarians fighting each other on Europe's blood-drenched battlefields understood that the real enemy was at home – something which the October Revolution would help to make clear.

When it did not, and irrespective of Stalin, the dominant trend in the ruling party following Lenin's incapacity was to leave history to look after itself and to concentrate upon the enormous enough task of coping with Soviet affairs. This Trotsky could not accept, though he accepted of course that Soviet affairs had to be managed – but ought to be managed, in his view, with reference to the 'permanent revolution'. There existed an intrinsic flaw in such a judgment of reality. The flaw was not in the assessment of the capitalist order as highly unstable and volatile, both in its metropolitan heartlands and in the colonial and semi-colonial regions of the Third World. The flaw was rather in the perception that a repetition of the October Revolution was likely or even possible on the territory of the developed nations. The misjudgment was in the end of the 'subjective factor' – the willingness of industrial workforces with long traditions of 'peaceful' and 'constitutional' practice to commit themselves to revolutionary enterprises – even when such an attempt would actually have been in their immediate material interests, as in Germany in January 1933. There developed a generic picture, which went back to the failed German insurrection of 1923 and was applied to the developments in Spain during 1936,[7] of a spontaneously militant working class ardent for revolution and straining at the political leash who were restrained and defeated only through the betrayal of treacherous leaderships. All subsequent events were read against the template of Europe between 1917 and 1919 and there developed an incorrigible tendency, apparent even in Trotsky's own lifetime, to take limited and partial developments such as major strikes or government crises for signals that the masses were ready to move into revolutionary action.

Trotskyism after Trotsky

The onset of the Second World War did not take Trotsky by surprise. He had in fact predicted the Hitler-Stalin Pact of August 1939, arguing that Stalin's fear of military confrontation with the German dictator, particularly following the former's massacre of his own officer corps in the Great Purges, would induce him to make a deal enabling Hitler to seize large areas of Central Europe. He argued moreover that this fear sprang from Stalin's understanding that if an anti-Nazi victory followed from an alliance between the

USSR and the Western democracies, the Soviet working class would without fail settle accounts with the bureaucratic usurper.

One might imagine then that when such a correlation of circumstances actually did arise and the USSR became involved in an anti-Axis military coalition, Trotsky's followers even out of purely tactical considerations, would have been inclined to support the war effort. This did not happen. They continued to treat the conflict, even following the entry of the USSR, as an inter-imperialist war (which of course in part it was) on the model of the First World War and to hope that it might issue in another 1917. They instigated or supported strikes, including ones in war-related industries and advocated, so far as they had the opportunity, not a relentless military assault upon the Third Reich but winning the German working class to overthrow it from within.

The war's outcome, far from resulting in the political overthrow of the Stalinist regime strengthened it enormously, and was followed by the extension of Soviet power over Eastern Europe and subsequently the Chinese revolution. Developments such as these posed major theoretical puzzles and dilemmas for the Fourth International which at the time, excluding the peculiar case of Ceylon, amounted to a few thousand individuals at most. According to the Programme and the accepted common position of Trotskyism, Stalinism was wholly and irredeemably bankrupt, its role could be nothing other than counter-revolutionary. Nor was that all. Without question, in the aftermath of the Axis debacle the European proletariat had recovered dramatically from the defeats of the 1930s and made gigantic advances, while simultaneously the colonial empires were in turmoil. Yet the Fourth International was no stronger and no more influential than when it had been formed, let alone come forward with dramatic access of support to lead the upsurge.

Effectively, everything had been staked on a particular historical expectation which had gone spectacularly wrong. The result not unnaturally was recrimination and fragmentation. There were some who abandoned the tradition altogether, made their peace with the class enemy and re-emerged as leading spokespersons on the right-wing of liberalism. Such was the case with a number of prominent New York literary intellectuals such as those around the journal *Partisan Review* who placed their well-honed anti-communist talents at the disposal of the Cold War institutions and won renown as the proponents of a manichean, irreconcilable conflict between the 'free world' and 'totalitariainism'.[8] They had transformed their politics but not their political temperaments.

In the main though, and for some years, the Fourth International attempted simply to live with the contradiction it could not reconcile between its evaluation of Stalinism and what was actually taking

place in Europe and Asia – speculating meantime in its circles and
publications on the likelihood of a world slump which would
transform capitalist recovery into crisis, discredit Stalinism and open
once more the prospects of revolution along the original Bolshevik
lines. The precedent of 1917 was very much in mind, particularly
in the expectation that groupings consisting of no more than a few
hundred individuals might blossom within months into revolutionary
forces capable of overthrowing bourgeois or Stalinist regimes.

Catastrophism was inherent in the Fourth International's world-
view and in 1951 there appeared an article by the head of its
International Secretariat Michel Pablo (not his real name of course)
of extreme catastrophic tendency, predicting world war[9] and
international revolution (rather than annihilation) in the none-
too-distant future. However, projecting from post-1945
developments he also argued that this fresh wave of revolution would
be led by the Stalinist parties and that for the indefinite future the
correct approach for Trotskyists was to operate within them as
concealed groupings (a strategy known as entryism). This minimal
concession to realism was eventually deemed heretical by an
important section of the FI's following and occasioned in 1953–4
the first major split, with the establishment of a rival Fourth
International (the International Committee of the Fourth
International) which included the largest and most important
Trotskyist organisation in the developed world, the US Socialist
Workers' Party (not to be confused with the entirely different
Socialist Workers' Party, or SWP, later formed in Britain).

Notoriously, the world of Trotskyist politics constituted a peculiar
and separate political universe. Its meat and drink consisted of intense
and constant doctrinal faction fights, splits, anathemas, expulsions,
recombinations – producing throughout the years an expanding and
bewildering plethora of minuscule organisations, each proclaiming
itself to be the only true standard-bearer of the faith and the vehicle
of world revolution. Particular styles might vary enormously, from
the sinister gangsterism of the organisation led by Gerry Healy
(latterly the Workers' Revolutionary Party) to the relative political
sophistication and pragmatism during the 1960s of the International
Marxist Group. Nevertheless there was universal commitment to
a form of practice whose essence was usually concealment from
the general public (and frequently the rank and file membership
as well) with invariably authoritarian centralisation, personalised
vendetta and stigmatising of political or organisational disagreement
as the expression of alien class viewpoints or possibly secret service
penetration.

In only one part of the world did Trotskyism succeed in becoming
a mass movement, namely the island of Ceylon, and the manner
in which this came about is indicative. A number of Ceylonese

students, having become adherents of Trotsky while studying in the universities of the colonial power, Britain, returned to their homeland and provided the ideological framework around which coalesced a significant part of the emergent labour movement there, forming a party whose Sinhalese initials were LSSP. The LSSP following Ceylon's independence found itself facing the dilemma that attends all organisations with a significant following and mass constituency when they uphold a rhetoric of intransigent revolutionism in long-term non-revolutionary circumstances. The LSSP before long went the way of the pre-1914 SPD or the post-1956 CPI, it became pragmatic and adjusted itself to the realities of pursuing limited objectives. In the late 1950s its majority entered a coalition government (a move Trotsky would certainly have denounced), was expelled from the branch of the FI to which it was attached and soon ceased to be a political actor of any consequence. In an even remoter part of the globe, the Andean state of Bolivia, Trotskyists were involved in a more than marginal fashion in the revolution of 1952, but were unable to build a significant movement out of their participation. Certain activists also succeeded in establishing a presence in colonial Vietnam but were physically destroyed by their communist rivals after 1945.

The two principal foci of Trotskyist politics during the postwar years have been Britain and the United States. In the latter country Trotskyism found more of a political space than in other developed countries thanks to a politically very weak CP rival[10] and the absence of a hegemonic party of labour. Nonetheless it never amounted to more than a few thousand members. The Socialist Workers' Party, founded principally by Trotsky's disciple James P. Cannon, has subsequently remained the largest of these groupings (and the largest orthodox Trotskyist party outside Ceylon). It has occasionally achieved some marginal industrial influence and has been centrally important in all the splits and regroupments which occurred thereafter in the Fourth International.[11] In 1953 Cannon aligned with Healy and his group in Britain against the International Secretariat located in Paris. Healy's refusal ten years later to participate in a reunification process constituted the largest split in the then international movement, such as it was.

Despite the disruption of the LSSP a measure of growth for international Trotskyism commenced in the 1960s. At that time the communist regimes and parties continued routinely to denounce Trotskyism, but no longer with the virulence that had characterised the Stalin epoch – the accusation of being fascist agents was quietly discontinued. Trotsky's ideas and record were attacked as ultra-left, petty bourgeois and so forth,[12] but the fact that they continued to be given this attention was in itself indicative – the ideas had not died. The single-handed endeavour of rehabilitation engaged in by Isaac Deutscher was of the utmost importance in restoring the true picture of what Trotsky had been and thought, through his biography of Stalin (by implication),[13] and later his monumental and meticulously researched three-volume biography of *The Prophet Armed/Unarmed/Outcast*, all of which possessed a weight and credibility that the sectarian pamphleteers could not hope to match.[14] The 1960s was the decade of revolutionary romanticism (see below) and Trotskyism, in spite of the hard-faced veterans who ran its fragmented organisations, unquestionably belonged to that species.

The surge of Trotskyist sentiment which reanimated existing splinters and gave birth to new ones rendered the movement organisationally less rather than more coherent. The founder's posthumous influence, which undoubtedly grew, was more a matter of permeating certain segments of the left intelligentsia than conjuring into being mass movements – or even credible political formations. The influence too was more in the form of a diffuse recognition of Trotsky's strengths than widespread acceptance of particular theories or ideological positions. It became generally recognised that in the Russian Revolution he had been a figure whose importance had been not far short of Lenin's, and that his critique of Stalinism was well-founded and the essential starting point for any structural analysis of the regime – but 'Permanent Revolution' and 'degenerate workers' state' remained distinguishing markers for an esoteric brand of politics rather than an idea whose time had come – even in a half century of nearly continuous revolutions and Stalinist-type regimes.

The moment of truth for Trotskyism as a revolutionary theory and form of practical politics – as distinct from a mode of historical interpretation – arrived with the fall of the Soviet bloc. This surely was the long-awaited moment when the bankruptcy of Stalinism and neo-Stalinism was made evident and the time had arrived for the Soviet and East European masses to defend the achievements of socialised property relations and to return to the fresh roots of the revolution by carrying through the political revolution to restore genuine Soviet power[15] and the workers' possession of the supposedly workers' state.[16]

Trotskyist groupings did indeed come into being as the regimes' power dissolved, but the impact of the doctrine or its followers upon events was even less than might have been expected – in effect absolutely zero. Virtually no one in the chaos of the communist collapse showed any interest in replacing the discredited version of revolutionary socialism with a purer and more authentic variety. There was no mass perception that the original revolution had been hijacked and that the conceptions of 1917 should be made real once again. By the bitterest of ironies the commonplace view of Trotsky, now that he could be openly discussed, was that he was no more than a failed Stalin, whose politics were in no way essentially different and who would have followed a similar path had the power struggle gone his way. A substantial number of citizens wanted to preserve what was already in existence against the avalanche of the uncontrolled market in economics and politics; a lesser proportion showed an interest in social democratic solutions; but the majority wanted to get as far away as possible from any articulated conception of socialism, particularly among the non-Russian nations.

Among the Western Trotskyist parties and grouplets, reaction to the cataclysm varied enormously. The British SWP, though not strictly Trotskyist, was one of the formations which had enormous hopes of a revolutionary sort invested in the processes which began in 1989. The fall of 'state capitalism' was welcomed unreservedly, but when the expected workers' revolution failed to materialise the group's theoreticians and publicists did not permit their complacency to be disturbed. They have continued to regard the end of the Soviet regime and the Soviet Union as opening up new vistas of opportunity for revolutionaries both on the territory of the former bloc and in other parts of the world. They have attributed the total refusal of history to conform to theoretical expectations to the absence or weakness of revolutionary leadership rather to a mass rejection of anything purporting to be revolutionary socialism. At the other end of the Trotskyist spectrum the Sparticists, a group based principally in the US but with a British affiliate, have stridently denounced the developments as a bourgeois counter-revolution and, in relation to Russia, despite their minuscule numbers, called upon the masses to defeat and overthrow the Yeltsin government and preserve whatever could be saved of the old order.

The Trotskyist factions have always presented an irresistible and unmissable target for caricature and satire, never more so than at the end of the twentieth century. Their elevation of political doctrine into cast-iron dogma, their theological hair-splitting, their propensity to organisational splits over abstruse theoretical disputes, their obsession with the details of long-forgotten and insignificant controversies,[17] the abyss between their pretensions and the actualities of their situation[18] all contribute to an impression of risible and preposterous irrelevance. At present there exist at least three 'Fourth Internationals'. It would, however, be an error not to take seriously the Trotskyist tradition, let alone Trotsky himself. Its appeal has been to the hopes and aspirations that were alive and widespread in the revolution's early days, summed up in John Reed's text *Ten Days that Shook the World*. That appeal has been reinforced by the associated conviction that following the correct theoretical guidelines will enable revolutionaries to repeat the experience and restore the aborted promise of the first four Comintern congresses.

Trotskyism (and the quasi-Trotskyism of Tony Cliff's followers in the British SWP) has posed itself as a science of revolution in opposition to the apparently immovable but supposedly hollow strength of the capitalist state and the degenerate caricature of socialism represented by the Stalinist tradition. In short, it has constituted a tradition of embalmed Leninism – or rather a horde of rival and contradictory Leninisms – made possible only by the fact that it has been incapable of mobilising a mass movement and never, with the exception of Ceylon, had to face the responsibility of relating to a mass constituency.[19] Notoriously it has tended to replicate within its sects all the worst features of Stalinist centralisation and authoritarianism – minus of course the power to inflict death and imprisonment. The pattern has been repeated with such unfailing regularity that it cannot be seriously doubted that it springs from the Leninist heritage. Organisational tactics and forms of control which may well have been appropriate and justified under the police repression of the Tsarist empire or the emergency of civil war, when transplanted to other environments become pathological and deadly.[20] Trotsky's much-quoted remark at the founding congress of 1903, which, much as he subsequently tried to repudiate it, continued to haunt him throughout his career – that the party envisaged by Lenin will come to substitute itself for the masses, the central committee for the party and finally the dictator for the central committee – was extraordinarily perceptive, the more so when it was Lenin's or his own epigones who were in charge.

Mike Waite has suggested[21] that the historic fate of Trotskyism merely foreshadows the breakdown of the Marxist-Leninist regimes in the sense of that form of politics proving to be a historical dead-end. If this analysis is accepted the further question which suggests itself is whether any alternative entrance is available to 'the realm of freedom' and any other solution available to the barriers of class rule and dominance which were correctly identified by Lenin and Trotsky. The ambiguity is well summarised by Deutscher:

> If the view were to be taken that all that the Bolsheviks aimed at – socialism – was no more than a *fata morgana*, that the revolution merely substituted one kind of exploitation and oppression for another, and could not do otherwise, then Trotsky would appear as the high priest of a god that was bound to fail, as Utopia's servant mortally entangled in his dreams and illusions. Even then he would attract the respect and sympathy due to the great utopians and visionaries – he would stand out among them as one of the greatest. Even if it were true that it is man's fate to stagger in pain and blood from defeat to defeat

and to throw off one yoke only to bend his neck beneath another – even then man's longing for a different destiny would still, like pillars of fire, relieve the darkness and gloom of the endless desert through which he has been wandering with no promised land beyond. And no one in our age has expressed these longings as vividly and sacrificially as Trotsky.[22]

Maoism

At the height of the Sino-Soviet dispute in the early 1960s, it was not unknown for the Soviet polemicists to accuse their adversaries of being crypto-Trotskyists. Nor was it exceptional for Trotskyists and Trotskyist sympathisers to read into the events then occurring in China a revival of the revolutionary impulse, which might run far beyond the original intentions of the party leaders who evoked it and draw them eventually towards a genuinely Trotskyist understanding. Even Deutscher was to express hopes of this kind.[23]

These the hopes were totally misplaced and any resemblances that there may have been were wholly coincidental – apart from the tendency towards doctrinal dogma and authoritarianism among the true believers. Trotskyism, whatever its shortcomings, rested upon a highly sophisticated albeit erroneous understanding of historic development and the unfolding of the world revolution, Maoism mostly upon a set of slogans. Maoism as an extension and development of Marxism lacked both strong social roots and intellectual credibility. That of course has to be distinguished from Mao Zedong's insights in establishing the direction and strategy of the Chinese revolution up to its spectacular triumph in 1949. He was undoubtedly a pre-eminent revolutionary – but not necessarily a Marxist in any sense that Marx would have understood. The Chinese Revolution was in essence a titanic peasant revolt, indeed the greatest in all history in terms of its scope and success. Leninism provided its leaders with a rational perception of social relations and a model of organisation and discipline which channelled the revolution's energies and saved them from being dissipated in the manner of its innumerable predecessors.

The revolutionaries did not take over a what was a 'backward' country in any absolute sense. The most populous nation on earth possessed an unbroken literate culture over two millennia old and a scientific tradition of immense sophistication. It had enjoyed a peak of civilised attainment coinciding in time with the European dark ages. Its script and culture had formed the basis for the civilisations around its periphery, Korea, Vietnam and most importantly Japan.[24] What the new rulers did face was a shattered society ravaged by centuries of indescribable poverty and decades

of colonial incursions, invasion, famine, civil war and economic disorganisation; largely bereft of twentieth-century industry and
machine technology – suffering in other words the classic stigmata
of backwardness as the West and the USSR understood them.

If Leninism had supplied the prescription for revolutionary
success, Stalinism at first did likewise for industrial development.
During the early 1950s agrarian collectivisation and centrally
planned concentration on heavy industry according to the Soviet
model were not very successful and the Chinese leaders grew
dissatisfied, as they did with Stalin's hard bargains and his
overbearing and patronising attitudes – though he avoided
interference in Chinese internal affairs. The alternative path of
development embarked upon under Mao's guidance in 1957 proved
to be even worse, indeed disastrous. The 'Great Leap Forward'
aimed to exploit the advantage of China's human numbers by
substituting extensive for intensive industrial development – a
myriad of steel-producing furnaces in peasant backyards. The
disruption was such that the resulting famine outdid in its severity
those that had occurred during the worst phases of the earlier
times of troubles. Meantime, as described in Chapter 3, relations
with Stalin's successors had deteriorated into poisonous enmity.

Two Phases

What came to be known as Maoism developed in two distinct phases
– excluding the practical innovations and theoretical writings of Mao
as a revolutionary leader in the time of Stalin and the immediately
following years. Maoism proper constituted the attempt to transform
the CPC and its leader into directing centres of world communism.
The first phase was an argument, intertwined with the breakdown
of relations between Moscow and Beijing, pursued – within the
confines of the existing communist movement – around a political
offensive by the Communist Party of China aimed at winning the
parties to its position, or at least of splitting them and creating
substantial pro-Maoist rivals. Naturally the polemic was not
conducted in the unvarnished terms that I have reconstructed
above, but was given a theoretical gloss. The Chinese critiques
centred on 'revisionism', to which the objects of these denunciations
were accused of capitulating. The paradigm case of revisionism was
alleged to be Tito's Yugoslav regime, for its relative political and
social liberalism and, ironically, its break with Stalin in 1948. The
Soviet leaders were reproached for maintaining friendly relations
with it at the expense of the embodiment of Stalinist orthodoxy,
Enver Hoxha's Albania, now China's ally and zealous ideological
partner. The leaderships of the Italian and French communist
parties were castigated for lurching in a revisionist direction and

summoned to mend their ways. Evidently if an internal coup should place either or both of these large and important parties within the Chinese camp the political balance within the European communist movement would be dramatically shifted. Finally the polemic moved from the lesser parties and the CPSU was accused directly not merely of revisionism but of sacrificing all the gains of the October Revolution and restoring capitalism within the Soviet borders.

The central indictment levelled in the accusatory material which the CPC began to propagate was that the Soviet leadership had restored capitalism in the USSR and adopted a line of foreign policy in keeping with a capitalist great power. The nature of this alleged reversion to capitalism or how it was supposed to have come about was never specified in detail – the Chinese confined themselves to gibes about the consumer emphasis Khrushchev wanted to impart to the Soviet economy and to cultural manifestations which were claimed to demonstrate a falling away from socialist values – they objected to imaginative creations representing anything other than a relentlessly didactic emphasis on zealous commitment and unquestioning revolutionary fervour.

Serious though they were, these were lesser manifestations of the purported revisionism and regression to capitalism. Far worse was the pretension of the CPSU to dictate to the rest of the movement and thereby lead it down a counter-revolutionary path. The favourite metaphor used in these contexts was that of an orchestral conductor and references abounded to the Soviet 'baton'. The longstanding resentment and bitterness of the Chinese leaders at their political subordination and enforced deference now erupted without inhibition.[25]

Worst of all however was the actual line along which the Soviets wanted to lead world communism, that of peaceful co-existence and socio-economic co-operation in place of military competition. This perspective was denounced as nothing less than capitulation to US might and intimidation, a sell-out of the world revolution to the chief counter-revolutionary force on the planet. Chinese propaganda urged instead an actively confrontational stance on all matters of East–West dispute and a ready willingness to deploy nuclear force.[26] They dismissed with contempt the argument that a strategy of this sort was likely to lead to universal holocaust and destruction, alleging that imperialism was a paper tiger which would slink away if resolutely faced up to, but that in the last resort nuclear warfare was not so terrible anyway and that if it took place imperialism would suffer final destruction and a 'beautiful' socialist world would be quickly reconstructed.[27]

The CPC's concept of 'revisionism' related primarily to a willingness to accept the doctrine of peaceful co-existence, as implying that there could be some long-term accommodation between socialism and imperialism, thereby diluting in theory and practice the commitment to class struggle. This corrupting right-wing deviation was held to lead in addition to the relaxation of Leninist norms in internal party structures and the corrosion of communist discipline, not to speak of addiction to material rewards. In Maoist eyes the Soviet leadership had succumbed to this corruption, and although it possessed state power and a nuclear arsenal, revisionism meant that through fear of the consequences of all-out conflict the USSR lost its willingness to confront imperialism in the shape of the US, sought to make rotten deals and so allowed imperialism the initiative in Third World conflicts. Regarding the latter, the theorists of the CPC advanced a novel interpretation of the current phase of the general crisis of capitalism, drawn from their experience of the Chinese Civil War and revolution. The communists in China had initially established their power in the countryside while the cities remained in the hands of the Kuomintang. As the reactionary power collapsed in defeat, the communist armies had surrounded the cities and captured them. The claim based on this analogy was that the epicentre of class struggle had moved to the Third World, the global 'countryside', where the victorious revolution would surround and advance upon the imperialist metropoles, the global 'city'. Overall, the essentials of Maoism in this phase were the promotion of ascetic communist rectitude and contempt for the Western fleshpots combined with uncompromising revolutionary militancy.

This phase of Maoism and the general political line of the CPC evoked some interest outside the ranks of the communist parties (the split of course was sensational public news) for example in the independent left US journal, *Monthly Review*, but as might be expected of such an esoteric and factually unconvincing collation of doctrines, its general impact was not very great. For the communist movement it was intensely disruptive, and indeed amounted to an irreparable fragmentation of the movement. To the Stalin revelations was now added the realisation that authentically Marxist-Leninist parties and regimes (for the Chinese party and state were never denied that title by the parties which refused their support) could attack each other in the most vituperative manner and rupture their relations. What now became of a world-historic process in which failing imperialism was overborne suddenly or gradually by the global socialist movement whose unity was among its cardinal assets?

The impact was felt most severely in Asia. The Indian CP was split into a Soviet-attached and a Maoist-inclined wing. The Indonesian CP aligned itself with the CPC, an option which was to produce horrific outcomes for its leaders and members.[28] The North Korean regime and the strong Japanese CP declined to commit themselves definitively either way, though inclining towards the Soviet position. One other Asian CP which did adhere firmly to the Chinese line (and split as a result) was that in New Zealand, but it was scarcely of major importance. No Warsaw Pact member defected, although the dispute did enable the regime in Romania to assume a more independent posture in foreign relations. In most of the West European CPs small pro-Chinese grouplets announced their appearance but remained for the most part wholly insignificant:[29] the only party in which they managed to secure any considerable following being the small Belgian one. In Latin America too, no more than minor fragments separated themselves from the official pro-Moscow parties. The Cuban regime, whose adherence would have been a major coup and whose revolutionary boldness might well have inclined it towards the CPC was much too dependent on Soviet material support to ever adopt such a standpoint. The Beijing leadership unquestionably saw itself as leading an alternative and genuinely world revolutionary communist movement, ready to confront imperialism at every juncture, in opposition to the 'revisionist' Soviets,[30] but it was a stance closely bound up with an outlook of national superiority inherited from Chinese cultural traditions. Their optimum outcome would have been a palace revolution in the Kremlin replacing Khrushchev with a leadership willing to acknowledge Chinese doctrinal superiority, amend its foreign policies accordingly and supply China with nuclear armaments. The palace revolution certainly occurred, but Brezhnev and his colleagues were no more willing than their predecessor to make any concessions. The CPC's actions had succeeded in bringing about an irreparable rupture in the unity of world communism, but had failed to displace Moscow as the leading influence in its major component.

The Cultural Revolution and its International Impact

What we may term the second phase of Maoism, or more accurately Maoism proper, derived less from the Sino-Soviet dispute than from the political hurricane which devastated China in the mid-1960s. This cataclysm had purely internal origins, its roots lying in divisions affecting the CPC leadership and in particular the attitudes and personality of Mao Zedong himself. The evidence scarcely allows any doubt that his revolutionary sentiments were genuine, however perverted. Had he simply been the power-crazed sex maniac depicted in some current interpretations, he was comfortably placed to enjoy both appetites to the end of his days without any need to throw China into repeated murderous upheavals which might easily have culminated in his own destruction.

Mao's concern appears to have been with the degree of proliferating bureaucracy in both party and state which he associated with attempts being made to sideline him in the party leadership. He responded by using his enormous prestige and acolytes in the military leadership to mobilise millions of school students under the designation of 'Red Guards' and send them to attack, arrest, humiliate, demote and from time to time murder public officials and party leaders under the pretext that they were 'taking the capitalist road'. This process was characterised by intimidating mass rallies, the descent of the red guards (in transport supplied by the military) upon towns and villages throughout China to terrify and punish local authorities, and by the release of fanatical mass emotion. A ferocious juggernaut rolled across the land and terrorised citizens jumped aboard whenever they could to escape being crushed beneath its wheels. Thus the Cultural Revolution propagated itself, the structures of the party organisation were flattened and their remnants remodelled in a manner more to Mao's liking.

He appears to have been convinced that at least part of the reason for the developments that disturbed him, and which the Cultural Revolution was designed to eradicate, was that the traditional Confucian culture was reasserting itself and contributing to the hardening of Chinese society. An explicit attack on Confucian values of subordination and respect for authority was therefore central to the Cultural Revolution, and used to justify the appeal to the young and the behaviour of the red guards and their incitement to rebellion in Mao's name against the lower levels of the hierarchy. This aspect in fact was the reason for using the designation of 'Cultural Revolution'. From any other perspective 'cultural counter-revolution' would have been more appropriate; for science, learning and formal education were denounced and disparaged, universities and colleges shut down, frail old academics 're-educated' by being dispatched to punitive labour in remote villages, and everything worth knowing alleged to be contained in 'Mao Zedong thought' or even the phrases culled from his writings and printed in the notorious 'Little Red Book'.

> ... read aloud in waiting rooms, in airplanes, in railway stations, read before others who repeat it in chorus, read by taxi-drivers who stop their cabs to read it to passengers – a hallucinating collective catechism which resounds from one end of China to the other.[31]

The international standpoints adopted by the CPC during the period of the break with the CPSU were maintained by the Maoists in the cultural revolution and indeed voiced with ever-growing stridency. Relations with the Soviet Union broke down calamitously, with red guards besieging the Soviet embassy in Beijing and incidents of armed conflict on the disputed border of the Issuri River. Moscow's pretensions to the leadership of the world revolutionary process led to it being designated as the principal enemy, justifying the Chinese rapprochement with President Nixon's United States on the principle of allying with the lesser satan against the greater one.[32] That did not exclude continued adherence to the concept of the exploited world countryside surrounding, besieging and finally annihilating the imperialist world city. The Maoist style – the choreography of monster demonstrations under massed red banners and slogans screamed in unison, the radical simplification of politics to slogans heavy with metaphor,[33] the denunciation of intellect or reasoned dialogue, total repudiation of individualism,[34] the personality cult around a semi-divine leader – not a copy of Stalinism but springing from similar roots – was calculated to appeal to an unsophisticated peasant audience. The Great Helmsman's conception of world politics was one of a global peasant revolt.

The Cultural Revolution phase of Maoism did evoke a small number of peasant risings under its banners, for instance in Peru and under the name of the Khmer Rouge in Cambodia – though these were initiated and led by urban intellectuals – but the most striking echo in global terms was heard in the educational institutions of the bourgeois-democratic West. Countless ardent – and rival – groups sprang into being[35] seeking the Maoist franchise. No doubt the Chinese embassies welcomed their existence, but seem to have made no effort to co-ordinate their activities and probably regarded them as very peripheral to the Chairman's objectives. For a short time in the 1960s Maoism was serious politics on the student left throughout Western Europe, above all in France.[36]

Its appearance in this role is not too difficult to explain and derives from exactly the same considerations as the contemporaneous expansion of the Trotskyist sects. It was the epoch of the revolutionary left in the student milieu but a time too when many participants sought alternatives to the hard-line bureaucratic conservatism of official communism – even before that was further discredited by events in Czechoslovakia. The Cultural Revolution made China appear as a nation in the grip of radical left mass insurrection, of power being seized not merely by the masses but by the youth, of returning to the wellsprings of revolutionary politics. Maoism's advantage over Trotskyism in the eyes of such potential adherents, despite its infinitely inferior theoretical grasp, was that it *also* represented the politics of a great world power, was embodied in a state that could make its international presence felt and serve as a pole of attraction. Even so, it is hard to comprehend how trainee intellectuals could embrace uncritically such an evidently obscurantist and philistine creed, however explosively radical it might appear. Some Maoist publications were nothing but sloganising pastiches of the Cultural Revolution style, although others did try to make coherent analyses of their own national politics by a stretched application of Maoist notions.

The country in which Maoism of this sort reached its most developed form was France, and the luminaries there who subscribed to it in whole or in part, such as Sartre or Louis Althusser, assisted in its re-export as an intellectual style to other parts of the world. In Britain the intellectual journal *New Left Review*, relating the Chinese guerrilla experience to the concurrent student upheavals in British higher education, wrote of establishing 'red bases' in British academia. Where Maoism did briefly achieve real political resonance was among the student revolutionaries of the May 1968 events in Paris (see below). If there was any mainstream current flowing through that revolt it was an anarchistic one, but Maoism was well represented and in any case the two were not so far apart in Maoism's European manifestation. In the aftermath, Maoist groups continued to receive publicity, particularly after Sartre took up their cause, believing them to be the only proclaimed revolutionaries who were actually trying to *do* something, and hence the ones most energetically persecuted by the authorities.

Even before the Chairman's death Maoism outside China and certainly in Europe had virtually exhausted itself and, having seen no success and possessing, unlike the Trotskyists, no longstanding tradition to fall back upon, quickly became moribund. With the repudiation of the Cultural Revolution and arrest of the 'Gang of Four', the high priests of the Mao cult, Maoism became as dead as its founder. Most of its leading French adherents moved over to the right – they had not lost their instinctive anti-Sovietism. By the end of the decade it was extinct, apart from some bizarre and sinister offshoots such as the Serendo Luminoso of Peru and the Khmer Rouge, the latter in any case repudiating communism, as part of its diplomatic manoeuvres. Maoism in the final analysis was a national – and nationalist – phenomenon, relating to Chinese circumstances. It briefly became a world one because it emerged in a country which was at the time the second pillar of a world communist fraternity, which made its authors seek to advance their quarrel with Moscow by deploying it upon a world stage, and because its incoherent ultra-revolutionary doctrines succeeded in catching a radical mood among a dissatisfied social stratum in the capitalist West.

Eurocommunism

If both Trotskyism and Maoism promoted themselves by hyping their revolutionary credentials, by being 'prolier than thou',

Eurocommunism by contrast was an endeavour to resolve the impasse of communist politics, evident after 1968, by questioning the formulae and assumptions by which the Soviet-aligned international movement had lived up to that point.

The term was one which was coined and applied to certain political positions by outside commentators – its objects employed it only with a degree of diffidence and embarrassment, some indeed denied its appropriateness. It was first used by a leading communist spokesperson, Santiago Carillo, the General Secretary of the Spanish CP, in a book entitled 'Eurocommunism' and the State, and even there he put the term in quotes. Nor did the adoption by communist parties of the kind of perspectives which were summarised in the term usually mean sundering relations with the CPSU, though it certainly strained them and in all cases led to internal conflicts – not surprisingly, for the word was consciously intended to draw a contrast with Soviet communism. The Eurocommunist CPs were all located within Western Europe.

By and large the parties to which the label came to be applied were the ones which had objected vociferously to the Warsaw Pact invasion of Czechoslovakia in 1968. (This did not include the PCF, which did pronounce its dissent but without great enthusiasm or conviction.) 'Eurocommunism' meant an explicit renunciation of the Leninist party-state, in favour of political pluralism[37] – renunciation in practice had occurred much earlier. They committed themselves to the bourgeois-democratic norms of action and practice, such as acceptance of open electoral verdicts even when they did not favour communist parties, continuation of civil liberties and the rule of law under putative future socialist regimes.

> These constituent elements of a communist third road were never actually synthesised into a theoretical framework; they added up to a cautious and uneven search for a political strategy grounded in the conditions of advanced capitalism rather than any fixed model.[38]

Early Bolshevism had stood unrepentantly for a very different form of government structure and ethos, a quasi-syndicalist framework to the workers' state, guided by a vanguard political organisation – though possibly, under ideal circumstances, not for long, for original Bolshevism was conceived of as an instrument for overthrowing class rule, not subsequently administering the society which followed.[39] In Lenin's own time, whether because of the circumstances prevailing in shattered Russia or on account of its own intrinsic flaws, it had become something very different – a party-state of intolerant and autocratic temper. Stalin had actually moved back towards the bourgeois-democratic formalities in the Stalin Constitution of 1936 (largely drafted by Bukharin). Window-dressing of this sort became the standard form of the 'People's Democracies' of Eastern Europe following the onset of the Cold War, for these, other than in the respect of being single-party regimes[40] with political opposition proscribed, were technically parliamentary democracies – though not of course in any meaningful sense. In communists' internal rhetoric they could be held up as demonstrations that popular fronts of progressive political forces under communist leadership could make parliamentary assemblies – with extra-parliamentary backing – effective instruments to achieve the transition to socialism.

In their unregenerate Stalinist days the Western CPs had applauded that model as appropriate not only for Eastern Europe but for all developed states. Bit by bit they had moved away from it, whether explicitly or implicitly. The change meant acceptance, usually implicit, that the democratic pretensions of the People's Democracies and by extension the USSR were a hollow sham, and they allowed it to be understood that they, by contrast, would treat democratic practice with the utmost seriousness and would never exploit a democratic mandate for nefarious purposes. In short they accepted the generally understood meaning of democracy and abandoned the attempt to win popular credence for their own previous redefinition, which, unlike the original aspiration to non-parliamentary government by soviets, had dishonestly used the name while intending something very different. A transitional stage of major importance was the move made within the Italian CP towards rejection of the Soviet model – articulated under the title 'polycentrism' by its general secretary, Palmiro Togliatti.

The Western parties faced a series of obstacles, each one of them apparently insuperable. In the first place, apart from the UK, manual workers nowhere comprised a majority of the electorate. Secondly, significant segments of that population were not class-conscious in political terms – they failed to vote or voted for other than workers' parties. Thirdly, except in Italy and to a lesser extent France, the CPs were not the dominant workers' party and no realistic prospect existed that they would become so. Fourthly, the electorates, including the working-class component, were overwhelmingly attached to traditions of political democracy and pluralism on the Western model – probably the most important single factor inhibiting the growth of the small CPs or the political breakthrough of the big ones. Fifthly, even in the unlikely event of a CP being elected to government office on its own or as dominant partner in a coalition, mechanisms – from economic destabilisation to military coup – were in place within the Western states to prevent a parliamentary majority being turned into social revolution, as the Chilean example hideously demonstrated.[41]

Adaptation, therefore, was essential and inevitable if these parties were to perform any meaningful political role. By retreating into an ideological fortress and concentrating upon industrial or community organisation and action they could make their influence felt from a position of pariah status, but in a consumer society that was a wasting asset. The problem was that, rejecting ideological pragmatism in principle and taking theory seriously, they had to find some way of reconciling the necessary shift in their politics away from proclaimed revolutionism with the ideological heritage of Leninism.

It was a question of bringing theory into line with practice, a process not so different in principle from that undertaken by social democrats in the course of the 1950s. In truth, the CPs of the European democracies – and of the underground Spanish Communist Party (PCE) – were moving to fill the political space being vacated by their social democrat counterparts. By the late 1960s they were, apart from certain peculiarities of their internal regimes and their fraternal links with the CPSU, to all intents and purposes nothing other than left-wing social democratic parties with some infusion from the new left. The new development of the 1970s was a more coherent and theoretically explicit articulation of their reformist practice combined with a further distancing of themselves from the Soviet party and the Soviet image.

Gramsci

Theorisation along those lines drew heavily upon the inheritance of Antonio Gramsci – whether or not that was misrepresented. Ernest Mandel wrote with hostile intent that 'For people who still call themselves communists it is obviously more comfortable to claim allegiance to Gramsci than to Kautsky.'[42] Gramsci was a subtle and profound Marxist thinker who was compelled to do the greater part of his thinking in Mussolini's prisons.[43] His focus was upon social consciousness, how it is formed and how it is altered in the dialectic between dominant and subordinated classes. From this derives the famous concept of 'hegemony', the condition through which, in Marx's phrase, the ideas of the ruling class become the ruling ideas of society. Class power can never be maintained for long by means of coercion alone – it requires in some measure the internal assent of the exploited to the system which exploits them; assent which is manufactured not only through the official media and educational systems but through the micro-relations of workplace, family, voluntary associations. Not that Gramsci, as the detractors of Eurocommunism were at pains to point out, was anything other than a Leninist revolutionary, convinced of the ultimate necessity of seizure of power by the working class.

What the Eurocommunists seized upon was Gramsci's appreciation of the necessity, if the seizure of power was to be accomplished, to construct a 'hegemonic project' in order to change the terms of understanding through which social reality was perceived; of recognising the many ideological fissures within the exploited classes and forming a 'hegemonic bloc' to incorporate its different sections in an organic rather than a mechanical fashion; of appreciating that it was a struggle which of necessity transcended politics and industrial conflict but penetrated to the very roots of intimate social relations. Above all it meant recognising that the horizon was necessarily a very long one, that what was involved was a 'war of position' rather than a 'war of manoeuvre', that no aspect of social practice, for example popular commercial culture, religious adherence or national sentiment, was to be dismissed as the irrecoverable domain of the class enemy but was to be treated as a site of contestation.

Eurofailure

Whatever the merits of the Eurocommunists' approach – and they were considerable – it is extremely doubtful that it could ever have culminated in anything that Gramsci would have recognised as a social revolution. It represented a more sophisticated and highly theorised version of the perspective of social democrats in the days when they were still serious about achieving socialism in gradual stages. The gibe that Eurocommunism was Kautskyism with a Gramscian gloss was actually justified. Its defence, if the Eurocommunist parties had been clearsighted about their project, would have been that the conditions in which they operated – and among those the political consciousness of their intended constituency was paramount – simply did not permit a Leninist-style revolution and was never likely to in the foreseeable future. The movement of history had made Leninism, let alone the Stalinism which shadowed it, a total anathema to the masses of Western Europe.

Adopting the new direction was one thing, making it work effectively amidst the complexities of West European society, politics and culture was quite something else, and must be accounted overall a dismal failure. The parties large or small which adopted it with any degree of enthusiasm all suffered splits and fragmentation. All had significant sections of their membership who refused to be taken along the new course, whether out of knee-jerk traditionalism or real insight into the likely difficulties. Further irresolvable tensions were generated by the actual application of the strategy when insuperable contradictions came to light and were exacerbated in some cases by the personal style of the party leaderships.

Not long after it emerged from illegality the PCE exploded in spectacular fashion, with Carillo left leading a rump from which, thanks to his ingrained Stalinist leadership habits, and in spite of his Eurocommunist politics, he was expelled in due course. He went on to set up yet another groupuscule – but not before he had effusively congratulated the monarchy for saving the newly-inaugurated Spanish democracy from a farcical attempt at a Francoist putsch. The PCI avoided breakup, although it suffered several breakaways which eroded its hegemony over the Italian left. In pursuit of the politics of 'historic compromise' however, it allowed itself to be swept along in the panic generated by the 'Red Brigades' terrorism and lent its voice and support to repressive legislation which severely encroached on civil liberties, strengthened the hand of the ultra-right secret services and had targets much wider than the terrorists themselves. In spite of this it failed even in its objective of governmental participation. Among the smaller parties the adoption of the new course caused those in Scandinavia, the Low Countries and Britain to split or fragment. Ironically, those which repudiated Eurocommunism, such as the Portuguese, which remained unrepentantly neo-Stalinist, or the French, where it had received only lukewarm assent and the leadership continued Stalinists at heart, survived much better – but only at the cost of intensifying isolation and growing marginalisation in their respective societies. Eurocommunism signally failed to produce an ideological consensus among the Western CPs which could have enabled them to survive the disappearance of the Soviet bloc.

Both Trotskyism and Maoism ostensibly and ostentatiously purported to be a continuation and application of Leninism – Eurocommunism to transcend it, amend its errors and to still pursue its essential objectives in a transformed historic situation which had outdated Leninism's political strategies and forms of party organisation. In reality, all three were responses in their different fashions to Leninism's corruption and failure, to the fact that the world had moved in a diametrically different direction from that projected in the days of hope of 1917 and the first four congresses of the Comintern.

CHAPTER 7

New Left, New Social Forces and Others

There are grounds for designating the twentieth century not only as the age of extremes but as the century of irony – in view of the extent to which the notion of 'winner loses' and 'loser wins' appears to apply to it. The most promising expectations (not only on the left) have been routinely confounded, triumphant victories have regularly turned to ashes in the longer or shorter term.

So far as the left is concerned, the principal irony has to be recognised in the fact that it is those parts of its tradition entrenched in the state and orientated towards political authority – regimes and centralising parties – which have collapsed most catastrophically and plunged into deepest historical discredit. The element of the left's tradition which in the 1990s appears to be most viable and healthy is that part which possessed no coherent structure, had been consistently marginalised, excluded from the centres of authority and confined to the role of criticising both the power structure and the 'orthodox' left's relationship to it.

Undoubtedly, the ghosts of anarchism do hover around the multiple strands of new left and the movements which have subsequently developed out of it. These are however a much more complex phenomenon than anarchism ever was, and with very different social foundations and agendas: what they share is a response to the challenge of modernity, its technology and its institutions – a response which takes the form of acute awareness not only of the incalculably expanded scope of authoritarian control and military slaughter but the potential for hideous techniques of destruction and tyranny lurking right at the heart of modernity's apparently most benign aspects.

Further back even than anarchism, affinities can be noted with the Romantic movement of the early nineteenth century, which confronted, in a rather similar spirit, a yet earlier phase of modernity. Variants of that Romantic sensibility were still around in both right and left-wing versions in the epoch that witnessed the technologies of the 'second industrial revolution' and the birth of a global labour movement. These shades of Romanticism are also related, albeit distantly, to the particular form of social and cultural critique that has flowered in the late twentieth century. The latter's main impetus however came from other sources. Three names which may be mentioned as particularly representative remain central to the current debate – Max Weber, Sigmund Freud and Friedrich Nietzsche.

Weber was above all an analyst of the social culture of modernity, which he viewed as the outcome of instrumental reason displacing a sacralised perception of the world. Bureaucracy, whether dominating the military, the educational system or the political party represented the application of instrumental reason to human affairs. Weber regarded the march of instrumental reason as both inevitable and progressive, but was acutely conscious of its two-edged character and considered 'the process of bureaucratisation ... the greatest danger to humanity in the age of industrial capitalism'.[1] Hence his antagonism to socialism, for

> While there might be many varieties of socialism, the only viable one, compatible with modern civilisation, was bound to be some type of centrally directed 'planned economy'. Rather than socially elevating workers, nationalisation would make social control even more extensive and oppressive. It would not matter to them whether these were private capitalists or a state managerial class. On the contrary, their chances of resisting the latter would be considerably reduced compared with the conditions under a market-orientated capitalist system with an independent government.[2]

In the context of 'actually existing socialism' who can seriously argue that he was mistaken? That workers are not actually much freer in conflict with a moneybags against whom they have some hope of winning than with a government against which they have none (though that of course begs the question of whether the moneybags have absorbed the government). The theme of oppression being located within modernity itself rather than in any particular structure of social relations is one which will recur throughout the development of this segment of the left.

The apparently unrelated doctrines – I use the word deliberately – of Freud and Nietzsche can likewise be traced to the same root. At one level this pair were no more than charlatans, but they are nevertheless supremely important, less so for the impact they have had on twentieth-century culture – although in the case of the former that has been incalculable – than for the fears they crystallised and articulated regarding the menace of the era that was about to overtake humanity.

There is no reason to treat Freud's substantive theories with any greater seriousness than those of his contemporaries, the spiritualists and the theosophists. The reason why his theories continue to flourish while the other two are reduced to the status of crank cults is not only because psychoanalysis presented itself in scientific guise, important though that was, but because its claims hit the rawest of raw nerves for a twentieth-century sensibility. It was not the pan-sexualist obsession which pervades the theory, though that undoubtedly enhanced its force, nor even the central contention that the ego is not a self-determining rationality, but merely the visible part of a mechanism propelled by unseen and unconscious drives. The really scary assertion is that personality formation for all of us is the outcome of a painful and traumatic childhood process of repression and internal terrorism – *in which the victims themselves are complicit.*

We co-operate (if we are to be well adjusted citizens) in the mutilation of our spontaneous libidinal impulses, accept and internalise the repressive codes. Freud regarded the process with weary resignation as the essential precondition for civilised existence. He assumed likewise that it held true for all times and places, but its actual resonance with a vision of bureaucratically conditioned and controlled human units of production and consumption, stripped of all autonomy, not by coercion but by their own acceptance, is only too plain to see.

In Nietzsche's case we have not acceptance but its opposite. Bertrand Russell's discussion of Nietzsche in his *History of Western Philosophy* is not very profound, but his encapsulation of Nietzsche's outlook in the phrase 'aristocratic anarchism' could scarcely be improved. Heroic transcendence, whether as a warrior, artist or thinker, is the ultimate attainment – 'the *goal of humanity* cannot be in its end but only *in its highest exemplars*' – but is open to few men (and no women). Nietzsche's writings contain an 'offer of subjectivity, greatness and immediacy'.[3] Such is the theme to which this philosopher eternally returns – a passionate demand for authenticity and individual realisation against all the odds and a scorching critique of the modernity which has made them impossible, 'the threatening sameness, everydayness and fear of the "fellah society" ',[4] the 'growing rigidity of abstract rationalism, and the concomitant standardisation of individual existence that characterised life under advanced capitalism'.[5]

'Western Marxism'

The diffuse current loosely referred to as 'Western Marxism' emerged out of the defeated revolutions following 1918, no doubt among the reasons for its lively appreciation – almost a defining characteristic – of modernity's ambiguity and two-sidedness, its pessimistic cast of thought and its attention to Hegel and Freud as well as Marx. In a sense the work of the Western Marxist luminaries[6] constantly referred back to that defeat – in the form of an extended exploration of the culture which stabilised capitalism and kept it in being. In the interwar years cross-fertilisation occurred on occasion with Trotskyism and even the mainstream communist movement. As professing Marxists, the writers in this current could not but embrace modernity and yet they were compelled to subject it to a searching critique, for in the twentieth century, if the unreflecting confidence of Stalinists and Trotskyists was rejected, history appeared to consist of little other than wrong turnings. Walter Benjaman's celebrated image of the blown-away angel was emblematic, as was his remark that 'there is no document of civilisation which is not at the same time a document of barbarism'.[7]

On the Marxist side the critical interrogation of modernity was most consistently undertaken by the group generally referred to as the Frankfurt School, dispersed mostly to the United States following Hitler's takeover. Modernity's perceived threat and the fear that accompanied it was at the same time being portrayed artistically, above all in the novels of Franz Kafka, with their dreamlike miasma of arbitrary and incomprehensible bureaucratic mazes. At a more popular level it surfaces in the dystopian novel; with H. G. Wells's *The Time Machine* as a precursor, followed by, to mention only the most celebrated, Yevgeny Zamyatin's *We*, the model for *Nineteen Eighty-Four* (the most influential of them all), Aldous Huxley's *Brave New World* and E. M. Forster's *The Machine Stops*. Less serious, but not without its influence, was the artistic movement of surrealism, deliberately organised as a caricature of a revolutionary party, and whose leader (who considered himself a communist) foreshadowed a distinctive 1960s school of psychiatry by regarding insanity as a liberating state of being.

Political conditions in the years following the Second World War were far from favourable to any alternatives on the left between the barrack-style but confident reality of world communism and US-aligned social democracy.[8] Outside tiny circles Trotskyism was a dying memory. By the 1950s however, with the geopolitical stability of the mature Cold War well entrenched and the long boom gathering momentum, the term 'new left' first came into use in France. Subsequently it was taken up by the movement which formed in Britain after 1956 in opposition to the instrumental rationalities of Stalinism on the one hand and consumer capitalism with nuclear bomb culture on the other. In character a loose amalgam of many different left positions, its main distinctiveness from the 'old left' was to be found in its anti-bureaucratic style and its perception of popular culture in all its facets as centrally important to the comprehension of modern reality. With the Campaign for Nuclear Disarmament it had links to a mass movement, but in

general its initial influence was very limited, and it survived only
a few years. Far from dying with it however, the *concept* of a new
left soon acquired a concrete reality of mass dimensions, above all
in the United States.

Devil's Decade?

It is no accident that the years of the 1960s feature so strikingly in
the demonology of the right.[9] In the course of that decade there
emerged a 'new left', with considerable political and social impact.
That in itself however, was no more than the political expression
of a monumental shift, a cultural revolution in the true sense, in
attitudes towards authority, hierarchy and deference. It was, as
revolutions generally are, identified with and located among the
young.[10] In a variety of different countries it pushed at the boundaries
of orthodox politics, influenced them, ruptured them at particular
points – but failed to dissolve them and in due course provoked
backlash and counter-revolution.

In a wholly unpredictable fashion the left during the 1960s
renewed itself. Indeed, the inability of the old and new lefts to
assimilate to each other proved to be one of the cardinal strengths
of the right in the years which followed. For reasons which are not
difficult to understand the new left remained an exclusively 'Western'
phenomenon – in the political and mostly in the geographical
sense as well, although it also affected Japan. This new left however,
was itself no more than the starting point for what became loosely
known as the 'new social forces' which developed out of it in a
dialectic of extension and contradiction.

It is no secret that revolutionary developments are not advanced
by general immiseration, but through combinations of circumstances
in which impoverishment or declining material standards in sections
of the population may act as one ingredient in an explosive mix –
but that it is generally the existence of an intolerable gap between
attainable aspiration and perceived reality among strategic social
elements which acts as the detonator. Political revolution however,
is a dangerous and potentially life-threatening business, entered into
by the masses only under the most urgent of imperatives when
passivity looks like an even less attractive option.[11] Cultural
revolutions, though by no means free of risk to those who participate
in them, do not as a rule carry the same potential for sudden death,
torture or lengthy imprisonment. Paradoxically, if they succeed in
taking root their long-term significance tends to be greater than those
of the purely political variety.[12]

The cultural revolution of the 1960s was a product of affluence
rather than deprivation. Keynesian-style demand-management

policies were in full flower and, in combination with US Cold War-related expenditure, had given rise to a world boom of unprecedented historic length and intensity with only occasional minor glitches, one in which living standards for the average population in the industrialised West had climbed and continued to climb. Since the late 1940s economies running indefinitely at full stretch had generated an exceptional demand for labour, with wide-ranging consequences. Competition among employers, combined with strong labour organisation, bid up wage rates and earnings – and high earnings in secure employment was the ultimate secret of the amazing consumer boom. Labour shortage also produced migration and demographic shifts, giving a multi-ethnic and multicultural character to European states and intensifying that already existing in the US.[13] Most significantly in respect of the cultural revolution it enabled a group previously excluded from the universe of high earning power now to enter it – namely young adults[14] of both sexes – thereby creating a previously non-existent market segment and, again from the 1950s, enabling this social group to develop distinguishing subcultures and lifestyles. The teenager had arrived.

Other features of the postwar social transformation tended in a similar direction. The expanding system of welfare provision incorporated wider access to higher education, propelled and justified moreover by the requirements of expanding economies. In Europe and the US the expansion gathered speed in the course of the 1950s then accelerated tempestuously during the 1960s, transforming the character and situation of student populations. Economic growth, labour shortage and higher education all promoted social mobility and the expectation of it by succeeding generations, each reinforcing the other.

The most dramatic transformation of Western lifestyle, with which the 1960s are inseparably associated in popular memory, is that of sexual attitudes and practices.[15] Contrary to myth, it did not happen overnight or without considerable resistance. In the succeeding decades however the extent of the change is apparent for the majority of young heterosexual individuals male *and* female – most markedly in the ranks of the lower middle classes and with the spread of higher education in this social group a major contributing factor. Marriage, though hardly less practised as an ultimate status, ceased to hold the existential value that it had possessed for a 1,000 years since the Church imposed its norms in the early Middle Ages. Premarital sexual experimentation became the acknowledged norm rather than a furtive source of condemnation, and permanent unions lacking formal marital status a matter of unremarkable routine. Single parenthood failed any longer to merit social ostracism.[16] Without doubt the principal agent of the sexual revolution was the availability of cheap and reliable

contraception, with the contraceptive pill as its central element –
although it is essential not to ignore the importance of running water
and private bathrooms, as Simone de Beauvoir pointed out in *The
Second Sex*.

As profound a transformation as this certainly was, more
exceptional still was the challenging, though not the overthrow, of
heterosexuality as the only legitimate norm of sexual disposition
and conduct – though this was resisted much more fiercely at
official level, in the media and on the streets than the liberalisation
of heterosexual relations – and still in the 1990s constitutes an
ongoing struggle. Nevertheless, though constantly besieged and
under attack, gay culture succeeded in establishing and holding its
bridgeheads in the public sphere, in coming out of the
underground.[17] Accompanying and underpinning all of these
developments was the opening up of the public arena, in all forms
of the media and communication, to the discourse of sexual themes
and sexual information. Submitting taboos to public inspection and
discussion was always a necessary and sometimes a sufficient
condition for making them fall.[18]

Maverick commentators such as Wilhelm Reich (and George
Orwell in *Nineteen Eighty-Four*) undoubtedly had a point when they
linked sexual authoritarianism in particular with authoritarianism
in general – a point also well understood by reactionaries – and the
overthrow of the former was likely to lead fairly directly to a
weakening of the latter. The Western youth rebellion of the 1960s
and its aftershocks up to the present, though concentrated upon
sex and consumption, was diffused as a general defiance of adult
regulation and control in the private sphere. In the eternal conflict
of youth and maturity the terms of the engagement moved
significantly in favour of the former in the second half of this
century. Naturally most of it was expressed in individual and
wholly non-political terms and ran into the channels of the
proliferating range of youth cultures and subcultures, hermetically
sealed against adults and largely impenetrable by them. Music
was and is of course central to those, the more raucous and ear-
shattering the better, as the evolution of this type of music, from
rock and roll through to the present, testifies. Since the 1960s drugs
of various fashions, having the double virtues of sensory modification
and illegality,[19] have figured as another near-essential component
of the 'youth scene'.

New Politics

However, during a large part of the 1960s and for some years into
the following decade, youthful anger, resentments and a sense of
the possible assumed a political identity among significantly large

numbers of that generation. From the same milieu sprang critiques of society, culture and the limits of the 1960s revolt itself, which became the founding charters of the 'new social movements'.

Although the signs had been present from the later 1950s, it was in the 1960s that the frozen international polarities of the Cold War began visibly to break up – indeed it became possible to interpret the Cold War itself as a pseudo-conflict, a system designed to maintain the power and authority of the elites on both sides of the divide. On this interpretation the real enemies of the White House and the Kremlin were not each other, as official pronouncement would have it, but the populations over whom they ruled. That interpretation might be refuted by what had nearly happened in 1962 as a result of the Cuban missile crisis – but on the other hand nothing could have demonstrated the irresponsibility and caprice of the governing elites to an appalled and helplessly watching generation better than the near-destruction of civilisation.

Shortly afterwards the two principals of this nuclear drama abruptly departed the scene. The great fissure in the communist bloc opened up and the apparent economic and technological dynamism of Khrushchev's regime, which, had things turned out otherwise, might have constituted a focus of attraction, faded back to unimpressive levels. Equivalent failures of promise occurred in the US, Britain and Europe. John Kennedy was turned into an icon not only because of the manner of his death and his film-actor appearance, but because his curtailed presidency seemed to promise achievements in social policy and foreign affairs which would in fact have been impossible to deliver. His successor, elected with an unprecedented majority in the belief that he would complete Kennedy's presumed intentions, brought rapid and brutal disillusionment. In the UK a parallel process of renegacy turned the premier Harold Wilson into a hate figure among precisely the people whose support he most needed to win. In France, Germany and Italy 'economic miracles' exposed the gap between private affluence and the public corruption and squalor generated and maintained by authoritarian or even criminal political systems.

In such circumstances orthodox communism, at least of the sort practised in the USSR, was unlikely to offer much appeal to an emerging politically-minded and affluent Western generation, even if the former's politics had been able to surmount, in the US, the entrenched anti-communism of both official and popular culture. In the countries where CPs were well established, the most adventurous and imaginative of the rising youth, if they found such parties unimpressive, were unlikely to join with the intention of transforming them from within – a possible option with social democratic parties – because of the tight system of internal discipline the communist parties maintained. Exercising the option with social democrat parties (though the youth movements of some, especially in Germany, did take on a very radical complexion) was likely to appeal only to those very committed, with a high tolerance for bureaucratic manoeuvring and who found attendance at endless committee meetings a life-enhancing experience.

The tendency was rather for this developing radicalism to be mobilised outside formal party structures, as indeed had the anti-nuclear weapons movements of the late 1950s and early 1960s, the precursors of the 1960s radicalism. The first real manifestation of the new wave made itself felt in the US in the shape of the civil rights movement's attack upon segregationist practice in the southern states, which not only had considerable significance for US politics itself, but provided an inspiring example, with martyrs to underline it. Inspiration was to be found too in other, at first glance rather unlikely, places. The first of these was Cuba, even though its leaders were becoming steadily more dependent upon the Soviet bloc for economic and military support and were evolving in their own politics more and more towards an imitation of orthodox Soviet methods. Nonetheless, the regime's uncompromising defiance of the US monolith on its doorstep continued to evoke admiration well beyond the circles of Soviet-aligned communist parties.

The development of the Vietnamese conflict was to prove even more portentous – indeed it was central to the concerns of the new radicals, and in the United States there was a straight carry over from civil rights activities to anti-war agitation. Again, there is an element of paradox in that the Vietnamese regime was much more strictly within the orthodox communist tradition than the Cuban one and even continued to regard Stalin in a positive light.[20] It is hard to imagine anything better designed to show up the United States in a bad light than the behaviour of its governments towards the Cubans and the Vietnamese, particularly at a time when its international credentials were coming increasingly under scrutiny and the automatic ideological deference it could expect from the educated Western public in the 1940s and 1950s was no longer to be found.[21] Outrage at criminal aggression against what Gladstone in the nineteenth century had termed 'peoples rightly struggling to be free' need not necessarily take a politically focused form, but when it did it linked the new left with an approach which already characterised some of the more adventurous Trotskyist groupings, had been adopted by numerous unattached leftists (including the original British New Left) and had some affiliation also with Maoism.

This outlook had gained the name of 'Third Worldism' and referred to the conviction that the contemporary Third World revolutions and independence struggles constituted the form which the general crisis of capitalism had assumed.[22] It was held that these had become the 'central contradiction' of the present era and *their* success, rather than the class struggles of the developed world, would fatally undermine and cumulatively defeat global imperialism, whether by a slow process of erosion or through the build-up to an apocalyptic crisis. No doubt this was, from the stance of classic orthodox Marxism, a deviation which was seen as attractive because the deadlocked confrontation of the two power blocs, Moscow's diplomatic caution, and relative passivity of the industrial working classes within the Western sphere, seemed to preclude any resumption of the forward march of revolution in the First World.

1968

No political structure is stable unless it can reproduce itself down the generations, by recruiting new drafts of participants, functionaries and activists who carry on its traditions and practices. It is a point that applies equally across the spectrum, from marginal political sects to the framework of politically pluralist societies. By the latter years of the 1960s it could appear that Western political society was threatened with breakup as a consequence of massive alienation on the part of the politically conscious young. The conventional political structures and parties, left or right, whether in the US, Britain, France, Germany or Italy appeared terminally exhausted, bereft of dynamism or credible purpose and the governments they sustained increasingly irresponsible and malevolent.[23] It is not surprising that this was the era of renewal for the Trotskyist groupings, of the eruption of Maoism and even of a modest revival for the historically sidelined anarchists. It is significant nonetheless that the above (though they secured sufficient to renew themselves for another generation and achieved an impact way above their numbers), were minority trends within the complex of developing youthful radicalism. It was suggestive and of the greatest importance that by and large the old left failed to win behind it the mass of the young radicals.

The year 1968 is sometimes compared with 1848 in the previous century, a failed revolution, the turning point at which history failed to turn. The comparison is not too far-fetched, though in both cases it considerably understates the importance of the respective events. The political revolutions of 1848 may have failed, but the consequences of their happening rolled on through the remainder of the century and beyond. Similarly with 1968 – no governments were overthrown in Europe, but both American and European politics were profoundly affected and – with even greater long-term effect – it became the starting point for a cultural challenge and conflict of the most far-reaching sort, one which was to have seriously adverse consequences for the left.

The political events of that year were the most resounding between 1945 and the Soviet bloc collapse, and in their geographical spread even more extensive. The Tet offensive in Vietnam by the NLF seriously undermined the United States' military credibility and ended any expectation that its forces could win the war outright. The repercussions in the US itself intensified the level of anti-war protest and deterred the President, Lyndon Johnson, from seeking a second term in the elections of that year. In Europe, Paris and France exploded in the May *evenements*, and massive, if less publicised, protest erupted in Germany and Italy, lasting through to 1969. Even Britain experienced an unusually intense wave of student protest and rising industrial dissension, along with the beginnings of re-emerging Scottish nationalism and permanent crisis in Northern Ireland. The Eastern bloc was not exempt, and underwent its own crisis with the Prague Spring and subsequent invasion. The wildest hopes and enthusiasms were ignited and for many of those who were involved it was not too difficult to imagine that capitalism itself was in mortal and imminently terminal crisis.[24] The Vietnamese and Cuban revolutions with the highly romantic death of Che Guevara in South America and the image of the Chinese Cultural Revolution, all helped to connect this first world upsurge to the Third Worldism which had formed a significant component of left-wing perceptions for about a decade.[25] The theory of the guerrilla 'foco', articulated by Regis Debray, was advanced as a surefire strategy for bringing down all the anti-popular Western-dependent regimes throughout the third world. The foundations of oppression throughout the world appeared ready to crack and crumble.

Radical oppositional politics were inevitably influenced by the novel lifestyles of the 1960s, and even the communist parties did not escape being affected. A great deal of the novelty was no more than an aggressively flaunted hedonism, the extreme edge of a range of stylistic innovation in more conventional life-patterns ranging from dress to childcare arrangements; but philosophical underpinnings were in due course produced. At the time the most publicly visible of such theorists were individuals who had come out of older traditions to appear as philosophical guides and exemplars to the new forces. Herbert Marcuse was perhaps the most unlikely of those, an individual in his eighties with a background in the Frankfurt School, and a heavily Freudian slant to his writings. Others such were the Beat poets and writers like Norman O. Brown, who wanted 'man [to be] ready to live instead of making history',[26] and Paul Goodman.

The centrally proclaimed insight or – on a less favourable reading – obsession of those interpreters (all of them resident in the United States) was the alleged radical incompatibility of technological civilisation with the potential for spontaneous human joyfulness, release of libidinal energies and non-alienated human relationships.[27] The revulsion extended to science per se and rational modes of discourse. Various brands of neo-paganism were plucked from the ideological supermarket shelves of previous centuries and promiscuously adapted to the twentieth-century youth culture.

> ... but also in attendance ... were contingents of 'witches, warlocks, holymen, seers, prophets, mystics, saints, sorcerers, shamans, troubadours, minstrels, bards, roadmen and madmen' – who were on hand to achieve the 'mystic revolution' ...
>
> ... the central event of the day [the October 1967 picket of the Pentagon] was a contribution of the 'superhumans': an exorcism of the Pentagon by long-haired warlocks who 'cast mighty words of white light against the demon-controlled structure', in the hope of levitating that grim ziggurat right off the ground.

The quotation is from the highly sympathetic commentator Theodore Roszak. His observations were made in articles appearing in the influential *Village Voice* in 1968, later assembled into a book under the significant title of *The Making of a Counter Culture*, and its even more revealing subtitle *Reflections on the Technocratic Society and its Youthful Opposition*. Across the Atlantic the rebellious Parisian students were at this stage more renowned for their inventive slogans ('It is forbidden to forbid!': 'be realistic – demand the impossible!' for example) than a worked-out theorisation of their attitudes and actions; though classic anarchism and Trotskyism were trying to accommodate and come to terms with the new developments. Maoism too proved a popular form of political focus, drawing such veteran leftists as Sartre into its orbit. However, what then appeared as a marginal irrelevance and crack-brained gesture – the phenomenon which had adopted the name 'Situationism' as far back as 1957, and distinctly reminiscent in both outlook and organisation of the surrealism of an earlier era – was probably the most accurate prefiguration of the postmodern sensibility.

The immediate revolutionary hopes of 1968–9 quickly foundered,[28] and in doing so threw a shadow over the meaning of the decade of which they had provided the climax. Disillusionment led in certain instances to sinister consequences, for the political movement having failed, a number of the romantic revolutionaries turned to undirected terrorism in the desperate hope of igniting a popular response to attack the detested state power. The Red

Army Fraction or Baader-Meinhof gang in Germany, the more formidable Red Brigades in Italy and the Weathermen and more obscure groups in the US were the most serious examples.[29] The terrorism was bad enough, even worse was the pretext it furnished to authorities only too eager to take advantage of it, for annihilating civil liberties in the states affected and screwing down repression against all sections of the left. By the mid-1970s the impetus of the 1960s in terms of the attack on governmental structures was largely exhausted, but its continuing influence was felt in other directions, for it had provided the starting point for differentiation into the varied forms of the 'new social forces'.

New Nationalisms and Ethnic Identity Politics

The rise to prominence of 'identity politics' has to be reckoned one of the most striking features of the later twentieth century. In one sense all modern politics is identity politics – participation in a political process of any sort, even to the extent of casting a ballot, gives the participant an elective affinity with others aiming to achieve similar objectives through political mechanisms. Since the nineteenth century, particularly in stable developed states, that identification has in general taken the form of class and parties have either represented particular classes, sections of classes or class coalitions. The second major dimension of politics was the state: all parties operated within a state framework and the Comintern was the only political party ever to be established across state frontiers.[30] The third dimension of social identification was the nation, and consequently tensions of varying severity were generated wherever state and nation failed to coincide and the lack of coincidence was viewed by large numbers as a major source of grievance. Political movements related therefore either to class or to nation, and this configuration did not change significantly before the 1960s.

The left has had difficulties with nationalism ever since it became clear in the later part of the nineteenth century that this form of 'imagined community', regarded since the French Revolution as a progressive force in opposition to dynastic states, could be co-opted for the purposes of conservatism and reaction. In the Second International debates raged as to how it should be related to the socialist project, and indeed whether it possibly could; of which the polemic between Lenin and Rosa Luxemburg is only the best-known instance. The Bolsheviks believed they had found the appropriate strategy for linking nationalism to revolutionary politics, and success in the civil war appeared to confirm their judgment – as at a later date did the Partisan strategy in wartime Yugoslavia. The Marxist-

Leninist tradition distinguished two sorts of nationalism: reactionary and oppressive, compared with progressive and liberating,[31] and it was a formula which worked well enough for the purposes of the Soviet bloc and the communist movement. Communist parties always proved strongest and most successful where they could combine their class appeal with a national one – in occupied Europe or in Vietnam or China.

Among the novelties of the 1960s and early 1970s was the upsurge of a clutch of hitherto unregarded nationalist movements in Western Europe[32] – expressions of minority discontent founded on economic disadvantage, language or culture within the historic states of the region, both democratic and otherwise. They included Irish, Scottish and Welsh nationalism in the UK, Basque and Catalan in Spain, Corsican and even 'Occitanian' in France. They had in common the fact that they tended to lean towards the left in their social agendas, and in politics, though they did not recognise these models, tended to replicate either brands of social democracy or forms of action parallelling the Castroite urban guerrillas of South America. They have also had the effect (except for the Basque ETA during the Franco era, when it could be admired unreservedly) of discomposing and dividing the established left, putting it at odds over the question of whether to treat them as progressive forces challenging the old order or manifestations of reactionary sectionalism dividing the working class.[33] In any event, though none has (as yet) achieved its primary national objective, they have had very significant effects upon the countries in which they are located.

Clearly linked to nationalism, yet nonetheless categorically distinguished from it, are the political organisations or pressure groups formed inside a society by sections of it who are separately identified on cultural or ethnic grounds but do not occupy a particular historically recognisable territory. The most immediately apparent of such populations is the blacks of the United States. The Comintern (and the Fourth International for that matter) had difficulty in arriving at a theoretical evaluation of the situation and political strategy for that population. This was evidently a group undergoing an identifiable form of joint oppression that was equally not of a straightforward class nature. Could they therefore be regarded as potentially forming a national community? The Comintern (and Trotsky) decided tentatively that they could and proposed the demand for a separate black state, though nothing much came of this and the idea was soon quietly discarded.[34]

It did however prefigure the kind of black American identity politics which were to arise spontaneously at a later date. These too had deep roots. Black lobbying organisations of orthodox politics, like the National Association for the Advancement of Colored People, had existed for many years, as had forms of black separatism, associated especially with the figure of Marcus Garvey. Their back-to-Africa orientation had similarities in principle with the Zionist movement of the same era, but the Zionists, with their specific territorial focus on Palestine, resembled more the orthodox forms of nationalism. In the 1960s the mainstream black movement was focused upon the civil rights campaign, but on its wings a current of revived black separatism brought into prominence the syncretic religion of the Nation of Islam, and its charismatic breakaway leader Malcolm X. Meanwhile new left revolutionary politics produced the Black Panthers, regarded by the authorities as especially menacing, and therefore exterminated by police action.

It was clear as far back as the 1960s that only a profound social transformation, amounting to a revolution in income distribution and employment patterns, could substantially and permanently amend the economic subordination of the black American population – otherwise civil rights would prove a disheartening mirage and benefit only a very narrow stratum. Such a change of course did not take place, the circumstances deteriorated if anything, particularly after the Reagan administration and its successor had gone to work on the welfare system, and central and local governments cut budgets for inner-city rejuvenation. By far the greater number of African-Americans remain locked into ghettoised, physically crumbling urban environments, beset by poverty and hopelessness, persecuted by criminal gangs and by racist police forces. It is not to be wondered at that the demagogues of separatism and identity politics[35] find responsive listeners in their appeal to an apocalyptic hope on the one hand and for a retreat into existing or newly manufactured black communal networks on the other; for if capitalism is the only viable system it sounds attractive to establish a black capitalism while waiting for divine fire and blood to descend upon the white race. Political mobilisation on an ethnic foundation has been a long-term feature of American life – it is the addition of separatist ideologies and a militant concern with ancestral roots which is novel. It is being copied by other low-status ethnic minorities in the US, such as Latinos and has extended across the Atlantic,[36] where it has appealed to ethnic immigrant-descended minorities in the major states of Western Europe, particularly Britain and France. [37]

The past two decades have witnessed a corresponding change in certain Third World nationalist movements with the rise of militant Islam as an international phenomenon, its coming importance announced with explosive force in the Iranian revolution of 1979. Since then it has made enormous inroads in terms of popular adhesion, at the expense of the secular nationalist parties which had dominated the scene since at least the end of the Second World War. Partly, but only partly, it is a matter of resources, the Iranian regime and its Islamist rivals, the deeply reactionary rulers of Pakistan and Saudi Arabia having spent freely to promote their own colour of politics throughout the Muslim world, but far more important has been the inability of secular nationalism throughout the area, whether in or out of power, to complete its agendas. Uncontrollable poverty and corruption have alienated the Algerian and Egyptian regimes from their peoples, so that they on the one hand and the PLO on the other – forced to accept a hopelessly mutilated peace deal with Israel – find themselves mortally threatened by Islamist enemies. The Iranian revolution after all, unlike the secular nationalists, was successful against all comers and achieved the unique distinction of humiliating the Great Satan, the US.

Not that secular nationalism is disappearing from the world – on the contrary, in the former USSR and Soviet bloc, above all in what was Yugoslavia, it is resurgent in a far more virulent form than ever before. One should not imagine it for a moment as an unchanging entity, dormant but waiting its opportunity throughout the decades of the communist era, rather that it has been resynthesised out of traditional materials by intellectual and political elites as a form of identity and politics to fill the space left by the bankruptcy of the communist project.[38]

The pattern is replicated with the rising strength of caste and communal politics in India; the effective collapse into total anarchic violence of certain African states; or even the appearance of entirely new forms of exclusivist separatism in Western Europe, such as the Northern Leagues in Italy. A common thread unites them. When hope is lost on all sides that the world is moving in the general direction of solving its most pressing problems through the extension of industrial technology and representative forms of government, when the promise of the Enlightenment appears to be comprehensively betrayed, it is entirely understandable that humans fall back upon the basic collectives and networks which have the appearance of greatest permanence and security – those of kinship, of locality, of community, of shared language (in both the literal and metaphorical senses) and venerable traditions. Thus the outsiders and strangers, the Others, take on the appearance of enemies, competitors for scarce resources, to be excluded always, subordinated where possible and destroyed where necessary. In such a climate more fragile and benign forms of identity politics are likely to go the way of internationalism in 1914, an outcome never dreamt of in the imaginations of those who in the 1970s welcomed the arrival on the scene of the articulate 'new social forces'.

Sexual Politics – Feminism

The relationship of national and ethnic identity politics to the movements of the 1960s is an ambiguous one and easily evolves in directions which lose all semblance of contact with recognisably left-wing positions. The same point can be made about another form of identity politics, a far-reaching and impressive offshoot of the political stem which grew out of the 1960s, the revived feminist movement. Feminism was far from being an historically new phenomenon: its ancestry went back to at least the late eighteenth century, with Mary Wollstonecraft's *Vindication of the Rights of Women*. Formally the socialist movement since its emergence in the nineteenth century had been committed to sexual equality,[39] but that, not surprisingly, did not necessarily correspond with the reality. Engels wrote speculatively about the historical processes of the distant past which had led to the subordination of women and Bebel, early in the twentieth century, produced a text intended as a definitive statement of how socialism aspired to liberate women as a distinct and specially oppressed part of the population. The Bolshevik regime in its early days actually tried to translate its sexually egalitarian principles into legislation aimed at some of the social roots of female disenfranchisement, with abortion on demand, collective childcare facilities and provision for easy and immediate divorce – provoking horrified accusations abroad of a regime of sexual debauchery, allied to the negation of property rights.

If all this showed greater enlightenment than was to be found in polite society, the difference nevertheless was a relative one. Marx not only neglected, and concealed the existence of his illegitimate child, the son of his maidservant, but presumed to exercise patriarchal interference in his daughter's private affairs.[40] Nicky Hart has argued convincingly that the politically rightward disposition of British women in the early century was related to a deep-seated misogyny and male chauvinism prevalent in working-class households and transferred into the organised labour movement, exemplified by its gender barriers in many skilled trade unions and the exclusively male workingmen's clubs concentrated in the north of England.[41] The Jacobin tradition, which was part of the French political left's inheritance even when formally repudiated, had a strongly anti-female dimension – but so did the rival syndicalist tradition with its focus upon the muscular male worker. Anarchism's founding intellectual Proudhon had also been a vehement misogynist. Women were perceived as deficient in intellectual capacity and hence particularly open to the wiles and snares of the priest and the bourgeois propagandist. During its existence the Third Republic, whether governed from the right or the left, did not extend the electoral franchise to Frenchwomen, who did not receive it until 1945. In the historical actuality throughout Europe and the US the initiative to defend women's interests and to extend their citizenship rights was taken by female pressure groups organised by and composed in large measure of bourgeois women.

The postwar shift in social relations throughout the developed world, issuing from the era of expanding mass consumption and welfare priorities, provided, as in the case of youth generally, the ground for a feminism to emerge ultimately which was built on a different foundation from those which had characterised past generations. The originating text in this case was Simone de Beauvoir's *The Second Sex*, an examination of the female condition with its thesis summed up in its title. Subsequent celebrated explorations like Betty Freidan's *The Feminine Mystique* or Germaine Greer's *The Female Eunuch* have been essentially repetitions and expansions of themes propounded in de Beauvoir's work. The earlier waves of feminist activism had focused upon demands for the removal of legal discriminations and the concession of full citizenship rights. By the 1950s that struggle had largely met with success and formal equality was in place throughout both the Cold War blocs – at which point it became evident that the emancipatory process, far from being accomplished, had barely begun.

The legal proscriptions which disbarred women from civic participation or occupying positions in the public domain might have fallen: it stood out all the more clearly that, aside from legal controls upon fertility, and subordination entrenched in family law, the barriers of custom and practice remained as high as ever. Women simply failed to be considered except in the most token capacities for elevated employment in politics, industry, commerce, the professions, academia. Even supposing these obstacles to be surmounted, a further level of confinement, a deeper layer yet of custom and practice, would still prevail, for women would remain enormously disadvantaged in taking advantage of the opportunities theoretically available.[42] The comparatively minuscule number of women who sought to pursue occupations of the kind traditionally associated with powerful males (the term 'career woman' is instructive) might be one thing: the overwhelming majority were seen to fill – both by the first sex and by themselves – a natural caste role as a low-wage labour resource in some employments but principally ones as domestic drudges, childminders and/or sexual conveniences. Traditionalist males preferred their partners not to exercise any other; the ostensibly more enlightened were willing that they should do so – but only on condition that they continued with the primary roles in addition.[43] The progressive character of the socialist movement in this sphere consisted in the main in improving and enhancing facilities for women to perform their traditional gender duties.[44] The ideology of the male breadwinner and the family wage was thoroughly ingrained in every national labour movement and the practice of industrial relations in the days of full employment and a seller's market for labour – the very language in which it was conducted – was structured around that assumption, taking little account of the specific and particular needs of women workers. The male industrial worker in factory, mine or transport with a dependent wife and family was presented invariably as the archetypal proletarian. The socialist movement of whatever stripe, not least because of pride in its commitment to formal sexual equality, was among the most reluctant to recognise that profound inequalities of a more subtle sort were built into its very institutions and ideologies.

The sexual revolution of the 1960s failed to overthrow these categorisations. Its emphasis was on attacking traditionalist restrictions on heterosexual activity and the deliberately cultivated ignorance and taboos which upheld them. That the advances made represented positive gains for both sexes is not to be doubted but it is equally clear that the principal benefit was appropriated by the male activists of the revolution, and Western men more generally, for it occurred within the framework of inherited unequal gender (as well as sexual) relations so that male priority continued as an unquestioned assumption and the women participants were on average expected to continue to subordinate themselves both sexually and socially.

In retrospect it seems therefore very much to be expected that the critique elaborated by de Beauvoir would be taken up and extended in political directions, added to, altered and adapted as the appreciation sank in that the world and its social reality was made for only one half of the human species. Around the turn of the decade the women's liberation movement emerged. Like the radicalism of the 1960s it evolved in an unstructured and many-sided fashion: on principle there could be no central co-ordination or leadership, no charismatic dominant figures, no universally accepted credo – although the concept of patriarchy, the general structure of male ascendancy and female subordination was common to all.[45]

If this new-wave feminism had any central principle it was the one expressed in the formula 'the personal is political'. The normal, taken-for-granted separation of these spheres was observed to reflect not merely a regrettable failure of perception on the part of the left, but to mirror the structural gender imbalance of social and cultural reality – for the demands of 'the political' were framed in such a manner that they could be accommodated only by men – or women willing to mimic the culturally-conditioned male indifference to personal considerations. Moreover the province which 'the political' was held to relate to was mostly the concern of men. 'The personal' by contrast constituted the residue, the less important – in other words the field that was left to women and the one for which in their secret consciousness even the most enlightened of male activists believed women to be better emotionally equipped.

It was pointed out for a start that the routines of meetings, conferences, agendas and resolutions, focus upon platform speakers and suchlike, when not geared towards the cultivation of dominant egos were alien to most women, whose ingrained conditioning since childhood ran contrary to such forms of performance and whose responsibilities in 'the personal' had anyway usually left them with insufficient time and opportunity, not to speak of inclination, to master such dubious arts. The normal units of the women's movement took the character of small relatively intimate circles, functioning in a formally unstructured manner and with only the sketchiest of networks and structures reaching beyond the basic groupings. The intention was to avoid the creation of hierarchies or dominant leaders. Attempts within these conditions to achieve long-term co-ordination over wider areas or upon national bases were not notably successful, and the movement had not been in existence very long before it began to experience irreconcilable ideological fissures.

Unquestionably the women's liberation movement had its origins in the left, but that category itself, along with the concept of socialism, soon came under question and was stigmatised by those sections which rejected it as being simply one more part of the male political universe. For the left, the division which opened up along this line[46] was by far the most significant. On one side stood what came to be termed the 'radical feminists', the side of the movement which regarded women in general on account of their gender roles as an oppressed class and feminism as a self-sufficient principle which would only be obscured by diversion into questions of property relations. They were able to point out that a change of property relations in itself was unlikely to do very much for women, and certainly had not done so in the Soviet bloc or China. This stance tended to be accompanied by one of female separatism, applied in practice by the groups which adhered to it and recommended as a principle for womankind in general, based upon the proposition that women's oppression, both social and, more especially, sexual, benefits *all* men. Logically the position led on to one of political lesbianism. This was the standpoint, accompanied as it usually tended to be by distinctive styles in dress and personal deportment, which generated the media stereotype associated with militant feminism.

By contrast, the socialist feminists attempted to integrate the insights of new wave feminism into gender relations with those of socialism into economic exploitation, class relations and institutional hierarchies.

The constitution of the individual worker as an individual appearing on the market with his labour-power to sell presupposes a work organisation 'behind the scenes' which is not articulated directly to the market process but appears as a personal service to the individual worker. That individual depends upon domestic labour as the central basis of his capacity to sell his labour-power to the capitalist, hence to appear as an individual in the marketplace.[47]

For better or worse this particular perspective proposed a more complex and differentiated understanding of various categories of oppression than did the standpoint of the radical feminists. In the competition between the two outlooks that was not necessarily an advantage – a simple and less nuanced message was more readily understood and lent itself better to striking slogans and interpersonal theatre. There are overtones here of the earlier competition between nationalism and socialism – with its all too predictable winner. Additionally, in the 1980s as the worldwide socialist project began to founder or at least appear to sink, the potential for upholding a specific socialist version of feminism seemed drastically to narrow. By that point however the organised feminist project itself was reaching an impasse.

A measure of success was attained in altering cultural consciousness throughout the developed world. By the 1990s it was, if not common, at least not sensational to see women occupying the top of hierarchies that not so long beforehand would have been regarded as exclusively and inherently male preserves – such as the boss of spy agencies. Throughout the world the number of female premiers and elected heads of state was moving into double figures. Although the numbers of women directly affected was infinitesimal, such developments were the surface indicators of more far-reaching subterranean movements, which were nonetheless still painfully slow and inadequate in relation to the accumulated centuries of patriarchal privilege and presumption. New opportunities had certainly come into existence, but it was women who were already relatively privileged in terms of background and education who were best placed to exploit them. That too was reflected in the acceptance which feminism had achieved at the level of the academy within a range of disciplines in the field of human sciences, particularly in the US.[48]

Despite its emphasis upon loosely structured institutional arrangements, pluralism and prefigurative practices, the women's movement was not spared the theoretical conflicts, organisational fractures, animosities and fragmentation that had traditionally plagued the male left. It is clear that this regrettable outcome was not due to the personalities involved nor to the clash of opposing theoretical positions within the movement but was an expression of the material contradictions which could neither be theoretically accommodated nor resolved in action. The radical/socialist feminist rupture was not the only one. 'Over the 1980s the interests and worldview of white heterosexual professional/managerial women continued to dominate mainstream feminism.'[49] That hegemony was subjected to challenge when issues of ethnic identity, sexuality and class were placed on the agenda. 'They spoke as women of an oppressed class, or race, or community, while the feminist movement spoke of Woman.'[50] That rethinking did not proceed without bitter struggle and division – 'although the mainstream organisations have made efforts to recruit and promote women of colour within their organisations, they have proved quite resistant to sharing power with organisations of women of colour'.[51]

The comments cited above apply to the US but the route followed by feminism across the Atlantic did not differ in essence. The movement in the US did indeed leave an important institutional legacy, not replicated elsewhere, in the shape of the National Organisation for Women (NOW) but that had changed according to Johanna Brenner from a movement into a lobby.

> Feminism in advanced capitalist countries today is much more a network of organisations for lobbying than for grass-roots organising. The membership provides money, sometimes votes, sometimes letters and phone-calls, but very little local activism.[52]

By the 1990s the term 'postfeminism' came increasingly into current usage. The social climate too of the long recession, with deteriorating resources available for social welfare, had grown increasingly hostile to any far-reaching transformation in the state of gender relations. Past gains came under threat from governments and from grassroots conservative mobilisations.[53] What remained of the women's movement was pushed onto the defensive, trying to hold onto rights previously won, such as affirmative programmes, abortion rights, maternity leave and public support for single parents.

In the sphere of theoretical debate the disillusionments of feminism, as with others of the new social forces, link up with the disillusionments of the generation of 1968 activists. With the dreams and hopes embodied in that year ultimately blighted, a significant number moved over to the right, whether the conservative right, like David Horowitz in the US or the right-wing of social democracy, such as Paul Hirst in Britain.[54] In France squads of former Maoists defected to become ideologues of the 'New Right', transforming the traditional colour of the French intelligentsia.[55] It was however the prophets of poststructuralism, whom the aftermath of 1968 had also brought centre stage, who were to bear the strongest influence upon feminism's ebb tide. A common focus existed in the concern with language that was manifested in the 'linguistic turn' identified with poststructuralism; the philosophy of power relations developed by Michel Foucault, and the adaptations of Freudian speculative theology in which the milieu of poststructuralism and postmodernism was steeped, but exemplified in its most bizarre version by the psychoanalyist Jacques Lacan. In this philosophical undergrowth feminist theoreticians searched for clarification regarding the issues of identity, personality formation, and patriarchal power, and in the writings of such as Hélène Cixous, or Luce Irigaray feminism turned full circle. *The Second Sex* had opened with the declaration 'One is not born a woman: one becomes one', repudiating the notion of an essential femininity inherited with the female anatomy and so justifying a separate (and inferior) role. Now these writers advanced, by speculative reasoning divorced from substantive evidence, arguments for the existence of a particular female essence expressed in language and shared by all women which should (naturally) be valued as highly as that of its male counterpart but which nevertheless posited an ontological barrier between the two genders. It was an updated and theoreticised version, presented in largely impenetrable language, of the ancient claim of a straightforward link between the character of the genitals and the functioning of the mind and would doubtless delight the opponents of female ordination in the Catholic Church if they were able to understand it.[56]

Whatever the disputes and fractures among conscious feminists a far graver source of concern arises from the deep division between conscious feminists and all other women. However good or bad the theoretical accomplishments of the former and whatever the diffused influence of feminism over the past quarter century, the fact remains that most women even in the countries of its strongest impact would repudiate the identification however much they might remain attached to the social and personal gains which have followed from that impact. Feminism emphatically remains a minority position and shows no likelihood of changing in that respect for the discernible future. These same gains, when not menaced by a reactionary backlash, show every sign of being diffused and absorbed into the general culture, ceasing to have any radically oppositional edge. Outside the developed world the feminist impact, though not altogether invisible[57] has been even more diluted and indeed easily dismissed as the hobby of the affluent and educated female middle class. In the former Eastern bloc women are losing or being forced to fight strenuously to preserve the laws and facilities of the communist regimes that were intended to confer formal sexual equality and enable women to enter the workplace. In the Islamic world the rise of rabid religious fundamentalism has already dramatically reversed the scope of female emancipation and threatens to bring on a grim night of medieval repression.[58]

Sexual Politics – Gay and Lesbian Liberation

For understandable reasons the gay liberation movement, coinciding in time with revived feminism, has been of lesser significance in that it has involved a much smaller segment of the population. A degree of overlap has of course been visible in respect of the lesbian component, though the two have tended to run in parallel rather than in an interlinked fashion. Unlike feminism however, gay liberation was something dramatically new. The most advanced thinkers of the past had confined their public declarations in favour of liberated sexual relations to heterosexual ones only.[59] D. H. Lawrence had damned homosexuality (though he himself was certainly not without some element of homosexual disposition). Wilhelm Reich, regarded in his time as the last word in theoretical sexual libertarianism, had viewed homosexuality nevertheless as linked to authoritarianism and reactionary politics.[60] The fact was that throughout nearly the whole world homosexuality was, either literally or in terms of social ostracism, an outlaw sexuality and the analogy drawn between the position of gay people at large and Jews in anti-semitic cultures was a wholly valid one.[61]

It is likely that the intellectual foundations for the liberation movement were laid by writers such as James Baldwin and Jean Genet, whose novels portrayed homosexuality not necessarily as a sympathetic lifestyle but as a valid choice of being; but the possibility of politicisation and militant rejection of the attribution of shame, in short of 'gay pride', was made possible by a climate of thought which for the first time in modern Western culture was capable of extending demands for heterosexual diversity to previously unacceptable forms and which consciously conjoined sexual liberation (in whichever form) with left-wing politics.[62]

Although militant campaigners were always a minority of the gay community and those consciously on the left a smaller minority still, such left-wing orientation was doubtlessly reinforced by the never-concealed lust on the part of the right to engage in homosexual persecution, with determination to stigmatise and isolate the orientation as a mark of depravity and the imminent collapse of civilisation, assisted by the moral panic surrounding the AIDS epidemic. It was possible to develop out of the gay sensibility a critique of the social order and identify 'heterosexualism' – insistence on heterosexual identity as the only legitimate one – as emblematic of repressive power relationships at large. Something of this sort can be seen in the enterprise of Michel Foucault, and the argument has been developed at a more popular level by various commentators and activists such as Peter Tatchell. By and large however, male gay politics has been mostly about fighting its own corner, resisting gay-bashing on the streets or in the legislature. A notable success has been in largely defusing the incipient categorisation of AIDS as a 'gay plague' concentrated in the homosexual community but nonetheless threatening everybody else; but what impression it has made on public culture has related more than anything else to the question of style in dress, accoutrement and interaction. The politics of lesbian separatism have been more explicit in challenging a male-dominated social order and in identifying heterosexual relations as inherently oppressive whether in bed or in more extended forms of intercourse – but in practical terms they have achieved little more than the creation of a stereotype and can in any case hardly be said in any recognisable sense to belong to the left.

Environmentalism

By contrast, the 'new social force' which has achieved the most effective penetration in traditional political terms has been the environmental movement, not least in the fact that established parties of both the right and the left have hastened to take over its agendas – in presentation if not in substance. Not only that, but it has generated its own parties, which in certain states have significantly affected the governing political structures. Beyond that it has also brought into being non-party political pressure groups which have achieved an if anything still greater impact. More fundamentally still it has succeeded in reaching and shifting the public consciousness throughout the world into a lively awareness of the global dangers emanating from the contemporary form of human interaction with the biosphere. None of which means that it will necessarily realise its fundamental aims or avert the predicted global catastrophe.

Environmental concerns go back a long way,[63] and local environmental calamities have occurred, affecting considerable populations. What distinguishes the environmentalism that has made its appearance since the 1970s is the perception that uncontrollable population explosion and increasing pace of globalised industrial production threatens to bring the human adventure to a premature and horrific conclusion, or at least divert it into radically different and even worse channels than those it has followed hitherto. Three main lines of concern, separate though connected, are to be identified. The first is that of resource depletion, most noticeably of fossil fuels, being used up at an accelerating rate and threatened with exhaustion in the course of the next century, but also of wood, water, soil, fish stocks, rain forest and the species of plant and animal life which inhabit the endangered environments. Secondly it is clear that apart from the long-term damage they do, these inimical processes are being conducted principally by the First World nations at the expense of the Third. Most menacing of all is the possible consequence of environmental pollution – the phenomenon of global warming, the large-scale and long-term effects of radioactive or toxic chemical discharge, the possible stripping away of the ozone layer – developments which singly or in combination are certainly capable of rendering the planet uninhabitable.

There is a bitter irony in the circumstance that the lifting of the fear of imminent annihilation by nuclear weapons has only served to highlight with greater emphasis that of destruction from ecological collapse – although this joint reality could possibly be a sign that the present character of human existence is unsustainable. Effective response to the danger is inhibited by a broad range of interlocked factors, of which two in particular stand out. The first is the slow and cumulative manner in which the individual forms of deterioration progress – by the time they are recognised and accepted as a problem they have become hard to reverse. For millennia the biosphere has served as a limitless resource and as a perfectly adequate receptacle for human-generated wastes – it is hard to transform such an ingrained assumption. How can global fertility, soil erosion, forest destruction or greenhouse gas generation, occurring over such a wide span under numerous individual sovereignties at so many points be controlled? How is it to be recognised when a critical point has been passed? The second factor is even less manageable. The citizens of the First World have grown accustomed to a lifestyle which is affluent beyond the imagination of previous generations. Not only are they understandably unwilling to give it up, they have acquired an expectation that it will continue not just to be sustained but to be continuously expanded. The citizens of the remainder of the globe aspire, not surprisingly, to emulate the fabulous society of abundance that has been erected in the G7 nations. To do that (assuming it to be politically feasible) requires not merely sustaining but stepping up the pace of industrialisation and accelerating the rate of economic growth. In other words, what the world's population values most highly is at the same time the encroaching agent of its likely demise.

It is a contradiction far more profound than the political polarisation of the Cold War ever was, despite the latter's more immediate threat, and it would be inconceivable that it should not produce a strong political reaction – the surprising thing is that this has not been even stronger. In a number of European countries

Green parties have emerged, though none has succeeded as yet in overturning their national political systems or of assuming a politically determining role within them. The most successful to date have been the German Greens, *Die Grunen*, who have elected considerable numbers of deputies to local and regional governments and secured a bloc in the Bundestag itself. Why the Federal Republic should have proved so comparatively favourable to Green politics is unclear, nothing to the same extent occurred in other European countries and in France it was virtually absent, despite having administrations among the most cavalier towards environmental concerns.[64]

The internal style of Green parties has been that of the new politics rather than the old. Like all the inheritors of the 1960s new left they have tended to shun tightly organised and hierarchical structures and to emphasise and apply grassroots participatory democracy. Indeed, they have thereby given occasion, because they have actually sometimes been in a position to make the political choices which typify orthodox parties of potential government, to enable a judgment to be made on the strengths and weaknesses of their novel structures and modes of action.

Regrettably, the weaknesses have been more in evidence than the strengths. The Green Party in Britain has never managed to win a parliamentary election, but its difficulties in this respect have been due to the first-past-the-post system. It has gained local councillors and recorded a very impressive 15 per cent in the European elections of 1990. Not long after this triumph it quickly fell apart, its conferences distracted by infighting over strategy and tactics for which no agreement could be found, nor any mechanism for arriving at a commonly accepted conclusion. Its officials complained that they were unable to do their jobs on account of the absence of any workable national controlling structures and because they were subject to constant hostile invigilation by unaccountable groupings and factions among the rank and file.

The Greens in Germany exhibited the same tendencies towards splitting and fragmentation, and for similar reasons, but were the more publicised and serious on account of the greater standing and responsibilities carried by that party. As in the British example, accusations of power-lust and ego tripping were thrown at the spokespersons and Bundestag representatives, particularly the most charismatic of Green political personalities, Petra Kelly, and were responded to with bitter complaints that the rancour and suspicion directed against them made any concrete political strategy impossible to develop, or even any effective day-to-day tactical interventions.

The principal line of fissure was emblematic of the central strategic problem which has confronted every element of the new left since it made its appearance – or indeed of the historic left ever since it emerged to structure the shape of modern politics. The question was the perennial one of relating means to ends. It has been a principal distinguishing feature of the new left in its many varieties to hold that the subordination of the means to ends characteristic of the old left, the indifference to the broken eggs required to cook the omelette, had been one of the main, if not *the* main source of its problems and historic disillusionments. Consequently the new left has adhered to a passionate conviction that the style of political or quasi-political action practised by it in the here-and-now should prefigure the ultimate society and culture that such action was intended to bring into being. Distrust or outright rejection of hierarchy, tight organisational structures and traditional political manoeuvring and bargaining has therefore featured prominently in its ethos. Once involved in a functioning political system however, the difficulty of maintaining such scrupulous principles inevitably became all too apparent.

Along this line of fracture the German Greens divided themselves into two broad camps, styled respectively realists and fundamentalists, or in their own terminology, 'realos' and 'fundis'. The former wanted to use the party's electoral successes more effectively to promote specific but necessarily limited environmental improvements and at regional or national levels to enter working alliances with Social Democratic administrations or oppositions wherever these were willing to adopt some part of the green agenda. The fundis scorned such dilution of the essence of the green vision of an ecologically transformed world, pointed out that the SPD was no less committed than the power elite to limitless economic growth and warned that the tempting but crippling compromises favoured by the realos would result only in cosmetic improvements and do nothing to retard the global slide towards an environmental armageddon. Between the two positions, with the realos naturally suspected of also wanting to take personal advantage of the sweets of power, the party was torn apart and rendered ineffective at either level – whether as a pragmatic environmental protection agency or as a beacon for the future.

The electoral success of the German Greens and their lesser counterparts in other countries was a demonstration that the formation of these parties responded to a strongly experienced popular sentiment. It remains, however, an unresolved question whether green movements ever acted sensibly in taking on the shape of political parties, thereby becoming part of structures which have evolved to manage and perpetuate the existing state of things rather than to transform them and which are designed to frustrate as much as to register the popular will. The party identity in itself immediately sets in motion the kinds of strain and contradiction most likely to destroy the organisation. Since a green party is never likely to be more than a pressure group – and in the almost unimaginable event of actually forming a government would be faced with fatal and unresolvable dilemmas – it may make more sense to unreservedly insist on that status and work from outside formal political structures. Such at any rate would appear to be the lessons of organisations like Greenpeace and Friends of the Earth which have unquestionably had far greater success both in practical achievement and international consciousness-raising than any green party has ever done. The drawback of course is that they remain forever dependent on influencing governments which administer economic systems diametrically hostile to environmental concerns.[65]

The worthy but limited attainments of the environmental pressure groups hardly seem to answer the urgencies attending the plight of life on earth. As happens very frequently in cases where major necessary transformations are blocked, symbolism appears as a substitute for real advance. What cannot be accomplished in practice can be asserted nevertheless in fantastic manifestations. Similar tendencies have been evident within the women's movement. In fact the two have linked up at a number of points and inter-penetrated with pressure groups and subcultures in the domain of 'animal rights'.[66] At the comparatively sober (but more sinister) end of this spectrum are elements which would make a virtue of necessity and welcome the extinction of the human species on the grounds that its existence is fatally harmful to all other forms of life, sentient or otherwise, the earth would be a better place without its intrusion and the sooner it goes the less irreparable damage will be done. The best known tendency of this sort is the US group Earth First!, not to be confused with the UK group of the same name, which remains human-centred.[67]

Still, if only just, within the sphere of rational discourse, is the 'Gaia hypothesis' propounded by James Lovelock, which defined the biosphere (under the name 'Gaia', the ancient Greek deity) as a single complex living organism capable of responding as a unity to far-reaching change or attack in any of its parts[68] – it is unclear whether it is also supposed to be a sentient one. It is not however too difficult to take that additional step, whether through Lovelock or some other route, and arrive at a destination of nature-worshipping (in the literal sense) mysticism. This has not only occurred but has extended into an international subculture prevalent both in the US and Britain, easily assimilated to neo-paganism, occultism and the more exotic shores of 'animal rights' ideology.

The growth of such practices, to an extent that they get taken seriously in their own terms by academic writers, marks not merely a slide into superstition but deliberate reversion to the most primitive forms of animism in which natural objects – seas, mountains, trees or whatever, have projected onto them attributions of sentience and intentionality, or even that that they harbour a spirit which possesses these characteristics. If however, it is contended that no system of belief can be regarded as demonstrably superior to any other; and if the customary tests which have been held to do are shown to be invalid – e.g. Western intellectual culture undoubtedly generates technological advance: but what's so definitive about technological progress? – then the approach and ideology of the nature worshippers is no worse and may indeed prove more effective than that of the conventional political campaign. Not all such implications would be accepted by the adherents of postmodernism (though I believe that they do logically follow) but the influence of this climate of thought, not least on the left, has been of a much wider quality than that embodied in the above extremes.

Postmodernism

The terms 'poststructuralism' and 'postmodernism' are evidently related, though they do not mean quite the same thing. The latter refers to what is more a climate of feeling, a cultural ambience, the former to a comparatively articulated and identifiable philosophical standpoint. Postmodern approaches can apply to anything from news reporting to architecture – indeed to any kind of social or communicative practice including politics.

It relates to shifts in the forms of economic and social organisation, to changing patterns of employment, the ending of jobs-for-life assumptions, the fragmentation of workforces linked to the emergence of core and peripheral workforces, the further blurring of class boundaries, the implications of information technology – above all in its expanding capacity to manipulate images. In short, to a rupture of boundaries and enhanced fluidity in all hitherto stable life processes, making taken-for-granted categorisations increasingly difficult or impossible to sustain, particularly those between truth and fiction. It heralds the supersession of the classically 'modern world' structured around 'Fordist' systems of manufacture associated with the mass-production industries of the earlier twentieth century, hierarchical, disciplined political parties with coherent goals, and the presumption of progress in history – to all of which, liberalism, social democracy and Marxism have been wholeheartedly committed.

Poststructuralism has purported to be and in some respects can be rightfully viewed as the theoretical annunciation of the above developments. According to Ellen Meiksins Wood '... there is a direct line from Maoism to post-modernism, and from "cultural revolution" to textual deconstruction'.[69] The reality is however more complex. Poststructuralism has almost as many dimensions as the cultural climate which it interprets (if the notion of interpretation can be meaningfully applied to poststructuralism), but the central term in its vocabulary is that of 'deconstruction' – the deconstruction being of the overt meaning of any text – which can include not merely texts in the usual sense of something (written or otherwise) made to be communicated, but institutions and cultural practices. Deconstruction exposes the text beneath the text, except that it also carries a denial that any final determinate meaning can ever be established. Going further, it can be asserted that the establishment of meaning is not a neutral procedure, but is bound up with power relationships, so that, for example, the categories 'homosexual' or 'schizophrenic' are not descriptive classifications but means of stigmatising groups and individuals who exhibit socially unapproved behaviours; or, more subtly, that all 'discourses', particularly those of sexuality, are inherently power-structured. '[For Foucault] regimes of power constitute us to our very roots, producing just those forms of subjectivity on which they can most efficiently go to work.'[70]

These approaches are associated with and reinforced by what is termed the 'linguistic turn' that poststructural and postmodernist modes of thinking have espoused in the human sciences. Again, the contention is that language is not a neutral medium for conveying information but is actually constitutive of the narratives and discourses which are embedded in it and even of the subjects which use it. All description, all narrative, is actually rhetoric – and moreover it is not the users but the recipients who determine whatever meaning may be attributed to it. It follows therefore that communities of speakers, whether arising from traditionally inherited modes of discourse or emerging out of particular collective modes of using language, have a truer reality than collectives based upon location in the labour process or experience of exploitation. For example, if we want to understand the mid-nineteenth-century Chartists or the 'amalgamated' unions which arose upon their defeat, the thing to study is their respective political discourses, not the materialities of class which have usually concerned labour historians.

The historian (or sociologist or political scientist) would therefore be constructing a narrative about a narrative, and on a postmodernist interpretation this is all that can be legitimately done. Any issue of general concern in the past and present is accorded its status by the discourses through which it is constructed. There may in any instance be a generally accepted narrative, but potentially there are a multiplicity, of greater or lesser compatibility. No 'objective' external reality exists against which competing narratives can be evaluated, the most that is possible is to make a comparison for coherence and internal consistency. In the most thoroughgoing versions of the doctrine these considerations are held to apply not only to the human sciences but the natural ones as well – physics and biology are judged to be as much social constructions as are history or literary criticism.[71] The philosophical move which abolishes objective reality, and is normally referred to as 'idealism', is a traditional one of ancient vintage, though the metaphysics of discourse gives it a contemporary twist. Postmodernism is perhaps really innovative and original in that it purports to abolish subjective reality as well. The poststructuralist and postmodernist writers have all been heavily influenced by Freudianism, the original version of 'the dissolution of the subject', which specifically rejects the concept of a stable autonomous consciousness whose transparent will creates the meaning which it wishes to convey. In the Freudian universe things are never what they seem to be, everything is symptomatic of something else; in the same manner that texts do not have a fixed ostensible meaning but are infinitely interpretable. Jacques Lacan has developed a fully theorised (and wholly speculative) account with Freudian roots of the manner in which the individual subject is actually constructed by the symbolic order of language.

The especial target of postmodernist denunciation is that of universalist claims to knowledge or ethical prescription, all such claims being viewed as no more than particularistic, constructed discourses illegitimately masquerading as modes of access to universal realities. Particular venom is reserved for the eighteenth-century Enlightenment as the fountainhead of error, a historic project which had as its purpose, successfully achieved, the universalising of Western scientific discourses and individualist values, which went on to serve as the rationalisation for misogyny, racism, imperialism, slavery and cultural or physical genocide. Of all objectionable discourses pretending to universal validity the most abhorrent is the 'grand narrative', which binds together into a single theme every element of scientific or ethical universalism. It is in essence the notion that history is going somewhere, that it has a specific destination – whether that might be in the world of globalised property-owning individualism or the classless society – and that the eventual improved state, made possible by the application of science, will express the culmination towards which all past development has been leading. In short, the notion of progress in history and the idea that the situation of the G7 nations today represents in any sense progress over that of past centuries.

In his sympathetic but critical discussion of poststructuralism, *The Logics of Disintegration*, Peter Dews observes that there has often been a de facto alliance between it and the left. This is certainly true, and expresses the continuing influence of 1968. The major French poststructuralist writers were all active well before that

date, but it was its backwash which carried them to the forefront
of the cultural stage and disillusionment with the aftermath which
gave their approach its peculiarly pessimistic note. In terms of
concrete political issues they did tend to lean towards the left, if
in a vague sort of way, but that was of minor importance. The
significance for the First World left of postmodernism has been
advanced both by positive and negative circumstances. In positive
terms it has offered a mode of analysis which deconstructs and
disintegrates the ideological legitimacy of established authority
and all the narratives which support it – including those which justify
the the position of the First World. For feminists in particular,
analysis of the discourses of domination demonstrates that they are
male ones and operate by silencing women and writing them out
of the script. Negatively however, its popularity has derived from
the helplessness of the left, especially the new left, in face of the
triumph of global capitalism, established elites and systems of
domination. It is, after all, more feasible to deconstruct discourses
than to deconstruct states or institutions.[72] In Dews's words
(though he distances himself from the assessment) 'post-structuralist
thought [is] itself a shattered mirror of the logic of disintegration'.[73]

In other words the response of the left to the postmodern
condition, if such it may be termed, has tended to be to retreat into
a form of hermetic analysis divorced from much purchase on
reality, a stance greatly reinforced by the collapse of the Eastern
bloc, the environmental crisis and the real or imagined discredit
of Marxism whether as a mode of analysis or as a guide to action.
Poststructuralism or postmodernism, it must be acknowledged, has
been responsible for valuable insights that identify major gaps and
weaknesses in the approaches of the left in particular and the
human sciences in general. Insistence on the importance of discourse
has been salutary: the significance of what has been said is only fully
understandable in the context of how it has been said and the modes
of saying prevalent at any given time and place. Disowning 'grand
narrative' in the sense in which the left has tended to uphold it, is
more salutary still: there is no reason to imagine that 'history is on
our side' or that the notion of automatic progress built into the
historical process has any validity. That argument was advanced
long before postmodernism came upon the scene, but its current
reformulation has not only caught the mood of the times but
encapsulated in the memorable term 'grand narrative' the source
of the error.

All the same, poststructuralist theory and a stance of embracing
joyfully the postmodern condition as advocated by Jean Baudrillard,
are likely to prove but sorry props to lean upon. The postmodernist
philosophic structure is an extremely rickety one[74] with a central
faultline in the denial that the concept of truth contains any

meaning. To assert that truth, except in the most banal sense, is always ambiguous and never complete can be taken as read, but to reject it altogether opens onto a totally different terrain and one wholly hostile to the left. If no discourse can lay claim to truth and all are of equivalent standing the same must apply ipso facto to postmodernist claims as well and leave no more reason for taking them seriously than any rival ones. Moreover, it is ontologically impossible to dispense with the concept, for *no* discourse can be taken seriously unless it is implicitly accepted as embodying truth in some sense, to appeal to a reality outside of the narrative. A genuine relativism would paralyse all action. Advertising and political manifestos, the most discredited of all narratives, produce their effects only because enough members of the public continue at some level to believe that their claims correspond to some kind of truth, all experience to the contrary notwithstanding.[75] Like a ghostly presence, a 'concealed premise', as Richard Webster puts it, truth continues to haunt the denial of its possibility. 'Show me a relativist at 10,000 metres,' Stephen Jay Gould has argued, 'and I'll show you a hypocrite'. The relativist by action if not in words accepts the truth of the mechanics which sustain the aircraft in flight.[76]

The spokespersons of postmodernism argue that the pursuit of universal truths and commitment to grand narrative is not only erroneous in principle but pernicious in effect. However the picture of the Enlightenment which emerges from these attacks is a grotesque caricature and it requires a considerable level of mis-representation to contend that the values of the Enlightenment thinkers justified, let alone motivated the atrocities of the modern era. The Spanish conquistadores did not require the Enlightenment to commit genocide upon the populations of the Caribbean, Mexico and Peru and subject the remnant to slavery, nor Genghis Khan to do similar things in Central Asia during an earlier period. These acts were committed by cultures with no pretensions to universalism (unless Christianity is to be regarded as such, in which case the root of the evil has to be sought a lot further back). If anything, Enlightenment writers were rather fond of contrasting Chinese or Persian culture (not to speak of the noble savage) favourably with that of the Europe of their own time because of their conviction that these exotic cultures better embodied the universal humane values they propounded. They were guilty of expressing such profanities as opposition to judicial torture, slavery, religious or racial persecution.

A logical corollary to postmodernism's insistence on the construction of reality by incommensurable discourse is that sharers in particular discourses, i.e. cultures, occupy equivalent moral space and that condemnation of particular cultural practices in the name of universal values is oppressive, unjustifiable, racist and a tactic of imperialist discourse. It does have the disadvantage that on this basis objection to practices such as female genital mutilation or burning widows alive is ruled out – and the latter position at least has been seriously upheld in recent times.[77] It also reveals a contradiction in that there is no justification to be found within postmodernism for condemning an imperialist culture either: oppressing and oppressed ones are on the same ontological level – indeed for followers of Nietzsche, as most postmodernists are, the oppressors, as exhibiting superior and more forceful will, would if anything seem to invite preference.

The above conclusion is not drawn however, let alone the extremity to which a wholly consistent cultural and ethical relativism inevitably leads. If cultures cannot be subjected to any outside standard and are to be judged only on their own terms, then the Third Reich too has to have the benefit of such ethical agnosticism. It was, after all, a distinct and recognisable cultural formation sustained by its own narratives and discursive practices. For Nazis, therefore, gassing Jews must be seen as a legitimate form of cultural affirmation. The conclusion is grotesque, monstrous and revolting, but, other than Richard Rorty's unconvincing sidestepping of the issue,[78] represents the only alternative to some species of ethical universalism.

Deconstruction claims to aim at the delegitimisation of institutional hierarchies, including those of knowledge-power. It is *only* in regard to the latter however that it achieves any impact and that is where it in fact finds its appointed resting place, in higher education and cultural institutions, given that other sorts of power and institution tend to be beyond its reach – the dying echo of 1968 whispers most loudly through the halls of academe, appropriately enough, since that it is where its thunder originally sounded. What gets deconstructed, pre-eminently, is not the ascendant ideologies of the right, embedded in immovable institutions and sanctified by political success, well able to ignore and disdain any deconstructionist critique which may come their way. The critical attack falls instead upon the vulnerable and outlawed universalisms of the left, easier targets insofar as they have lost their material embodiments and apparent historical rationale. The proclivity of the left to tear itself apart over theoretical issues is notorious and the deconstructionist weapon is one readily wielded in the arena of factional intellectual conflict. The left however can subsist only as a permanent *and universalist* critique of oppressive power and its foundations, by keeping in the forefront of its concerns, as Marx put it, 'the property question'. Relaunching its theoretical vessel on the foam of postmodernism is as sure as recipe as any for an early foundering, demoralisation and co-option by the right.

Assessment

Although in this chapter the new left, issue and identity politics have been treated separately for the sake of analysis, in reality, as anyone familiar with any of their aspects is well aware, they are intimately connected through multiple channels of discourse and practice. Do they possess any commonality? The argument presented here is that in their broad thrust they represent an attempt to establish an alternative tradition, a different way of doing left politics, to the deadlocked traditions of social democracy or Leninism whether in their mainstream or marginal guises.

Hilary Wainwright in *Arguments for a New Left* proposes a different although not incompatible form of coherence, namely that these movements are grounded in a conception of social knowledge which stands in opposition to the all-knowing, all-responsible centralised party or state common to both historic Leninism and bureaucratic social democracy, as well as to the property-related atomistic individualism peddled by Hayek's acolytes as the constitution of liberty. Instead – and one section of the volume is headed 'A new politics of knowledge' – the new movements work through a diffuse and spontaneous combination of theoretical, practical and experiential knowledge, often difficult to articulate and always impossible to codify, but shared and participatory. She suggests that the future of the left, if any, lies in developing along such a direction.

> In effect, many of the organisations produced through these movements presume that instead of acting on definitive, predictive social laws, they are themselves engaging in a form of experimental activity; with every significant action, they are revealing new clues to the character and contradictions of the institutions they are trying to transform ...
> ... the contradictory and the common interests, for instance, of low-paid casualised women workers and the higher paid male employees of the same corporation; the common economic bonds alongside cultural differences between white working class women in Europe and black women in Asia working in the textiles, electronics and other industries.[79]

Perhaps this is too romantic a view and the expectations associated with it utopian, but it seems difficult to imagine that the old left has any more promising perspectives to offer.

Conclusion – The Winter Landscape

If Karl Marx were alive in the 1990s he might be able to derive some bitter and sardonic consolation from the confirmation of his basic methodological premises, while he reflected upon the utter confounding of his social and political hopes. Marx's approach and perspective was above all a dialectical one and he was peculiarly sensitive to the reality that entities change their content and reverse their character as their inner contradictions are released and unfold. He was therefore the last person to be impressed with the continuity of names, and would have been intensely conscious that what ended its career a century after the institution of the Socialist International resembled only symbolically the 'dictatorship of the proletariat' that he and Engels had envisaged as the necessary next act in the drama of human progress.

Not that Marx expected any sort of uninterrupted straight-line development. *The Eighteenth Brumaire of Louis Bonaparte* is renowned for the remark about historical tragedy repeating itself as farce, but it also contains the following:

> On the other hand proletarian revolutions, like those of the nineteenth century, criticise themselves constantly, interrupt themselves continually in their own course, come back to the apparently accomplished in order to begin it afresh, deride with unmerciful thoroughness the inadequacies, weaknesses and paltriness of their first attempts, seem to throw down their adversary only in order that he may draw new strength from the earth and rise again, more gigantic, before them, recoil ever and anon from the indefinite prodigiousness of their own aims ...

Marx would not have been surprised, though he would have been appalled, at the turn taken by the SPD and the other socialist parties in 1914, especially when it is recalled how in his own lifetime he privately assailed what he regarded as the SPD's vacillation, weakness and failure of political understanding.[1] He would have regarded it as a product of the bourgeois values and attachments of which the workers' parties had failed to rid themselves. He would have been confident that in the long run the experience would produce a proletarian movement more capable of rising to its 'indefinitely prodigious' tasks. Would he also have endorsed the course taken by Lenin and have applauded the

Bolshevik revolution? The answer is almost certainly yes, for he would not have failed to notice the parallel between the bourgeois Provisional Government of 1917 and the French one of 1848. In other words, whether or not in accord with Lenin and Trotsky's analysis, he would have shared their perspective of establishing a workers' state in Russia as a way of bringing about a revolutionary proletarian regroupment in the warring nations; of breaking the imperialist chain at its weakest link. But like Rosa Luxemburg, from a position of solidarity he would have been a severe and searching critic of the early Soviet regime, and subsequently the Comintern. Thereafter, it can be surmised, Marx – unlike all the old Bolsheviks, the parties of the International and much earlier than Trotsky – would have appreciated, as in bourgeois ideologies, that words were being employed to conceal realities and that these realities were in utter contradiction to the purposes of the revolution and to those he had identified in the nineteenth century as being inherent within the proletariat and its dictatorship.

He would have repudiated with anger and shame the pre-Stalinist as well as the Stalinist regime, and would have expressed his fury by analysing the contradictions which had given such a shape to events, concluding no doubt that the isolation of backward and economically crippled Russia had ensured that there would be no alternative to the degeneration. What we cannot know is whether he would have drawn conclusions – from that isolation, from the absence of proletarian revolution in any advanced nation and from the character of what social democracy had become – that would have led him to rethink his own premisses regarding the proletariat's historic destiny, or of how he would have defined the social character of the regime which eventually took over on the territories of the former Russian empire.[2]

We cannot speculate more conclusively on whether historical developments during the remainder of the short twentieth century would have caused Marx to re-evaluate more categorically his presumption of the proletariat as the revolutionary agent that would be obliged out of its own nature to strive towards the classless society. What we can say is that the passage cited above from the *Eighteenth Brumaire* is written out of a vision of hope and certainty, a confidence that whatever detours or obstacles may be in prospect the ultimate destination is secure. It breathes, from a different vantage point, the same passion for the future world which Condorcet expressed in the shadow of the guillotine 60 years earlier. In one sense or another that hope and confidence has been the hallmark of the left.[3] Down to the end of the short twentieth century the hope remained alive, sustaining the left in all its variants, even if the confidence had been wearing thin in recent decades.

The novelty of the present is that the hope is all but extinct and the confidence has certainly vanished.[4] On this interpretation capital has gained not merely a major battle but scored a decisive victory – it has won the war. Celebratory volumes are already upon the bookstands; that with the biggest impact to date being Francis Fukuyama's *The End of History and the Last Man*.[5] This is sometimes classed under the postmodern rubric, but in fact is anything but postmodern. Its theoretical standpoint is Hegelian, and it embodies the grandest of all grand narratives – not merely that history is heading towards a particular destination *but that it has already reached it*. The destination in question is liberal capitalism (Hegel was of a similar opinion) and the fall of socialism (fascism having been mastered earlier on) signifies that the journey is at an end. Human existence will continue of course, but will hereafter proceed under a different sign, history having attained its culmination. The comment was made shortly after the book's appearance, that if history was at an end, in the Balkans energetic efforts were in hand to reinvent it. That however is to misunderstand the argument, which is not that liberal capitalism's triumph is comprehensive at this point – if all the world is in its economic orbit a lot still remains outside its cultural one – but that it is definitive: the rest will be mopping-up operations.

In fact the argument is similar to the soaring intellectual structures of neo-liberal economics, built around a single valid insight, elegant and impressive, but ultimately standing on air. Marx's insights into the nature of capital's reproduction and accumulation have never been bettered or displaced: his prevision of its future was extraordinarily percipient and impressively fulfilled. He was never a better prophet than when he insisted that capitalism was hastening towards its unavoidable destruction, that its internal forces carried it in a certain identifiable direction, which (*contra* Keynes) cannot be reversed or evaded. 'What capital produces above all is its own gravediggers.' Marx meant the working class, and he was mistaken. What looks more likely to be capitalism's executioner is capitalism itself – the problem is that everything else is practically certain to be entombed with it.

It is the merest of banalities to point out that the *present* level of the earth's resources are more than adequate to furnish every existing inhabitant of the planet – all 5 billion of them – with a basic sufficiency in nutrition, water, shelter, health care, education and sanitation. What sort of comment is it upon our socio-political structures that this modest aspiration takes on the character of a laughable utopia? The trend is precisely in the opposite direction, towards intensified polarisation, the concentration of misery, suffering, deprivation and hopelessness at the lower end of the scale, mirrored by exorbitant and unceasing accumulation at the other pole – though even the materially fortunate remain plagued with fear, insecurity and angst.

The wretched of the earth are at the end of the twentieth century more wretched even than than they were in the previous era of capital's supremacy, 100 years ago when the *Internationale* was composed; more wretched than was the case in the early 1960s when Franz Fanon used the phrase as the title for a polemic which foresaw some of the direction in which the newly decolonised Third World was about to move. And yet (*contra* Marx) the deprivation and oppression fails to generate a counter-movement, focused, articulate and of global dimensions, certain of its objectives and confident of its ability to realise them. Once again, *contra* Marx, philosophy did not and does not find its realisation in the proletariat, nor does the proletariat find its instrument in philosophy.

If one accepts the contention that in the absence of class consciousness a social grouping does not really constitute a class, it could be argued that working classes in the G7 nations hardly exist any more. To be sure the classic material conditions for new working-class formations are being established elsewhere, particularly in the rapidly advancing economies of Eastern Asia (including China) where male, female and juvenile workforces toil in Dickensian conditions, governed and controlled by regimes of management incomparably more knowledgeable and efficient than their Dickensian forerunners. Nobody seriously imagines that these new industrial workforces are going to replicate the careers of the European, Russian or even US working classes. One should perhaps not make too much of the Confucian authoritarian culture which is claimed by certain commentators to condition East Asian workers into reflexes of loyalty and bind them more indissolubly to their industrial and political masters than European ideologies ever could; for that would be to mistake existing quiescence for a permanent state of integration – discontent is likely to explode whenever it finds the opportunity. One should however be ready to make a great deal of the resources, both material and cultural, available to the rulers of these polities in the twenty-first century for preventing isolated outbursts of opposition from ever escalating into a more generalised national or transnational threat to the foundations of their property and their regimes.[6]

Generally speaking, alienation does not cease from systems of rule which reproduce, in constantly more extreme forms, the inequities of the world order, nor does militant opposition to them die. When however there no longer exists any creditable global framework of an organisational or ideological sort offering a convincing vision of a better order of things together with a believable programme for reaching them – and moreover when the previous such framework has fallen apart in calamitous infamy –

then the oppositional response may well assume virulent and obscurantist forms, easily manipulatable by cynical and reactionary elites.[7]

These forms are varied and multifarious and what Tom Nairn designates as 'ethnic nationalism' is only one of them. What they have in common are two things. In the first place a demand for conformity by the members of a designated group – nation or whatever – to standards of belief and conduct of a highly restrictive and inflexible sort, with stress, in the name of family values, nearly always on the subordination of women and their exclusion from the public sphere: and in the second place rabid hostility not towards the genuine authors of their woes but designated scapegoat communities, groups or individuals.

Besides ethnic nationalism there appear to be three main trends of this sort. The most comparatively 'civilised', originating in the US, is the 'communitarian' movement promoted by Amitai Etzioni. It urges, essentially, that the social and cultural devastation occasioned by the unconstrained operations of capital can be countered by rediscovering the virtues of the socially cohesive neighbourhood community, where in principle everybody will be responsible for everybody else's behaviour. Amid scenes of urban blight, lack of social standards and random violence the notion might appear to have a certain attraction, but it is apparent that the community these spokespeople have in mind is that of the middle-class suburb, in an idealised version at that.[8] More substantially, they are wholly indifferent to broader questions of power, property and privilege and appear to envisage communities where privacy and open choice of lifestyle would be at a discount, to say the least. The best that could be said for this approach are that its solutions are comparable to treating third-degree burns with sticking-plaster.

A much more terrifying manifestation is the phenomenon of militant religious fundamentalism; which has tended to be associated of late with Islam in particular, but is no less abhorrent when coming from other points on the map of traditional salvation faiths – Judaism, Christianity, Hinduism, Sikhism, Buddhism.[9] The claim to possession of a divine and exclusive revelation which is beyond investigation or argument easily convinces adherents gripped by their zealotry to view insubordinate unbelievers (and apostates even more so) as less than fully human. Conviction of divine approval is also among the most effectual motives known to history for the unflinching destruction of life, resources and culture by those so convinced. Traditionally, in grossly inequitable societies, fervent religious belief and observation has been employed as a drug – 'the opiate of the people' – by regimes which ostensibly share and uphold the values incorporated in the faith. However, when yoked to searing poverty, boiling social resentment and political exclusion and directed against political authority conceived of as illegitimate, it can take on the shape of an explosive revolutionary force.

The Iranian revolution of 1979[10] represented the first demonstration of this new phenomenon's potential energy and mobilising power. At the time of writing the secular governments of Egypt and Algeria are being rocked by and barely able to hold their own against so far irrepressible armed revolts conducted under Islamist banners. The strength of Islamist fundamentalism in the Arab world however, though fuelled by populist mobilisation, is also highly dependent upon being resourced, guided and encouraged by the Islamist regimes of Iran, Sudan, Saudi Arabia and to an extent Pakistan. Wherever these movements succeed in grasping state power their priority agenda is the imposition, regardless of cost, of their prejudices, superstitions, and lifestyle codes upon citizens who fail to share them, particularly women. Such a cultural counter-revolution is regarded in part as one means of addressing the social deprivations which have brought the fundamentalists to power; in part as a diversion from them. In southern Sudan a civil war of exceptional ferocity and destructiveness has been unleashed by the determination of the Islamist government in Khartoum to impose medieval Islamic law upon the Christian and animist population of the Equatorial region.

It is not by any means confined to the Islamic world. Buddhist fundamentalism linked to state power has achieved a bloodbath in Sri Lanka. The Indian government and the integrity of the Indian state are both threatened by the Hindu and Sikh variants. A combination of rival Muslim and Jewish fundamentalisms do their best to overthrow and extinguish any form of compromise between Palestinian and Israeli nationalisms. In this instance religious fundamentalism interlinks with ethnic nationalism on both sides, challenging the older secular tradition for command of the nationalist agenda.

Nor is it confined to the East, despite the media in the West having turned 'Muslim' and 'fundamentalist' into nearly interchangeable terms. The interpenetration of fundamentalist religion and ultra-nationalism is one component of late twentieth-century populist irrationalism's most terrifying manifestation of all, namely the revival of violent neo-fascism and associated forms of political behaviour. In Europe this link is certainly a weak one (although it is present in the Orange culture of Northern Ireland) but in general the skinhead gangs linked formally or informally to fascist groups in Britain or Western Europe require no religious justification to express their social frustrations in racist or homophobic violence. In the United States, by contrast, Protestant fundamentalism is closely associated with right-wing politics. Biblical literalism goes accompanied with a zeal for punishment, sexual repression and social control. The forces which gave rise to Prohibition in the 1920s are far from extinct, now focusing upon crushing the 'underclass' (particularly black single mothers), removing abortion rights and impeding female emancipation and gun control. This is the side which works within the existing political system and aims to seize control of the Republican party for ultra-right objectives. Other elements however reinforce the Ku Klux Klan, provide ideological justification for the unofficial militia movements – armed to the teeth, ultra-right in politics[11] and largely out of public control – a paramilitary force which only needs to find a politically capable and charismatic leader to become a major public order problem, although the deeply individualist ideologies of the militia adherents would make it very difficult for them to accept any leader. Still loopier brands of US Protestant fundamentalism establish sectarian churches on openly racist and anti-Semite platforms, and are involved with or are even the founders of avowed neo-Nazi organisations.

For the left the most disturbing characteristic of the neo-fascist revival is not even its extent and persistence, but the shift in the social base from the classic fascist movements of the interwar years. Although there is historical argument about particular examples, especially Germany (and an enormous literature has been devoted to this discussion) there is no serious dispute that the mass base of interwar fascism wherever it appeared was to be found in the petty bourgeoisie, the lower middle class on any reasonable definition. That is no longer the case, at least so far as Western Europe is concerned, whether in Germany, France, Scandinavia, the Low Countries, Italy or the UK, and is probably true of a great deal of Eastern Europe as well. The leaders of neo-fascist or neo-Nazi formations still derive from social strata similar to those of their pre-war counterparts, but the majority of their activists and followers now tend to come from predominantly working-class backgrounds, above all long-term unemployed white male youth trapped in areas of multiple deprivation and confronting a daily struggle for resources and status with rivals of frequently different ethnic background. The Nazi symbolism, it has been pointed out, may well be adopted initially as a means of generating shock and attention and displaying aggressive indifference to conventional etiquette, but the politics tends to follow on.

Depressing though this development is, it need occasion no great astonishment. The members of the working class are not endowed with any form of peculiar virtue which naturally inclines them towards the left and enlightened politics and which insulates them from the fascist virus. The career of the Protestant working class in Northern Ireland since the nineteenth century might have made that point. Sectionalism has in any case traditionally been the bane of socialist agitators trying to instil a working-class consciousness transcending particular interests. If large numbers of individuals from working-class backgrounds were to come to view their aspirations as being served by populist extreme right-wing politics, there is no *intrinsic* reason why they shouldn't embrace them as readily as anybody else. That historically they haven't done so has been due to the existence of labour movements (socialist or liberal) which became hegemonic in working-class culture at a time when the conflict of capital and labour was particularly raw and unconcealed and whose traditions persisted down the generations. This did not prevent the formation of reactionary attitudes among working classes at certain important levels – racism,[12] homophobia, misogyny, even jingoism, but it did keep these atavisms within bounds and ensure a general orientation towards enlightened politics in the organised labour movements. It is the fatigue of these movements both in Europe and the US which has provided the ultra-right with its opportunity to make inroads into a working-class constituency, or at any rate into its younger members, among whom historic traditions, under the assault of unemployment and the electronic media, grow weaker by the year.

A dismal scene unfolds itself of a world where capital, whether in the shape of the global banking system or the armed forces of the G7 powers, is immovably entrenched and can well afford to ignore perturbations at its outer edges; all proceeding under the shadow of threatened environmental catastrophe. Economic and social polarisation proceeds remorselessly, leaving the major part of an enormously inflated world population – most, though by no means all in the Third World – sunk in abject wretchedness, plagued with permanent hunger, recurrent famine, tyrannical regimes and no less tyrannical oppositions propelled by superstitious fanaticism. The only remaining universalism is the exchange mechanism, and the vision of the developed world too ceases to be one of equal citizenship and becomes instead one of differentiated and segmented communities each practising its own species of abomination upon its weaker members in the name of cultural integrity.[13] If you think enlightenment is a problem, wait till you've tried obscurantism.

Discussing 'The Ends of History' (a deliberately punning title) Perry Anderson[14] identifies three historical predecessors to the socialist project, Comintern or social democratic, which has ended in ruins. The first, though not in time, was the system of collective Amerindian communities established by the Jesuit fathers in eighteenth- century Paraguay. It was suppressed, leaving no memory beyond that of a historical curiosity. The second, more important, was the challenge of the Levellers and Diggers of the English Revolution, demanding respectively democratic rights and common property in land. That too suffered total defeat and was forgotten for a time, but another age revived it and found in it a pertinent inspiration. The third was the Jacobin Republic of the Year II, that 'terrible and glorious' episode when, in Eric Hobsbawm's words, all good citizens were equal in the eyes of the Republic and the people smote the traitors. Overthrow and defeat followed in this case as well, but this time the cultural thread remained unbroken and what had happened in 1793–4 was incorporated into the collective memory of the left of subsequent generations. Anderson speculates on which of these outcomes is most likely to mirror the fate of twentieth-century socialism, and the question is pertinent to the left as a whole. The implication, which is almost certainly justified, is that the left in its previous forms is beyond revival except as an antique curio, and that any inheritor of its universalist outlook may incorporate certain of the former left's traditions, but will need to transcend and surpass them in a manner responsive to a radically altered economic, social, and cultural universe.

The third millennium of the Christian Era is nearly upon us, but that accident of the date is scarcely needed to provoke very fundamental reflections and appraisals upon the past and the future. The written historical record extends to just over 5,000 years, but the existence of *homo sapiens* to something between 50 and 100,000. The coming millennium certainly, and the next century very probably, will fix the general line of development for the equivalent span into the future. One does not require any special insight to recognise three well-defined ranges of broad possibility. The first, and regrettably on present indications the most likely, is that the species will exterminate itself (and most, if not all, others) through misapplications of technology. The second is that the civilisation of high technology will prove to be no more than a passing episode in the human story, and that it will be cataclysmically destroyed by the collapse of the material web which sustains it, but before the ecosphere has been irretrievably damaged – in which case the surviving population will be compelled to depend directly or indirectly on subsistence agriculture as the dominant form of economic practice. In time subsequent agricultural civilisations sustaining the culture of the few on the servitude of the many might certainly appear, flourish and die, but it can be taken as read that the one just lost could never be reconstructed.[15] That too would mark an 'end to history', of a kind. The third scenario, but the least probable, is that the framework vision of the Enlightenment will after all be realised and that science and technology in sustainable and benign forms will supply the foundations for every inhabitant to enjoy the opportunity of realising the potential inherent in the human situation and the individual human being. It is worth recalling Trotsky's words: 'The average [person] will rise to the stature of Aristotle, Goethe, Marx. And above these heights new

CONCLUSION – THE WINTER LANDSCAPE 231

peaks will rise.'[16] Perhaps – although we would be content with something a good deal more modest. What we can assert with complete confidence is that the existing system is hurrying to its doom and that our descendants will be in a position to know one way or the other which of these paths into the future or extinction humanity is about to follow.

Any hope that the most favourable option might be realised is bound up with an effective successor to the nineteenth/twentieth-century left coming into being, and at no very distant date. The planet and species-threatening perils of the immediate future are not waiting to surprise us – they have been identified, discussed and warned against at length (though there may yet be others still to appear). The system that is globally dominant today will not address them – it is the main part of the problem. A great deal of oppositional energy does indeed exist, but it is dissipated, unfocused and some of it is running into depraved channels. I promised in the introduction to this volume that I would confine myself to analysis of what had happened, not being prescriptive or trying to expound the kind of spring which might follow the winter of our discontent. I will end merely by indicating three things that any credible renewal would be required to do.

In the first place any successor will have to understand and absorb the reasons which brought on the debacle at the end of the short twentieth century. That is no mean undertaking, but it is nevertheless the easiest of the three and this volume is intended as a minor contribution to that discussion.

The second is to establish a believable perspective of historic hope, to evolve a *convincing* alternative to the present, to demonstrate that human control can be grasped and asserted over circumstances and structures, and – even more formidably difficult – how it can be done.

The third is for the new project, whatever it might be, to achieve, I believe within the terms which Hilary Wainwright identifies, an intellectual – *not* organisational – hegemony over the present remnants of the existing left, from which it will have to draw the initial human resources for its endeavours. That of course is the most difficult of all, and time is not exactly plentiful.

Notes

Introduction

1. By the labour leader Ramsay Macdonald, for example. The 'eugenic' movement, interpreting evolution in a different sense, warned stridently of 'racial degeneration' but had little influence on mainstream discourse and none on public policy, except marginally in the US, while two notorious anti-Semitic episodes, the Dreyfus case and the Belis trial, ended with the repulse of the anti-Semites.
2. Stalin attempted to suppress this contradiction in respect of the movement which he controlled. Communism during his rule was supposed to have neither right, left nor centre but to be 'monolithic'.
3. Designation of these conservatives as 'right-wing' in BBC news bulletins annoyed conservatives in Britain.
4. This revolution was to prove in due course of the utmost world-historic significance, but in the immediate term, although its principles certainly made some impact in Europe, the early American Republic was located in a part of the world as yet distant from the centres of political power and cultural production.
5. See Albert O. Hirschmann, *The Rhetoric of Reaction,* Harvard University Press, 1991, for a historical survey.
6. This is not to deny that enormous populations, even in Europe, remained untouched directly by the transformations. These were however the prime reality of the epoch and very few, on any continent by the end of the nineteenth century, escaped their indirect consequences.
7. After 1945 only politically maverick right-wing regimes such as Francoist Spain continued to openly denounce democracy. The very similar example in Portugal adopted a pseudo-electoral window dressing. See Paul Preston on 'The Labour Government and Franco Fascism' in *Socialist History* 8, pp. 123–4.
8. Perry Anderson, *Arguments in British Marxism,* Verso, 1989, p. 20.
9. As did equivalent political formations in the Third World.
10. Particularly marked in relation to the communist parties in the countries of the former Soviet bloc, China or South Africa; exemplified from the social democratic side by various Western European parties but most emphatically by Tony Blair's New Labour.
11. Cliff Slaughter, in John Lea and Geoff Pilling (eds), *The Condition of Britain: Essays on Frederick Engels,* Pluto Press, 1996.

Chapter 1: The Matrix

1. Conservative and right-wing currents were engendered as well.

2. See Giovanni Arrighi, *The Long Twentieth Century*, Verso, 1994. My own model differs in detail. 'What has propelled the prodigious expansion of the capitalist world economy over the last five hundred years, in other words, has not been inter-state competition as such, but inter-state competition in combination with an ever-increasing *concentration* of capitalist power in the world system at large' (italics added) Arrighi p. 13. Unsuccessful challengers for world market hegemony were successively the Dutch, French and Germans.

3. '[From the mid-nineteenth century] only the United Kingdom was simultaneously involved in the politics of all the regions of the world and, more importantly, held a commanding position in most of them'. Ibid. p. 53.

4. Ibid. p. 87.

5. Miners or shipbuilders for example.

6. Christopher Hill, *The World Turned Upside Down; Radical Ideas during the English Revolution*, Penguin, 1975.

7. See for example George Rudé, *The Crowd in History*, Lawrence and Wishart, 1981.

8. And which they were of course likely to exercise in turn against their dependants.

9. The subversive *Rights of Man* by Thomas Paine had the largest circulation of any text in England during the 1790s.

10. As argued by E. P. Thompson in *The Making of the English Working Class*.

11. John Breuilly, *Labour and Liberalism in 19th century Europe*, Manchester University Press, 1994, pp. 96–7, which is overall an extremely valuable examination.

12. Or in collectives such as mining villages etc.

13. See for example John Foster, *Class Struggle and the Industrial Revolution*, Weidenfeld and Nicolson, 1974.

14. For example the Labour Churches founded by John Trevor (sharply distinguished from Christian Socialism). E. J. Hobsbawm, *Labouring Men, Studies in the History of Labour*, Weidenfeld and Nicolson, 1964, pp. 375–6.

15. Denial of the electoral franchise, for example.

16. The point applies in reverse. David Cannadine devotes considerable space in his *The Decline and Fall of the British Aristocracy*, Yale University Press, 1990, to aristocrats who joined revolutionary movements.

17. But see the argument advanced by Stephen Berger in *The British Labour Party and the German Social Democrats 1900–1931: A Comparative Study*, Clarendon Press, 1994.

18. See for example, Roger Magraw, 'The Peculiarities Of The French: Writing The Social History Of The French Working Class' *Socialist History* 9, April 1996; Richard J. Evans, *The German Working Class 1888–1933, The Politics of Everyday Life*, Croom Helen, 1992.

19. The importance of the spreading railway network cannot be underrated here.

20. Stanley Pierson, *Marxism and the Origins of British Socialism: the Struggle for a New Consciousness*, Cornell University Press, 1973, p. 121.

21. Used by Marshall Berman as the title of his book on the experience of modernity. The use of the term 'Industrial Revolution' is also indicative.

22. The socially disintegrative power of money, liquid wealth as contrasted to real estate, was recognised and portrayed much earlier, especially by Shakespeare.

23. Claude-Henri St Simon, Charles Fourier, Etienne Cabet and Robert Owen are the principal names associated with 'utopian socialism'. They were highly esteemed by Marx and Engels, particularly the last.

24. The name 'communist' was initially used to emphasise the distinction of a revolutionary group from the 'socialists', or thinkers who aimed to achieve their social objectives through intellectual persuasion.

25. Hegelian influences were very important in this respect. The proletariat and its historic objectives were perceived to develop according to an inner logic.

26. Marx however dismissed the working-class communist theoreticians such as Weitling with sarcastic contempt.

27. Marx and Proudhon co-operated briefly in the 1840s but quarrelled violently thereafter.

28. Although the working class was subject internally to innumerable material and ideological fissures which its enemies were well able to exploit.

29. Helga Grebing, *History of the German Labour Movement*, Berg, 1985; W. L. Guttsman, *The German Social Democratic Party 1875–1933*, Allen and Unwin, 1981.

30. Wolfgang J. Momsen, 'Max Weber and German Social Democracy', in Carl Levy (ed.), *Socialism and the Intelligentsia 1880–1914*, Routlege and Kegan Paul, 1987, p. 93.

31. Although he and Engels acclaimed what they regarded as progressive nationalist movements against politically reactionary overlords, e.g. in Poland or Ireland.

32. It was formally wound up in 1876.

33. Although anarchism continued to survive as a significant force into the twentieth century, particularly in southern Europe and Latin America.

34. See e.g. David McLellan, *Karl Marx: His Life and Thought*, Macmillan, 1973; Julius Braunthal, *History of the International 1864–1914*, Nelson, 1966.

35. A lineage which postmodern theory now denounces.

36. Though some individual socialist leaders such as Belford Bax in Britain were outrageously misogynist.

37. Such as Bernard Shaw's eloquent denunciations of imperial brutality in Egypt.

38. For example by James Connolly in his pamphlet *Labour Nationality and Religion*.

39. Though there were again variations. The Canadian syndicalists, who went so far as to officially entitle themselves One Big Union (for *all* employees) specifically rejected mere *industrial* unionism – see David Jay Bercuson, 'Syndicalism Sidetracked: Canada's One Big Union'

in Marcel van der Linden and Wayne Thorpe, *Revolutionary Syndicalism: An International Perspective*, Scolar Press, 1990.

40. In its first decade the International had very little organised structure and was known by a variety of different names.
41. The Labour Party (as distinct from trade unions and the ILP) was admitted to the International in 1908.
42. Sanitary reformer and architect of the nineteenth-century English Poor Law.
43. 'Beatrice [in 1887] was convinced that, if socialism ever became possible, the discipline and rigours of the workhouse would have to be many times more terrible than they were already.' Royden Harrison, 'Sidney and Beatrice Webb' in Carl Levy (ed.), *Socialism and the Intelligentsia 1880–1914*, RKP, 1987.
44. V. I. Lenin, *What the 'Friends of the People' are and How They Fight the Social Democrats'*, Progress Publishers, 1970, pp. 169–70.
45. These were the principal object of attack in Lenin's *What Is To Be Done?*
46. Formally the Second Congress, meeting in Brussels and London in 1902. The first attempt, in Minsk in 1998, was arrested by the Tsarist police.
47. Ironically, Stalin came nearest to a working-class origin.
48. It was advanced during 1905 revolution and has similarities with but is not identical to Trotsky's contemporaneous concept of 'permanent revolution'.
49. See Mike Davis, 'Why the US Working Class is Different', *New Left Review* 123, September/October 1980.
50. Which may help to account for Rosa Luxemburg's denial that concessions to national sentiment had any place in a socialist programme.
51. Quoted in F. L. Carsten, *The Rise of Fascism*, Batsford, 1982, p. 39.
52. Guttsman, *German Social Democratic Party*, p. 291.
53. Grebing, *History of the German Labour Movement*, p. 79.
54. In fact during the century between 1815 and 1914 European great powers fought each other on only four occasions. Each of these conflicts was localised, comparatively short and, by the standards of the twentieth century, relatively bloodless. They were also confined to the years between 1852 and 1870.

Chapter 2: Leninism and Stalinism

1. For example by Richard Pipes, *Russia under the Bolshevik Regime 1919–1924*, Harvill, 1994; Robert Blick, *The Seeds of Evil: Lenin and the Origins of Bolshevik Elitism*, Ferrington, 1993. Ernest Nolte in Germany has advanced similar arguments.
2. Pipes, *Russia Under Bolshevik Regime*.
3. 'The far-flung network of quasi-permanent overseas military bases put in place by the United States during and after the Second World War ... was without historical precedent; no state had previously based its own troops on the sovereign territory of other states in such extensive

numbers for so long a peacetime period', Giovanni Arrighi, *The Long Twentieth Century*, Verso, 1994, p. 21.

4. '... the world capitalist system could absorb the three trillion dollars of debt ... into which the 1980s plunged the USA... There was nobody, at home or abroad to take the equivalent strain on Soviet expenditure ... ', E. J. Hobsbawm, *Age of Extremes: The Short Twentieth Century*, Michael Joseph, 1994, p. 250.

5. Marcel Liebman, *Leninism Under Lenin*, Merlin, 1975, p. 261.

6. Engels specifically denied that his comments in *Anti-Dühring*, regarding the impossibility in the 1890s of classical barricade insurrection, was intended to preclude the possibility or necessity of violent revolution.

7. Which is probably why between 1903 and 1917 they tended to have more adherents than the Bolsheviks.

8. Its predecessor, the Kievan monarchy, had been founded by Viking slave traders – a symbolic relationship.

9. See Perry Anderson, *Lineages of the Absolutist State*, New Left Books, 1974.

10. One of Lenin's most important perceptions was that these could be allied with the industrial working class in a revolutionary bloc. 'The Workers' Party and the Peasantry', *Selected Works*, Vol. II, Lawrence and Wishart, 1944.

11. Liebman, *Leninism*, p. 242.

12. He compared it to a steel block.

13. In 1908 he shut himself away to compile a lengthy philosophical tract, *Materialism and Empirico-Criticism*.

14. The history of the German bourgeoisie in the nineteenth century offered an obvious precedent.

15. See R. Craig Nation, *War on War: Lenin, The Zimmerwald Left and the Origins of Communist Internationalism*, Duke University Press, 1989.

16. Liebman, *Leninism*, p. 147.

17. Robert Service, *Lenin: A Political Life Vol. 1, The Strengths of Contradiction*, Indiana University Press, Bloomington, 1985, p. 5.

18. As with Harry Pollitt, 'The thing that mattered to me was that lads like me had whacked bosses and the landlords and taken their factories, their lands and their banks ... These were the lads and lasses I must support through thick and thin ...', quoted in Kevin Morgan, *Harry Pollitt*, Manchester University Press, 1993, p. 177.

19. Liebman, *Leninism*, p. 334.

20. See Isaac Deutscher, *The Prophet Unarmed*, Oxford University Press, 1970, pp. 4–9 for an eloquent summary.

21. Ellen Wilkinson and Palme Dutt, who attended the formation of a student international around 1920 as delegates, found their perceptions dividing along such lines. See 'Reminiscence of Palme Dutt' (Anon), *Our History Journal* 11, January 1987, pp. 4–5.

22. These councils however were very plastic in their political outlook. Some decided to appoint representatives of the middle classes – in Heidelberg the representative was Max Weber.

23. Lenin himself had noted in October 1917 that in Germany '... *all* classes of the population [are] incredibly hostile to the idea of internationalism ... ' But see also below, Chapter 5.

24. Richard M. Watt, *The Kings Depart: The German Revolution and the Treaty of Versailles*, Penguin, 1973, pp. 245.

25. Paul Frölich, *Rosa Luxemburg*, Gollancz, 1940, p. 307.

26. See Watt, *Kings*, passim; J. W. Wheeler-Bennett, *Nemesis of Power: The German Army in Politics 1918–1945*, Macmillan, 1967, Chapter 1; Barker, Julius Braunthal, *History of the International 1914–1943*, Praeger, 1967, Chapter 5; Nick Howard, 'Shirkers in revolt – mass desertion, defeat and revolution in the German Army: 1917–1920', in Colin Barker and Paul Kennedy (eds), *To Make Another World: Studies in Protest and Collective Action*, Avebury, 1996.

27. It proved to be no less isolated when in 1923 the KPD for the last time attempted to stage an insurrection.

28. Especially with Germany. The two pariah states, despite their political differences, established a military symbiosis.

29. Although the term was enunciated by Stalin in 1924.

30. Consumer industries remained state owned, but were obliged to function according to market criteria. Petty production was privatised.

31. A great deal of administrative manipulation was also employed to ensure his defeat in the party, but it is unlikely that this could have succeeded on it own.

32. His own position had in any case been shaken in 1927 by the Soviet leadership's responsibility, via the Comintern, for advice which led to the massacre of Chinese communists.

33. The Soviet government were also in genuine fear of military attack from Poland encouraged by France.

34. This turn resulted in the marginalisation and posthumous disgrace of the country's leading historian, M. N. Pokrovsky.

35. For a detailed discussion of the consequences on the British CP, see Mike Squires, 'CPGB Membership during the "Class against Class" Years', *Socialist History* 3, Winter 1993.

36. Within limitations, workers were free to seek employment where they could find it; a military-style direction of labour was not adopted.

37. 'There is no need to dwell upon this phenomenon of sacralisation, aimed at transforming a substantive theory into a system serving to justify a particular established order.' Liebman, *Leninism*, p. 19.

38. Most notably the Webbs, who found in Stalin's Russia the imagined fulfilment of their Fabian aspirations, as they declared in *Soviet Communism: A New Civilisation?*, 1935. (The second edition omitted the question mark.)

39. Discourse theory might be relevantly applied to this phenomenon. See also Bill Moore, 'Why Did We believe?', *Our History Journal* 12, January 1988, pp. 18–21.

40. In *To the Finland Station*, written around this time, Edmund Wilson assumes that Marxism was historically exhausted.

41. See Braunthal, *History*, Vol. II, Chapters 4–7.

42. The Eastern European states which had been German allies however were stripped of useable plant and equipment to supply reparations to the USSR.
43. Though for appearances sake remnants of the Popular Front parties were allowed to continue ghostly existences as constituents of a communist-led Front.
44. In the US itself plans inspired by the wartime alliance to turn the CPUSA into a 'political association' were forcefully put into reverse.
45. It's organ had the astonishing title *For a Lasting Peace, for a People's Democracy*, allegedly so that Western broadcasters would have to pronounce that phrase whenever they mentioned the journal.
46. Anti-Semitic overtones were marked in this case. A significant number of the defendants were Jewish and were accused *inter alia* of conspiracy with foreign Jewish organisations.
47. The Hungarian, Bulgarian and Czech purges were the worst; the Polish and Romanian ones of lesser ferocity.
48. The British were able to exploit cultural divisions between the ethnic Malays and immigrant Chinese, among whom the main strength of the revolutionaries was to be found.
49. From 1949 this also included the former Soviet occupied zone of Germany, in the form of the German Democratic Republic.
50. All were excluded from public life in the states where they were located and the smaller ones subjected to witch hunts of greater or lesser intensity, with the CPUSA suffering most.
51. One of the principal accusations against the Yugoslav leadership was that they had dissolved the Yugoslav party into more broadly-based organisations.
52. Though to different degrees. The PCI, even during the Cold War, had a relatively 'liberal' reputation.
53. Except in the US. So anti-communist had the popular culture become that the semi-legal existence of the CPUSA probably served as a useful bogey for the authorities.
54. Following the dissolution of the Cominform in 1955 the only formal international institution remaining was the journal *Problems of Peace and Socialism* (*World Marxist Review*), published from Prague.
55. Though one might compare the relationship of the state of Israel with Jews outside its borders.
56. For example, the Soviet-sponsored Stockholm Peace Appeal of 1952.
57. Such was the basic conception behind the CPGB programme *The British Road to Socialism* of 1951.
58. There were however substantial Trotskyist parties in Ceylon and Vietnam. (See below, Chapter 6.)

Chapter 3: 'Actually Existing Socialism'

1. The phrase is actually prefigured in Simone de Beauvoir's novel, *The Mandarins*, written in the early 1950s and set in the immediate postwar era. One of the characters argues that Soviet socialism is the best in the world *because it exists*.

2. A more civil tone in private was also adopted towards the Chinese leadership.

3. This appears to have been the standpoint of the French CP Leader, Maurice Thorez.

4. They had been advised not to complete the Chinese revolution; Soviet diplomats accredited to the Kuomintang regime had been the last to evacuate its capital.

5. Although that notion sounds preposterous in the 1990s it was taken seriously around 1961 by commentators far removed from suspicion of communist sympathies.

6. Castroism maintained an analysis of Latin American society divergent from that of the orthodox communists, giving rise to different strategies. The CPs envisaged a bloc with the progressive local bourgeoisies giving rise to a revolutionary process which would not necessitate armed insurrection.

7. See Gilbert Rozman, *A Mirror for Socialism: Soviet Criticisms of China*, I. B. Tauris, 1985.

8. The Vietnamese leadership, owing to the country's particular situation, was able to avoid committing itself, though it leaned towards Moscow.

9. Vital statistics, which would have indicated the persistent failure of the regime to achieve its objectives, were subject to increasing censorship in the course of the Brezhnev era.

10. Temporarily preserving a window-dressing of revered national leaders, e.g. Benes and Jan Masaryk.

11. Trotskyists and Maoists acclaimed the developments, not because they approved of the Dubcek regime, but because for different reasons they saw it as a sign of a possible Maoist or Trotskyist revolution.

12. That may have been a utopian hope, but the important point is that the events were widely perceived in such a light.

13. There was however, in every CP, a minority who enthusiastically acclaimed the invasion.

14. Ian Birchall, *Workers Against the Monolith*, Pluto Press, 1974.

15. See Jung Chang's family autobiography *Wild Swans, Three Daughters of China*, HarperCollins, 1992, for a detailed personal memoir.

16. Except on far left, which regarded the Moscow-inspired constitutional policies followed by the Chilean left as responsible for the debacle. See Ralph Miliband, 'The Coup in Chile', *Socialist Register* 1973.

17. There is a striking comparison with the aftermath of the even bloodier 1965 coup in Indonesia, where the Soviet bloc remained more or less mute over the fate of the Maoist PKI.

18. Cyprus was however permanently, though illegally, partitioned as a result.

19. At the same time a US-backed fascistoid regime was under heavy pressure from left-wing guerrillas in nearby El Salvador.

20. And was revealed by the leftist academic journal *Critique*. Its analyses however were generally disregarded at the time.

21. Giovanni Arrighi, *The Long Twentieth Century*, Verso, 1994, p. 323.

22. The scheme was a wholly impossible one, but that fact did not make it any less relevant.

23. As had been accomplished a few years earlier in Jamaica by the use of economic pressures.
24. The Soviet-backed regime in Ethiopia was also destroyed by internal revolt, though in that case the outcome was due to its own inadequacies, and well deserved.
25. Attempts were made to close some of the gap by encouraging private agriculture at the margins of the collective system, but the latter was so intrinsically built into the Soviet economy as to be incapable (unlike the Chinese) of being reversed.
26. Stephen White, *Gorbachev in Power*, Cambridge University Press, 1990, p. 3. Hobsbawm notes that by the 1970s not only was economic growth lagging but basic social indicators such as mortality were ceasing to improve. E. J. Hobsbawm, *Age of Extremes: The Short Twentieth Century*, Michael Joseph, 1994, p. 472.
27. Larissa Lomnitz, quoted Arrighi, *Long Twentieth Century*, p. 329.
28. In the GDR the *Readers' Digest*-style Soviet journal *Sputnik* was banned as tending to undermine public confidence in the regime.
29. All Soviet constitutions had, in line with Lenin's views on nationalism, incorporated a formal right to secession for the subordinate republics. There were proposals to abolish it during the drafting of the last, Brezhnev, constitution but these were rejected.
30. The issue was not purely one of national self-determination. There were large numbers of Russians living in the Baltic Republics.
31. The restoration of the St Petersburg name to Leningrad was highly symbolic.
32. A lot of unanswered questions remain around the precise character of the events of August 1991, including Yeltsin's own role.
33. The original 'purges' were wholly non-violent proceedings and involved expulsion from the party but no penal consequences.
34. See Isaac Deutscher on the Bolshevik Old Guard, *The Prophet Unarmed*, Oxford University Press, 1970, pp. 21–2; 32–5.
35. See e.g. Carl Tighe, 'Partyspeak in Poland', *Our History Journal* 18, for an example. The prevalence of political jokes constituted a negative indication of the degree to which the propaganda was failing.
36. A point reinforced by the experience of Vietnamese society in its postwar era.
37. Hence the self-serving distinction made by the US State Department between 'totalitarian' regimes (theirs) and 'authoritarian' ones (ours).
38. The phrase originated from a remark made by Khrushchev on a visit to Hungary that a socialist society would not be well regarded by its citizens if it could not provide them with goulash.
39. See Arrighi, *Long Twentieth Century*, Chapter 4.
40. An argument has been advanced that Lenin never in any case envisaged a world revolution, but it is unconvincing. See Piero Melograni, *Lenin and the Myth of World Revolution: Ideology and Reasons of State*, Humanities Press, 1990.

Chapter 4: The Fragments

1. It's leader Y. Zyvgonov was Yeltsin's main rival in the 1996 presidential contest.
2. See Gavan McCormack, 'Kim Country: Hard Times in North Korea' *New Left Review* 198, March/April 1993.
3. Ibid., p. 39.
4. Ibid., p. 42.
5. Ibid., p. 27.
6. In the ferocity of the regime's treatment of its citizenry and enforcement of hermetic isolation, there are echoes of the Khmer Rouge. The differences are more significant however, for urbanisation and industrialisation are central to the North Korean perspective and Kimilsungism is, in however perverted a shape an ideology of modernisation. The Khmer Rouge by contrast represented an attempt to uproot and eradicate modernity.
7. Attempts are currently being made to develop market mechanisms in the economy though there is no question of pursuing a road to capitalism.
8. Gerard Greenfield in 'The Development of Capitalism in Vietnam' *Socialist Register*, 1994, conveys an extremely discouraging picture.
9. Although the events of 1989 in Tiananmen Square demonstrated that the potential for political disintegration certainly existed.
10. According to Bob Arnot, there is a frequently expressed wish in Russian elite conversation that the USSR had copied China in this respect.
11. Nor is there any likelihood of a Chinese workers' revolution establishing a genuine proletarian democracy. See Richard Smith, 'The Chinese Road to Capitalism', *New Left Review* 199, May/June 1993, for hopeful hinting at such a possibility.
12. *Big Issue in Scotland* No. 65. Monty Johnstone comments that bad though things are they are not quite so bad as that.
13. Developments of this kind did occur but proved unfruitful.
14. Comment by Bob Arnot.
15. But note that the official unemployment figure at beginning of 1996 was only 3 per cent – due to enterprises keeping on their books employees they are incapable of paying meaningful wages or salaries to.
16. The Orthodox Church was not behindhand in this endeavour. Proposals were seriously advanced for the canonisation of the last Tsar. It is not reported whether the same was advocated for Rasputin.
17. *Glasgow Herald*, 1 January 1996. However, according to Bob Arnot, labour unrest and strikes are growing significantly, and these are *ipso facto* political ones, for the ruling elites in contemporary Russia are much disadvantaged by a certain inheritance from the Soviet era – the lack of any veil of commodity fetishism. Social relations are too transparent, economic actions are viewed as the outcome of political decisions, not of impersonal market mechanisms.

18. The developments took on a similar, mostly peaceful character in most of the bloc states. The exception was Romania, where they were very violent, although brief.

19. Dubcek was resurrected from obscurity and briefly presided over the Czechoslovak parliament.

20. Yugoslavia proved to be the extreme example of this process – with horrendous consequences.

21. The ghostly minor parties of the communist-dominated 'Front' governments returned to independent life.

22. See Peter Gowan, 'Neo-Liberal Theory and Practice for Eastern Europe', *New Left Review* 213, September/October 1995; Janos Jemnitz, 'Labour and Politics: Hungarian Workers' Parties, Trade Unions and the State', *Socialist History* 2, Autumn 1993.

23. And their technologies, it soon became evident, had been responsible for environmental blight as bad as anything to be found in the capitalist world.

24. And were equally anxious to deter them from establishing economic associations among themselves, instead insisting that each should be linked individually to the West. See Gowan, Ibid.

25. See Hilary Wainwright, *Arguments for a New Left: Answering the Free Market Right*, Blackwell, 1994, Chapters 1–2.

26. These included Roger Scruton the ultra-right philosopher, who learned Czech especially for the purpose.

27. Quoted by Wainwright, *Arguments*, p. 43.

28. Ironically by a government which traced its origins to a trade union revolt.

29. In Slovakia, as with Croatia, there had existed unusually strong interwar fascist movements whose legacies had been far from wholly eradicated.

30. There are comparisons with Slovenia, the most developed of the six Yugoslav republics and which established its independence while escaping involvement in the civil war.

31. See Roger Griffin (ed.), *Fascism*, Oxford University Press, 1995.

32. See especially Branka Magas, *The Destruction of Yugoslavia; Tracking the Break-up 1980–92*, Verso, 1993.

33. Andrew Whitehead, 'Calcutta Compromise' *New Statesman*, 20 November 1992, p. 19.

34. Ibid.

35. The state government, though the target of the privately-owned Calcutta press, maintains good relations with local big business.

36. See e.g. various articles by R. W. Johnson in the *London Review of Books*.

37. KwaZulu in Natal however continues to be dominated by the violently antagonistic and virulently reactionary Inkatha movement uniting the White right and traditionalist chiefs, which Mandela has been obliged to incorporate precariously in his government but which is likely to prove a source of instability in the not too distant future.

38. In the case of the PCF (French Communist Party) even to accommodate unofficially to anti-Arab racism.

39. Causing it to lose the adherence of its one publicly notable figure, Angela Davis.

40. See Wainwright, *Arguments*, Chapter 7; D. S. Bell (ed.), *Western European Communists and the Collapse of Communism*, Berg, 1993.

Chapter 5: Social Democracy

1. Leaving aside agriculturalists.
2. Eduard Bernstein on the Social Democrat side, Max Weber on the bourgeois.
3. But avoiding membership of bourgeois governments.
4. The argument advanced in Lenin's *What Is To Be Done?*
5. Some socialist leaders were less naive in this respect, for example Jean Jaures.
6. Even in Russia. (Serbian socialists, though according to Lenin the only ones which might legitimately have supported their government, were the only ones apart from the Bolsheviks to denounce the war.) Attitudes were undoubtedly influenced by the expectation that the war would be short.
7. Except in Ireland.
8. Ebert was furious at a member of his government who demanded the dismissal of an officer who had described the government to his assembled troops as 'a bunch of crooks'. He declared, 'We are not going to dismiss so capable an officer just for that!' Julius Braunthal, *History of the International 1914–1943*, Praeger, 1967, p. 132.
9. See J. W. Wheeler-Bennett, *Nemesis of Power: The German Army in Politics 1918–1945*, Macmillan, 1967, Chapter 1; Nick Howard, 'Shirkers in Revolt – Mass Desertion, Defeat and Revolution in the German Army: 1917–1920,' in Colin Barker and Paul Kennedy (eds), *To Make Another World: Studies in Protest and Collective Action*, Avebury, 1996.
10. Richard M. Watt, *The Kings Depart: the German Revolution and the Treaty of Versailles*, Penguin, 1973, p. 304.
11. The SPD's strength was drawn principally from the more skilled and least unemployment-threatened sectors of the workforce.
12. It may appear peculiar that the intransigently constitutional SPD possessed a paramilitary force (the Reichbanner), but in the Weimar Republic every self-respecting party had one.
13. Wheeler-Bennett, *Nemesis*, p. 18.
14. As revealingly expressed by J. H. Thomas, the British railwaymen's leader, who when told by Lloyd George in 1921 that the trade union movement had the government at its mercy and challenged it to take power, replied that it was better for the movement to suffer utter defeat than for it to act unconstitutionally.
15. Adam Przeworski, 'Social Democracy as a Historical Phenomenon', *New Left Review* 122, July/August 1980, p. 49.
16. The Austrian social democrats, who were on the left-wing of the movement were able to preserve considerable institutional strength, in spite of the country's conservative semi-dictatorship, until they were militarily suppressed in 1934. Their Hungarian counterparts were the most abject, co-operating fully with the Horthy regime in return for the concession of being allowed to exist.

17. Finnish politics, following the civil war of 1918, were very different from the other Scandinavian countries. The social democrats were subordinated but not seriously endangered.

18. See e.g. James Fulcher, 'Sweden', in Stefan Berger and David Broughton (eds), *The Force of Labour*, Berg, 1995.

19. But not even in this case was industry collectivised. With the exception of the French armaments industry not a single company was nationalised in Western Europe during the interwar period. Przeworski, 'Social Democracy' p. 48.

20. Or at least their white populations.

21. See Mike Davis, 'The Barren Marriage of American Labour and the Democratic Party', *New Left Review* 124, November/December 1980, p. 69 for comment on this discussion.

22. See e.g. Stephen Baskerville and Ralph Willet (eds), *Nothing Else to Fear: New Perspectives on America in the Thirties*, Manchester University Press, 1985.

23. Peter Clarke, *The Keynsian Revolution in the Making 1924–1936*, Clarendon Press, 1988.

24. Przeworski, 'Social Democracy', p. 52.

25. Alan Bullock, *Ernest Bevin, Foreign Secretary*, Heinemann, 1983.

26. Even the German Christian Democrats in their postwar Ahlen Programme accepted the necessity of a substantial publicly owned industrial sector.

27. The 1946 world harvest was unprecedently bad.

28. 'Eventually the impasse was broken by the "invention" of the Cold War. What cost-benefit could not and did not achieve, fear did' ... 'The genius of Truman and of his advisers was to attribute the outcome of systemic circumstances which no particular agency had created or controlled to the allegedly subversive dispositions of the other military superpower, the USSR. By so doing, Truman reduced Roosevelt's vision of a global New Deal to a very shoddy reality indeed, but at least made it workable.' Giovanni Arrighi, *The Long Twentieth Century*, Verso, 1994, p. 295–6.

29. 'Perhaps an even more devastating outgrowth of modernisation was the decline of party systems as agencies of popular mobilisation and social change', Carl Boggs, *The Socialist Tradition*, Routledge, 1995, p. 77.

30. See Julius Braunthal, *History of the International, Vol. 3, World Socialism 1943–1968*, Gollancz, 1980, for a detailed account.

31. C. A. R. Crosland, *The Future of Socialism*, Jonathan Cape, 1956, p. 571.

32. Ibid., p. 27.

33. Part of the price was that the PSI renounced its local government agreements with the PCI and was now reunited with the more explicitly social democratic PSDI.

34. Goldwater's principal slogan was 'In your heart you know he's right!' The response to this was 'In your guts you know he's nuts!'

35. Kennedy had won the 1960 election partly on the promise to bridge a wholly imaginary 'missile gap'.

36. These tactics were brought to perfection under the Nixon administration, but had been initiated under Johnson.
37. The 1965 massacre of Indonesian communists with 500,000–1 million victims represented one of the most sanguinary episodes of the century.
38. Although the Greek party had already split.
39. Spain and Greece were the only European countries in which unmistakably civil wars were fought between the end of the Russian Civil War and the collapse of the Soviet bloc.
40. The anti-communist part of the populace also engaged in large-scale civil disturbances.
41. Strikingly, exactly a century after the collapse of 1873 which ushered in the 'Great Depression' of the Victorian era. Note, also no *absolute* decline or stoppage of growth.
42. Such as Andrew Glynn and Bob Sutcliffe, who demonstrated that the rate of profit in Britain was declining towards zero.
43. See Arrighi, *Long Twentieth Century*, Chapter 4.
44. Except to some extent by Japan, and Keynsian methods of deficit financing could still be used by government in a huge and dominant economy such as Reagan's United States.
45. Not to speak of Australasia.
46. Some such advantage was expected by many commentators at the time of the Soviet bloc collapse.
47. Liberalism was stigmatised by its enemies in the US as the 'L word'. This at a time when 'The US Census reported that between 1973 and 1989 the real income of male high school graduates dropped by a third; the income of those who didn't make it through high school dropped by 40 per cent.' Frances Fox Piven, 'Globalising Capitalism and the Rise of Identity Politics', *Socialist Register* 1995, p. 112.
48. Although this was cushioned to some extent by a far-reaching programme of regional aid.
49. Also indulged in by the British secret state.
50. The terrorism was directly the responsibility of peripheral groups dissatisfied with the political caution of the fascist party, the MSI, but the activists of both certainly overlapped.
51. The term 'transformisimo' had been current in Italian politics since the nineteenth century.
52. The party now reverted to its original name of Popolari.
53. Opinion polls and local elections suggested huge forthcoming gains for the left.
54. See Michael Salvati, 'The Crisis of Government in Italy', *New Left Review* 213, September/October 1995; Lucio Magri, 'The Resistible Rise of the Italian Right', *New Left Review* 214, November/December 1995.
55. An Asian Socialist (i.e. social democrat) Conference was established in 1953.
56. Braunthal, *History of the International, Vol. 3*.
57. Paul Cammack, 'Brazil. The Long March to the New Republic', *New Left Review* 190, November/December 1991; Emir Sader, 'The Workers' Party in Brazil', *New left Review* 165, September/October 1987.

Chapter 6: Trotskyism, Maoism, Eurocommunism

1. For example, Isaac Deutscher, Marcel Liebman, Ernest Mandel, C. L. R. James.
2. Bukharin was viewed by some, doubtless incorrectly, as the inspiration behind the Gorbachev reforms. For Bukharin see Stephen F. Cohen, *Bukharin and the Bolshevik Revolution: A Political Biography, 1888–1938,* Oxford University Press, 1980, though his estimate is contentious.
3. 'His extreme will to power and his insufficient intellectual equipment' 'A new idea must create its bureaucracy before Stalin can have any confidence in it.' 'Bureaucracy as bureaucracy is permeated through and through with the spirit of mediocrity Stalin is the most outstanding mediocrity of the Soviet bureaucracy.' L. Trotsky, 'Stalin', in *Portraits Political and Personal,* Pathfinder Press, 1970.
4. Ibid., p. 219.
5. See Deutscher's comment in *The Prophet Outcast, Trotsky: 1929–1940,* Oxford University Press, 1970, pp. 419–29.
6. Zinoviev and Kamanev, who argued passionately against the insurrection, turned out after all to be the most percipient of the Bolshevik leaders.
7. Or even in France that same year.
8. It is probable that they, picking up on Trotsky's characterisation of Stalin's regime, popularised the term 'totalitarianism' in political discourse during the Cold War. '... among the literary Trotskisants of the nineteen-thirties there were only a very few who would not be found at the head of the propagandist crusaders against communism of the late nineteen-forties and nineteen-fifties.' Deutscher, *Prophet Outcast,* p. 436.
9. To be fair, the international conjuncture of 1951 gave some reason for expecting the onset of global conflict.
10. Though the CPUSA in the 1930s and early 1940s exercised a more than negligible trade union influence.
11. It was compelled to resign its actual membership of the FI on account of the prohibitions of the Smith Act, but remained 'in solidarity' with its foreign co-thinkers.
12. In 1969 the CPSU published a lengthy text, *The Bolshevik Party's Struggle against Trotskyism.* An outline history of the Comintern published in Moscow in 1971 avoids mentioning Trotsky except allusively and negatively.
13. For which it was attacked vehemently in the communist press of the time.
14. Which did not prevent Ted Grant of 'Militant' characterising Deutscher as a 'philistine'.
15. Or, in the case of Eastern Europe, institute it.
16. Adding a particularly bitter flavour to Deutscher's words near the close of his biography: 'The open vindication ... will be more than a long-overdue act of justice towards the memory of a great man By this act the workers' state will announce that it has at last reached maturity, broken its bureaucratic shackles, and re-embraced the classical Marxism that had been banished with Trotsky.'

17. Despite its unflinching editorial sectarianism the journal *Revolutionary History* manages nonetheless to produce some very informative material on Trotskyist history.

18. The British 'Militant' sect, establishing its own 'Fourth International' in 1974 declared that this was 'the germ of a mighty workers' International which will *within the next decade* become the decisive force on the planet' (emphasis added).

19. Gerry Healy was renowned for the practice of splitting his organisation whenever it threatened to grow too big for him to control.

20. See especially the discussion in the Conclusion of Marcel Liebman, *Leninism under Lenin*, Merlin, 1975.

21. 'Trotsky in the Post-Soviet World', *Socialist History* 2, Autumn 1993.

22. Deutscher, *Prophet Outcast*, pp. 510–11.

23. Isaac Deutscher, 'Maoism – Its Origins, Background and Outlook', *Socialist Register*, 1994.

24. During the European Middle Ages Chinese seaborne expeditions reached as far as East Africa.

25. The CPC also wanted recognition of Mao as the prime living Marxist theoretician.

26. Given the extreme international tensions around China's relations with Taiwan this was a fairly immediate consideration.

27. Eric Hobsbawm notes that Mao is reported to have said to the Italian CP leader Togliatti 'Who told you that Italy must survive? Three hundred million Chinese will be left, and that will be enough of the human race to continue.' On the other hand, in its public statements the CPC always emphasised that resolute confrontation would certainly deter the US from launching a nuclear conflict. E. J. Hobsbawm, *Age of Extremes: The Short Twentieth Century*, Michael Joseph, 1994, p. 229.

28. Unconfirmed speculation suggests that the USSR connived at the destruction of the Maoist PKI.

29. One was founded in Britain led by an eminent trade unionist, Reg Birch.

30. A formal international organisation centred in Beijing was not created however.

31. J-P. Sartre, *Between Existentialism and Marxism*, NLB, 1974, p. 58.

32. This also involved good relations with any anti-Soviet regime. Consequently, after the Chile coup Maoists who had taken refuge in the Chinese embassy were handed over.

33. For example, 'the east wind will overcome the west wind'.

34. Such as compelling villagers to use common latrines.

35. Some British ones explicitly were Stalinist and/or looked to the Albanian regime.

36. In Germany too, according to Hilary Wainwright, who in *Arguments for a New Left: Answering the Free Market Right*, Blackwell, 1994, p. 93, claims that some of the later Green leadership emerged from a Maoist background.

37. Willingness varied on this point. All however discarded the phrase 'dictatorship of the proletariat'.

38. Carl Boggs, *The Socialist Tradition*, Routledge, 1995, p. 116.

39. Lenin's *State and Revolution* has to be understood in this sense.

40. As indicated above, incorporating token non-communist parties. The Bulgarian leadership after 1945 had actually wanted to join the USSR as a Soviet republic.
41. See R. Miliband, 'The Coup in Chile', *Socialist Register*, 1973.
42. Ernest Mandel, *From Stalinism to Eurocommunism*, New Left Books, 1978, p. 201.
43. During Stalin's lifetime Gramsci's prison writings were suppressed on the initiative of Togliatti. The purpose of this censorship was to protect Gramsci's reputation, for in the days of high Stalinism and the *History of the CPSU(B) Short Course* they would have been deemed to be intolerably heretical and their author posthumously denounced.

Chapter 7: New Left, New Social Forces and Others

1. Wolfgang J. Momsen, 'Max Weber and German Social Democracy' in Carl Levy (ed.), *Socialism and the Intelligentsia 1880–1914*, Routlege and Kegan Paul, 1987, p. 92.
2. Ibid.
3. Quoted in Lutz Niethammer, *Posthistoire: Has History Come To An End?*, Verso, 1992, p. 23. This volume examines the right-wing critique of modernity.
4. Ibid., p. 26 on Ernest Junger.
5. Martin Jay, *The Dialectical Imagination: A History of the Frankfurt School and the Institute for Social Research 1923–50*, Heinemann, 1973, p. 48.
6. Gramsci should certainly also be regarded as part of this current.
7. Jay, *Dialectical Imagination*, p. 177.
8. For example the RDR in France, with which Sartre was involved.
9. Attacks in this vein began early, with Christopher Booker's *The Neophiliacs* in 1969.
10. Compare E. J. Hobsbawm, 'Revolution and Sex' in *Revolutionaries*, Weidenfeld and Nicolson, 1973.
11. One may compare the situation and practices of the Scottish National Party on the one hand with Sinn Fein on the other.
12. It is the *combination* which distinguishes the really historic revolutions – compare the American or Irish with the French. (There are of course even deeper structures which a far-ranging cultural revolution might not touch, for which France again provides evidence.)
13. Britain, France and Germany all experienced considerable immigration.
14. For marketing purposes 'teenagers' were defined as individuals between the ages of 15 and 25.
15. This was generally true, but particularly marked in urban concentrations, less so in rural and small town environments.
16. The legal category of illegitimacy was abolished in Britain.
17. The discourse of AIDS exemplifies the contradiction. On the one hand it was presented as the 'gay plague', on the other it has evoked movements of solidarity around the importance of safe sex. World AIDS Week is being held as I write.
18. Illustrated in the famous opening line of Philip Larkin's poem 'Annis Mirabilis', 'Sexual intercourse began in 1963 ... '.

19. It might be plausibly argued that the kick of pleasurably illicit behaviour, now the concept of irregular sex has now all but disappeared in this age-group, has become attached instead to drugs.

20. The Vietnamese communists had also liquidated their Trotskyist rivals.

21. 'Revisionist' historians began to reinterpret the origins of the Cold War in a manner unfavourable to the US position, middle-class opinion was shocked by revelations of secret CIA funding to ostensibly independent anti-communist organisations, Noam Chomsky's critiques of US foreign policy made a strong impression.

22. Authors particularly important in this respect were Sartre, Frantz Fanon, Regis Debray.

23. Ken Livingstone remarked that when he joined the Labour Party in 1968 it felt like the rat *boarding* the sinking ship.

24. The left-wing US journal *Monthly Review* reflected these expectations. See also Tariq Ali (ed.), *New Revolutionaries, Left Opposition*, Peter Owen, 1969 – illustrated with a diagram of how to make a Molotov Cocktail.

25. Developments in South Africa and the Portuguese African colonies also played a significant role.

26. Quoted in Niethammer, *Posthistoire*, p. 43.

27. Marcuse's approach, though easily fitted in, was considerably more complex.

28. Not only in Europe – the assassination of Robert Kennedy and the riot at the Democratic Convention of 1968 were equivalent disillusioning experiences in the US.

29. These are not really comparable with the underground armed movements in Ireland, Spain and Latin America, the latter being defeated with indescribable brutality by US-trained repressive forces.

30. Apart from Nazi outgrowths in Austria and the Sudetenland.

31. It was usually easy enough to categorise any particular nationalism or national movement, but some, such as the IRA were ambiguous.

32. And in North America in the case of Quebec.

33. See the arguments advanced by Tom Nairn, especially *The Break-Up of Britain: Crisis and Neo-Nationalism*, New Left Books, 1977. The elements of the Trotskyist tradition have been bitterly divided on these issues.

34. This was not held to imply a need for a separate black CP.

35. Particularly Louis Farrakhan and his imitators.

36. In opposition to: ' ... the [universalist] view that relies on compliance of whites for its workability, [rejected because] Black people have waited too long', Claudette Purville, 'Spirit of Remembrance: Conflicting Theories in the Changing Vocabulary of Blackness', *Cultural Studies from Birmingham*, No. 3, 1994. The problem with this stance is that no minority, particularly one which is proportionately small, can hope to realise emancipatory objectives without mobilising support or at least assent in the majority community.

37. The German situation differs somewhat in that the Bonn government has historically pursued a policy of forcing its Turkish and Yugoslav immigrants to remain as migrants.

38. See Branka Magas, *The Destruction of Yugoslavia: Tracking the Break-up 1980–92*, Verso, 1993. Tom Nairn is at pains to distinguish between what he refers to as 'civic nationalism' and 'ethnic nationalism'. See his article in *New Left Review* 214, November/December 1995.

39. The Chartist movement in the 1830s and 1840s did not demand the franchise for women. Women (and children) were the particular object of factory legislation, partly because limitation of their hours also made adult male work impossible.

40. See Yvonne Kapp, *Eleanor Marx*, Vol. 1, Lawrence and Wishart, 1972, on the bourgeois ambience of Marx's household.

41. Nicky Hart, 'Gender and the Rise and Fall of Class Politics, *New Left Review*, May/June 1989.

42. '... women form fifty-two per cent of the world's population, perform two-thirds of the world's labour, receive one-tenth of the world's wages and own less than one-hundredth of its property'. Varda Burstyn, 'Masculine Dominance and the State', *Socialist Register* 1983, p. 45.

43. This situation was particularly apparent in the Soviet bloc, where highly traditionalist gender roles accompanied very high female participation in the workforce.

44. Creches and family allowance, highly progressive achievements, nevertheless had the effect (though in other circumstances they might have done the opposite) of further reinforcing gender stereotypes.

45. A remarkably percipient pamphlet written by Sheila Rowbotham at the dawn of the movement sketches not only all the major issues upon which it was to focus, but also the contradictions which were later to fragment it. Sheila Rowbotham, *Women's Liberation and the New Politics*, May Day Manifesto Pamphlet 4, no date but circa 1970.

46. There were others. See Johanna Brenner, 'The Best of Times, The Worst of Times: US Feminism Today', *New Left Review* 200, July/August 1993.

47. Dorothy E. Smith, 'Women, Class and Family', *Socialist Register*, 1983, p. 10.

48. Critiques of media representation of women have been a particularly important product of this development.

49. Brenner, 'Best of Times', p. 141.

50. Vron Ware, *Beyond the Pale, White Women, Racism and History*, Verso, 1991; Johanna Brenner, 'Feminism's Revolutionary Promise: Finding Hope in Hard Times' *Socialist Register* 1989, p. 249.

51. Brenner, 'Best of Times', p. 142.

52. Brenner, 'Revolutionary Promise' p. 248.

53. Particularly in the UK and the US, the attack being most severe in the latter country.

54. See Ellen Meiksins Wood, *The Retreat from Class*, Verso, 1986.

55. See R. Lew and J-P. Garnier, 'From the Wretched of the Earth to the Defence of the West: An Essay on Left Disenchantment in France', *Socialist Register*, 1984.

56. Cixous and Irigaray deny an essentialist standpoint but it is difficult to comprehend *ecriture feminine* or *parler-femme* in any other terms. See Myra Macdonald, *Representing Women*, Edward Arnold, 1995, p. 68.

57. For example in opposition to female genital mutilation.

58. Christian or Jewish fundamentalists would certainly do the same if they got the opportunity.

59. Edward Carpenter in the late nineteenth century is an exception. The Bloomsbury group can only with great reservations be regarded as being on the left.

60. See Wilhelm Reich, *The Mass Psychology of Fascism*, Souvenir Press, 1972, especially Chapter 7.

61. Simone de Beauvoir concealed her own bisexuality during her lifetime and *The Mandarins* contains disparaging remarks on male homosexuals. Doris Lessing in *The Golden Notebook*, published in the 1960s, is even more overtly brutal.

62. It had previously been conjoined in public perception with the right, through association with such institutions as the English Public Schools or the Nazi SA.

63. Among the nineteenth-century Romantics, for example. A pulp science fiction novel of the 1950s interestingly envisaged a post-nuclear world dominated by feminism, with subversive environmentalists called the Greens – thus incorporating a contemporary concern with two which were still in the future.

64. The presence or absence of convincing left alternatives is a possibly relevant consideration.

65. The Rio Summit of governments produced declarations of concern but very little else.

66. The concept of 'rights' is a contentious one if applied to sentient beings intrinsically incapable of articulating them.

67. 'Deep ecology' in another term used of groups which prioritise nature *against* humans. Also 'eco-fascism' – the notion of solving population and environmental crises in an authoritarian fashion.

68. Again, this idea has a precursor in 1950s pulp science fiction.

69. Ellen Meiksins Wood, 'A Chronology of the Left and its Successors, Or: Who's Old-Fashioned Now?', *Socialist Register*, 1995.

70. Terry Eagleton, *Ideology, An Introduction*, Verso, 1991, p. 47.

71. The writings of Thomas Kuhn, especially *The Structure of Scientific Revolutions* are often inaccurately bracketed with this genre. What Kuhn is actually discussing is the sociology of scientific endeavour. Paul Feyerabend was the leading irrationalist in this area.

72. In this regard the attack on 'the canon' – the texts which are generally held to represent the major achievements of Western culture – is particularly significant.

73. Peter Dews, *Logics of Disintegration: Post-Structuralist Thought and the Claims of Critical Theory*, Verso, 1987, p. 234.

74. Dews observes that is passe in France – but continues to thrive elsewhere.

75. The notion that incompatible world-views – e.g. science and superstition – can each be regarded as nevertheless embodying 'truth' for their adherents is reminiscent to an extent of the old Stalinist distinction between 'bourgeois' and 'proletarian' science.

76. John Dewey, the eminent philosopher of pragmatism, an earlier version of relativism, had a theoretical problem when denouncing the Moscow Trials as absolutely untrue, for his own philosophy did not admit the legitimacy of such a concept.

77. See Ania Loomba, 'Dead Women Tell No Tales: Issues of Female Subjectivity, Subaltern Agency and Tradition in Colonial and Post-colonial Writings on Widow Immolation in India', *History Workshop* 36, Autumn 1993, for a critique.
78. By attempting to have it both ways, both to condemn oppression on absolute grounds and yet sustain a relativist viewpoint. The argument is that being part of Western culture we rightly adopt its absolute standards. See Richard Rorty, *Objectivity and Truth*, Cambridge University Press, 1991 and Norman Geras, 'Language Truth and Justice', *New Left Review* 209, January/February 1995.
79. Hilary Wainwright, *Arguments for a New Left: Answering the Free Market Right*, Blackwell, 1994, p. 263–4.

Conclusion: The Winter Landscape

1. Particularly in the *Critique of the Gotha Programme* at the time of the party's formation.
2. Certainly not by the concept of 'state capitalism' applied to the regime of the five-year plans (as distinct from that of the NEP).
3. Compare Lenin's certainty that the debacle of the Second International in 1914 would become the springboard for international proletarian revolution.
4. Remnants still exist trying to assert the contrary, but few take them seriously.
5. A more penetrating examination is Lutz Niethammer, *Posthistoire: Has History Come To An End?*, Verso, 1992.
6. Particularly striking examples at present are the kleptocratic regimes in Indonesia, the Philippines and Thailand, the more so because these countries, unlike, say, Saudi Arabia, have a past history of powerful left-wing movements, now largely obliterated. See Benedict Anderson, 'Radicalism after Communism in Thailand and Indonesia, *New Left Review* 202, November/December 1993.
7. East Asian ruling elites, such as that in Singapore or Malaysia, have become adept at manipulating Western post-colonial guilt to justify their autocracies as expressions of an authentically different cultural norms.
8. Etzioni's presentations make the *Reader's Digest* appear sophisticated in comparison.
9. See Martin Marty and R. Scott Appleby (eds), *Fundamentalisms Observed*, University of Chicago Press, 1991.
10. This was not initially fundamentalist in every respect, but the most reactionary elements gained the upper hand.
11. The US form of ultra-rightism is distinctive, best described perhaps as right-wing anarchism.
12. Above all in the US.
13. Stephen Lukes' s fictional satire, *The Strange Enlightenment of Professor Caritat* expresses this well.
14. Perry Anderson, *A Zone of Engagement*, Verso, 1992.
15. Primarily because the fossil fuels and other natural resources essential to the first technological breakthrough would no longer be available.
16. Isaac Deutscher, *The Prophet Unarmed*, Oxford University Press, 1970, p. 197.

Select Bibliography

Place of publication London unless otherwise stated.

Adler, Alan (ed.), *Theses, Resolutions and Manifestos of the First Four Congresses of the Third International* (Ink Links, 1980).

Ali, Tariq (ed.), *The Stalinist Legacy: Its Impact on 20th Century World Politics* (Penguin, 1984).

Anderson, Perry, *Arguments in British Marxism* (Verso, 1989).

Anderson, Perry, *A Zone of Engagement* (Verso, 1992).

Anderson, Perry and Camiller (eds), *Mapping the West European Left* (Verso, 1994).

Arrighi, Giovanni, *The Long Twentieth Century* (Verso, 1994).

Barker, Colin and Kennedy, Paul (eds), *To Make Another World: Studies in Protest and Collective Action* (Avebury, Aldershot, 1996).

de Beauvoir, Simone, *The Second Sex* (Penguin, Harmondsworth, 1972).

Bell, D. S. (ed.), *Western European Communists and the Collapse of Communism* (Berg, Oxford, 1993).

Berger, Stephen, *The British Labour Party and the German Social Democrats 1900–1931: A Comparative Study* (Clarendon Press, Oxford, 1994).

Berger, Stephen, and Broughton, David (eds), *The Force of Labour* (Berg, Oxford, 1995).

Birchall, Ian, *Workers Against the Monolith* (Pluto Press, 1974).

Boggs, Carl, *The Impasse of European Communism* (Westview Press, Boulder, Colorado, 1982).

Boggs, Carl, *The Socialist Tradition* (Routledge, 1995).

Braunthal, Julius, *History of the International, 1914–1943* (Praeger, New York, 1967).

Braunthal, Julius, *History of the International*, Vol. 3, World Socialism 1943–1968 (Gollancz, 1980).

Brenner, Johanna, 'The Best of Times, The Worst of Times: US Feminism Today', *New Left Review* 200, July/August 1993.

Breuilly, John, *Labour and Liberalism in 19th Century Europe* (Manchester University Press, Manchester, 1994).

Carr, E. H., *The Russian Revolution from Lenin to Stalin 1917–1929* (Macmillan, 1979).

Claudin, Fernando, *The Communist Movement: From Comintern to Cominform* (Penguin, Harmondsworth, 1975).

Cohen, Stephen F., *Bukharin and the Bolshevik Revolution: A Political Biography, 1888–1938* (Oxford University Press, Oxford, 1980).

Crosland, C. A. R., *The Future of Socialism* (Jonathan Cape, 1956).

Davis, Mike, 'Why the US Working Class is Different', *New Left Review* 123, September/October 1980.

Davis, Mike, 'The Barren Marriage of American Labour and the Democratic Party', *New Left Review* 124, November/December 1980.

Deutscher, Isaac, *Stalin: A Political Biography* (Oxford University Press, Oxford, 1961).

Deutscher, Isaac *The Prophet Armed, Trotsky: 1879–1921* (Oxford University Press, Oxford, 1970).

Deutscher, Isaac *The Prophet Unarmed, Trotsky: 1921–1929* (Oxford University Press, Oxford, 1970).

Deutscher, Isaac, *The Prophet Outcast, Trotsky: 1929–1940* (Oxford University Press, Oxford, 1970).

Dews, Peter, *Logics of Disintegration: Post-Structuralist Thought and the Claims of Critical Theory* (Verso, 1987).

Evans, Richard J. (ed.), *The German Working Class, 1888–1933: The Politics of Everyday Life* (Croom Helm, 1992).

Ferro, Marc, *The Bolshevik Revolution: A Social History* (Routledge and Kegan Paul, 1985).

Foster, John, *Class Struggle and the Industrial Revolution* (Weidenfeld and Nicolson, 1974).

Geras, Norman, 'Language Truth and Justice', *New Left Review* 209, January/February 1995.

Glynn, A. and Sutcliffe, R., *British Capitalism, Workers and the Profits Squeeze* (Penguin, Harmondsworth, 1972).

Gowan, Peter, 'Neo-Liberal Theory and Practice for Eastern Europe', *New Left Review* 213, September/October 1995.

Gramsci, Antonio, *Selections from the Prison Notebooks* (Lawrence and Wishart, 1971).

Grebing, Helga, *History of the German Labour Movement* (Berg, Oxford, 1985).

Guerin, Daniel, *Anarchism* (Monthly Review Press, New York, 1970).

Guttsman, W. L., *The German Social Democratic Party 1875–1933* (Allen and Unwin, 1981).

Hobsbawm, E. J., *Labouring Men, Studies in the History of Labour* (Weidenfeld and Nicolson, 1964).

Hobsbawm, E. J., *Revolutionaries* (Weidenfeld and Nicolson, 1973).

Hobsbawm, E. J., *Nations and Nationalism Since 1780, Programme, Myth and Reality* (Cambridge University Press, Cambridge, 1990).

Hobsbawm, E. J. *Age of Extremes: The Short Twentieth Century* (Michael Joseph, 1994).

Jacoby, Russell, *Dialectic of Defeat: Contours of Western Marxism* (Cambridge University Press, Cambridge, 1981).

Jay, Martin, *The Dialectical Imagination: A History of the Frankfurt School and the Institute for Social Research 1923–50* (Heinemann, 1973).

Jemnitz, Janos, 'Labour and Politics: Hungarian Workers' Parties, Trade Unions and the State', *Socialist History* 2, Autumn 1993.

Levy, Carl (ed.), Socialism *and the Intelligentsia 1880–1914*, Routledge and Kegan Paul, 1987.

Liebman, Marcel, *Leninism Under Lenin* (Merlin, 1975).

Linden, Marcel van der and Thorpe, Wayne, (eds) *Revolutionary Syndicalism: An International Perspective* (Scolar Press, Aldershot, 1990).

McCormack, Gavan, 'Kim Country: Hard Times in North Korea' *New Left Review* 198, March/April 1993.

Magas, Branka, *The Destruction of Yugoslavia; Tracking the Break-up 1980–92* (Verso, 1993).

Mandel, Ernest, *From Stalinism to Eurocommunism* (New Left Books, 1978).

Marty, Martin and Appleby, R. Scott (eds), *Fundamentalisms Observed* (University of Chicago Press, Chicago, Illinois, 1991).

Merridale, Catherine and Ward, Chris, *Perestroika in Historical Perspective* (Edward Arnold, 1991).

Miliband, R, Saville, J. and Liebman, M. (eds), 'The Uses of Anti-Communism', *Socialist Register*, 1984.

Murray, Martin, *The Revolution Deferred, The Painful Birth of Post Apartheid South Africa* (Verso, 1994).

Nairn, Tom, *The Break-Up of Britain: Crisis and Neo-Nationalism* (New Left Books, 1977).

Nation, R. Craig, *War on War: Lenin, The Zimmerwald Left and the Origins of Communist Internationalism* (Duke University Press, Durham and London, 1989).

Niethammer, Lutz, *Posthistoire: Has History Come To An End?* (Verso, 1992).

Nettl, J. P., *Rosa Luxemburg* (Oxford University Press, Oxford, 1966).

Nove, Alec, *An Economic History of the USSR* (Penguin, Harmondsworth, 1972).

Padgett, S. and Paterson, W. E., *A History of Social Democracy in Postwar Europe* (Longman, Harlow, 1991).

Pethybridge, Roger, *The Social Prelude to Stalinism* (Macmillan, 1974).

Pierson, Stanley, *Marxism and the Origins of British Socialism: The Struggle for a New Consciousness* (Cornell University Press, Ithaca and London, 1973).

Piven, Frances Fox, 'Globalising Capitalism and the Rise of Identity Politics', *Socialist Register*, 1995, p. 112.

Przeworski, Adam, 'Social Democracy as a Historical Phenomonen', *New Left Review* 122, July/August 1980.

Reich, Charles, *The Greening of America* (Allen Lane, 1971).

Rozman, Gilbert, *A Mirror for Socialism: Soviet Criticisms of China* (I. B. Tauris, 1985).

Sassoon, Donald, 'The Rise and Fall of West European Communism', *Contemporary European History*, Vol. 1, Part 2, July 1992.

Service, Robert, *Lenin: A Political Life* Vol. 1, The Strengths of Contradiction, (Indiana University Press, Bloomington, 1985).

Service, Robert, *Lenin: A Political Life, Vol. 2, Worlds in Collision*, (Macmillan, 1991).

Service, Robert, *Lenin: A Political Life, Vol. 3, The Iron Ring* (Macmillan 1994).

Smith, Richard, 'The Chinese Road to Capitalism', *New Left Review* 199, May/June 1993.

Trotsky, L., *History of the Russian Revolution* [three vols] (Sphere, 1967).

Trotsky, L., *The Revolution Betrayed* (Pathfinder Press, New York, 1970).

Wainwright, Hilary, *Arguments for a New Left: Answering the Free Market Right* (Blackwell, Oxford, 1994).

Walker, Rachael, *Six Years that Shook the World: Perestroika – The Impossible Project* (Manchester University Press, Manchester, 1993).

Waller, Michael, *The End of the Communist Power Monopoly* (Manchester University Press, Manchester, 1993).

Ward, Chris, *Stalin's Russia* (Edward Arnold, 1993).

Ware, Vron, *Beyond the Pale, White Women, Racism and History* (Verso, 1991).

Watt, Richard M., *The Kings Depart: The German Revolution and the Treaty of Versailles* (Penguin, 1973).

Westoby, Adam, *The Evolution of Communism* (Polity Press, Oxford, 1989).

Westoby, Adam, *Communism since World War II* (Harvester Press, Brighton, 1981).

Wheeler-Bennett, J. W., *Nemesis of Power: The German Army in Politics 1918–1945* (Macmillan, 1967).

White, Stephen, *Gorbachev in Power* (Cambridge University Press, Cambridge, 1990).

Whitehead, Andrew, 'Calcutta Compromise', *New Statesman*, 20 November 1992.

Wood, Ellen Meiksins, *The Retreat from Class* (Verso, 1986).

Woodcock, George, *Anarchism*, (Penguin, 1963).

Yergin, Daniel, *Shattered Peace: The Origins of the Cold War and the National Security State* (Penguin, Harmondsworth, 1980).

Young, John W., *Cold War Europe 1945–1985* (Edward Arnold, 1991).

Index

(References to specific countries are under entries for political parties, wars or revolutions. Some general terms such as labour movements or trade unionism do not have separate entries).

AFL-CIO 139
AIDS 209, 210
Acton, Lord 111
African National Congress 123
Allende, Salvador 88
Althusser, Louis 180
Anarchism 9, 22, 26, 28, 29, 44, 186, 195, 197, 202
Anderson, Perry 9, 229–30
Andropov, Yuri 96
Anti-semitism 27, 40, 42, 100, 209, 228
    and German Workers' Party 37
    and *Pamyat* 117
Aristotle 230
Arrighi, Giovanni 16

Bakunin, Mikhail 22
Baldwin, James 209
Baltic Republics 100
Batista, Fulgencio 113
Baudrillard, Jean 218
Beauvoir, Simone de 192, 203, 204, 238n.
Bebel, August 27, 202
Benjamin, Walter 189
Berlusconi, Silvio 152–3
Bernstein, Eduard 27, 141, 144
    and Revisionism 31–2, 39, 133
Bismarck, Otto von 7, 24, 25
Black Panthers 144, 200
Blanqui, Auguste 22
Bonald, Louis-Jacques 5

Bolsheviks 25, 28, 34–5, 39, 44, 48, 52, 53, 59, 60, 77, 103, 104, 107, 129, 160, 181, 198, 202, (*see also* Leninism, Revolutions)
Bonaparte, Louis (Napoleon III) 7
    Napoleon 78
Braunthal, Julius 154
Brezhnev, Leonid 83, 96, 116, 177
Brown, Norman O. 196
Bukharin, Nikolai 57ff, 97, 102, 160, 181
Bulganin, Nikolai 76
Burke, Edmund 5
Byron, Lord 132

Callaghan, James 148
Campaign for Nuclear Disarmament 189
Cannon, James P. 169
Capital 23, 165
Carillo, Santiago 181, 185
Carr, E. H. 2
Carter, Jimmy 95
Castro, Fidel; Castroism 79, 113, 199
Cavour, Camilo 7
Ceausescu, Nicolae 82
Central Intelligence Agency (CIA) 140
Chadwick, Edwin 30
Chartists 18, 216
Chateaubriand, Francois-René 5
Chernenko, Konstantin 96
Chernobyl explosion 98
Chiang Kai-Shek 68
Christian Democrats (Germany) 119, 143, 151
Christian Democrats (Italy) 152
Christianity 3, 219

Churchill, Winston 64, 66
Civil Rights (USA) 194
Cixous, Hélène 208
Class identity 16–19, 21, 40, 137,
    198, 207, 225, 228–9
Cliff, Tony 172
Cobbett, William 18
Cold War 2, 8, 42, 66–72, 73, 74,
    79, 89, 102, 105, 111, 112,
    127, 152, 167, 182, 189,
    190, 211
  and Popular front governments
    66ff.
  and Berlin Wall 80
  and Cuban missile crisis 193
  and Social Democracy 137–40
  'Second Cold War' 92, 102,
    114
Collectivisation (in Soviet
    agriculture) 62
Communist Information Bureau
    (Cominform) 69–70, 73, 74
Communist International
    (Comintern, Third
    International) 49ff, 60, 63,
    69, 71, 73, 122, 126, 127,
    129, 131, 160, 161, 172,
    185, 198, 199, 223
  and 'united front' 51, 61
  and 'class against class' 61, 63,
    69
  and Popular Front 63
  dissolved 65
Communist Manifesto 6, 21, 22,
    23, 24
Communist parties in (see also
    Eurocommunism)
  Afghanistan 93ff.
  Albania (APL) 69, 81, 174
  Belgium 82, 177
  Britain (CPGB) 125, 126
  China (CPC) 56, 68, 69, 77,
    80ff, 113 15, 173–80, (see
    also Maoism, Cultural
    Revolution)
  Cuba 107, 112–13
  Czechoslovakia (CPCz) 70,
    120, (see also Prague Spring)
  France (PCF) 69, 81, 123,
    124, 125, 146, 174, 181

  Germany (KPD) 52–3, 61,
    131, 163
  Greece 146
  India (CPI) 80, 82, 176, (West
    Bengal) 122–3
  Indonesia (PKI) 82, 176, 239n,
    244n.
  Italy (PCI) 69, 81, 123, 124,
    125, 140, 143, 147, 152,
    169,174, 185, 238n. (PDS)
    125, 153
  Japan 176
  Netherlands 125
  New Zealand 82, 177
  North Korea 107, 111–12, 176
  Portugal (PCP) 89, 146, 147
  Romania 67
  Russian Federation 118
  South Africa 122, 123–4
  Spain (PCE) 147, 180, 183, 185
  USA 125, 139
  USSR (CPSU) 60, 62, 74, 76,
    77, 80ff, 97, 100, 101ff, 110,
    115ff, 152, 161,175, 178,
    181, 183 (see also Bolsheviks,
    Revolution)
  Venezuela 86
  Vietnam 113
Communist parties (Sino-Soviet
    split) 80–2
'Communist Refoundation' (Italy)
    125
Condorcet, Marquis de 223
Confucianism 112, 178, 225
Conservative Party 140
Crosland C. A. R. 140–3, 150
Cultural Revolution 86, 87, 107,
    177–80, 196

Daniel, Yuli 83
Debray, Regis 196
Democratic Party (USA) 135ff.
Deng Xiaoping 114
Disraeli, Benjamin 6, 7
Deutscher, Isaac 57, 64, 78, 165,
    170, 172, 173
Dews, Peter 217, 218

ELAS 66
ETA 4, 199

Ebert, Frederich 54, 130, 131, 132
Engels, Friedrich 17, 20, 26, 29, 31, 71, 133, 202, 222
Enlightenment, the 10, 21, 26, 27, 37, 41, 201, 217, 219, 230
Environmentalism 210–15
Erhart, Ludwig 142
Etzioni, Amitai 226
Eurocommunism 147, 152, 180–5
and 'polycentrism' 182
and Chilean example 182
European Community /Union (EC/EU) 119, 151

Fabians 27, 30, 32
Fanon, Franz 225
Fascism 8, 9, 47, 63, 83, 152, 224
'social fascism' 61
neo-fascism 121, 153, 227–9
as Bonapartism 165
Feminism 201–9
First World War 7, 38, 46–7, 48, 55, 91, 107, 127, 129, 161, 167
Five-Year Plan 62, 63, 80
Forster, E. M. 189
Foucault, Michel 208, 210, 216
Franco, Francisco 145, 199
Freemasons 18
Freidan, Betty 203
Freidman, Milton 119
Freikorps 54, 129, 139,
Freud, Sigmund; Freudianism 187–8, 208, 217
Frolich, Paul 54
Fukuyama, Francis 224

Gagarin, Yuri 96, 118
Gaitskell, Hugh 142
Garvey, Marcus 200
Galliflet, General 39
Gay and lesbian politics, culture 192, 209–10
Genet, Jean 209
Genghis Khan 219
Gladstone, W.E. 194
Glasnost – see Gorbachev
Goethe, Johann 230

Goldwater, Barry 144, 244n.
Gonzalez, Felipe 145, 151
Goodman, Paul 196
Gorbachev, Mikhail 96–101, 114, 116
Gould, Stephen Jay 219
Gramsci, Antonio 165, 183–4, 248n.
Green parties and organisations
German 212–13
British 212, 214
US 214
Greer, Germaine 203
Guevara, Che 83, 196

Hart, Nicky 202
Hayek, Friedrich von 119, 151, 221
Healy, Gerry 168, 169
Hegel, G. W. F. 188, 224
Helsinki Agreements 89
Hervé, Gustave 40
Hindenburg, Field Marshal 130
Hirst, Paul 207
Hitler, Adolf 61, 117, 163, 165, 189
Hitler-Stalin Pact (1939) 64, 166
Hobsbawm, Eric 10, 32, 68, 100, 101, 107, 120, 125, 127, 137, 230
Horowitz, Davis 207
Hoxha, Enver 174
Hugenberg, Alfred 152
Huxley, Aldous 189

IRA 4
Identity politics 198–210
ethnic 199–200, 207
feminist 201–9
class 16–19, 21, 40, 137, 198, 207
Independent Labour Party (ILP) 30
Indian National Congress 70, 122, 154
International Monetary Fund (IMF) 138, 148
Irigary, Luce 208
Islam 200–1, 226–27

Jaruselski, General 95
Jaurès, Jean 39
Jesuits 229
Jevons, Stanley 20
Johnson, Lyndon B. 143, 144, 196

KGB (Committee for State Security) 97, 100, 101
Kafka, Franz 189
Kagarlitsky, Boris 116
Kamenev, Lev 102, 161
Kapp putsch 54, 130
Kautsky, Karl 31, 33, 38, 40, 41, 183
Kelly, Petra 212
Kennedy, J. F. 143, 144, 193
Keynes, J. M; Keynsianism 10, 136–7, 141–2, 153, 190, 224
  and laissez-faire 91
  and postwar reconstruction 138
Khmer Rouge 3, 106, 179
Khrushchev, Nikita 76, 81, 82, 83, 85, 95, 96, 175, 177, 193
  and 'Secret Speech' 76–8
  and Hungarian revolt 78
  and Sputnik 78
  and 22nd CPSU Congress 79, 105
Kim Il Sung 111
Korean War 74
Kulaks 58, 62, 103
Kuomintang 68, 176

Labour Party 27, 29, 30, 63, 71, 132, 137, 139, 140, 142, 145, 146, 153
Lacan, Jacques 208, 218
Lassalle, Ferdinand 23
Lawrence, D. H. 209
Lenin, V. I: Leninism 32, 34, 35, 39, 42, 55, 57, 59, 68, 75, 80, 99, 102, 103, 104, 105, 107, 108, 118, 127, 128, 133, 159, 160, 161, 165, 166, 170, 172, 173, 174, 176, 183, 184, 185, 198, 220, 222, 223 (see also Marxism-Leninism)

Liberal Party 29, 137, 153
  (Liberal Democrats) 153
Liebknecht, Karl 53, 54, 130
Liebman, Marcel 43, 44, 47–8
Lombard Leauge (Northern Leagues) 152, 201
Lovelock, James 214
Ludendorf, General 130
Luxumburg, Rosa 31, 38, 39, 44, 53, 54, 130, 160, 198, 223

McCarthy, Joe 139
Macdonald, Ramsay 27
Maistre, Joseph de 5
Malcolm X 200
Malthusianism 6, 7
Mandel, Ernest 183
Mao Zedong; Maoism 56, 57, 68, 80, 82, 173–80, 185, 194, 195, 197, 215
  and 'Gang of Four' 87, 180, 207
  and 'Great Leap Forward' 81, 174
  and 'Hundred Flowers' 81
  see also Cultural Revolution
Marcuse, Herbert 196
Marshall Plan (ERP) 84, 138
Marty, André 66
Marx, Karl; Marxism 6, 15, 17, 20, 23, 26, 29, 30, 32, 33, 34, 35, 38, 43, 45, 46, 52, 57, 71, 72, 103, 112, 128, 131, 133, 136, 141, 142, 160, 163, 164, 173, 183, 184, 195, 202, 215, 220, 222ff, 230
  and 'Economists' 34
  and International Workingmen's Association (First International) 25, 40
  and League of the Just (Communist League) 22
  and 'Legal Marxists' 34
  Marxism-Leninism 10, 82, 87, 97, 98, 100, 147, 198–99
  Western Marxism 188–90
  Frankfurt School 189, 196
Medvedev, Roy 16

Mensheviks 34, 35, 39, 43, 44, 46, 53
Michels, Georg 103
Millerand, Alexandre 39
Mitterand, Francois 147
Modernity 2, 186ff.
Mother Theresa 123
Murdoch, Rupert 150, 152
Mussolini, Benito 183

Nairn, Tom 226
National Association for the Advancement of Colored People (NAACP) 199
Narodniks 33
and Social Revolutionary Party 34, 44, 53
National Organisation for Women (NOW) 207
Nationalism 6, 7, 38ff, 100, 198–99, 201
in France 199
in Ireland 196, 199
in Scotland 196, 199
in Spain 199
in former USSR and Eastern Europe 117–18, 121–22
in Wales 199
Nazism 37, 42, 61, 107, 131, 220, 228
'New Deal' (USA) 135ff, 143, 151
'New Economic Policy' (NEP) 58, 59, 60, 63, 103,
New Left 186ff.
and 1968 195–98
New Left Review 180
New Right 91, 95, 207
Nietzsche, Friedrich 7, 187, 188, 220
Nineteen Eighty-Four 111, 189 192
Nixon, Richard 89, 142, 179
North Atlantic Treaty Organisation (NATO) 99, 146, 151
Nove, Alec 10
Northern Ireland 37

Orange Order 227
Orwell, George 192

Pablo, Michel 168
Palestine Liberation Organisation (PLO) 201
Papendreaou, Andreas 146, 151
Perestroika see Gorbachev
Peter the Great 44
Pinochet, Augusto 88, 116
Plekhanov, Georgi 165
Postmodernism, poststructuralism 10, 207–208, 215–20
Prague Spring 83–6, 97, 121, 179, 181, 196
Progress 1, 2, 230–31
Proletariat 16–19, 22–3
Proudhon, Pierre Joseph 202

Racism 36–7
in Australian labour movement 36
in South African labour movement 37
Rathenau, Walther 130
Reagan , Ronald 92, 99
'Red Army Fraction' 197–8
'Red Brigades' 185, 198
Reed, John 171
Reich, Wilhelm 192, 209
Religious fundamentalisms 226–8
Revolutions:
Angolan 42, 90, 93
American 4
Bolivian 169
Bolshevik 8, 42, 47ff, 58, 63, 73, 108, 135, 161, 165, 166, 170, 175, 223
Chinese (1911) 36
Chinese (1949) 42, 68, 69, 70, 107, 167, 173
Cuban 42, 79, 80, 144, 194
English 229
Ethiopian 89
French 4, 5, 6, 15, 16, 21, 23, 26, 27, 41, 46, 198, 202, 230
German 52–5, 129ff.
Grenadian 90, 93, 154
Iranian 90, 200–1, 227
Nepali 154
Mexican 36
Nicaraguan 42, 90, 93

Mozambican 42, 90, 93
Portugese 89, 90, 146
Russian (1905) 33, 35, 36, 38, 46
Russian (March 1917) 48
of 1848 6, 17, 22, 43, 195, 223
0f 1871 (Paris Commune) 17, 25, 28, 39
Roosevelt, Franklin D 135, 139
Rorty, Richard 220, 252n.
Roszak, Theodore 197
Russell, Bertrand 188

Salazar, Antonio 145
Sandinistas 42–3, 90, 93
Sartre, Jean-Paul 180, 197
The Second Sex 203–4, 208
Second World War 2, 8, 64, 65, 107, 108, 137, 166, 167, 189
Resistance in 65, 73
Serendo Luminoso 180
Service, Robert 48
Sexual attitudes 191–2
Shaw, Bernard 20
Sinyavsky, Andrei 83
Situationism 197
Slansky, Rudolf 70
Smith, Adam 21
Soares, Mario 146, 151
Social Democracy 8, 9, 10, 37, 61, 69, 127–55, 215, 220
in Australasia 134
in Brazil (PT) 154
in France (SFIO) 32, 39, 139, (PS) 143, 145, 147, 148, 151
in Greece (PASOK) 143, 145–6, 151
in Italy (PSI) 125, 140, (PSDI) 140, 143, 152–3
in Germany (SPD) 23, 29, 31–2, 39, 40, 43, 46, 52ff, 128ff, 133, 137, 139, 142, 143, 145, 146, 148, 151, 169, 213, 222
in Jamaica 154
in Nepal 154
in Portugal 145, 146, 151
in Russia 1903–12 (RSDLP) 34, 39

in Scandinavia 8, 134, 148
in Spain (PSOE) 145–6, 151–2, 153
Socialist International (Second International) 15, 20, 25–41, 45, 74, 127, 130, 131, 146, 154, 159, 160, 198, 222
Socialist Labour Party 28
Socialist Workers' Party (SWP) [UK] 168, 171, 172
Socialist Workers' Party (SWP) [USA] 168, 169
Solidarity (Polish trade union) 95, 100
Soviets (councils) 35, 44, 51
Soviet Bloc, economic 'shock therapy' in 115–22
nationalism in 117–18, 121–2
Spanish Civil War 63, 145
Spartacus League (see revolutions, German)
Stalin, Josef; Stalinism 39, 55–75, 76, 77, 78, 81, 82, 83, 84, 96, 102, 103, 104, 124, 140, 160, 162, 164. 165, 167, 168, 169, 170, 171, 174, 176, 181, 184, 185, 189, 194, 223, 246n.
and 'socialism a single country' 57–63, 80, 105, 107, 108, 112, 116, 117, 127 163
and purges 63–4, 70, 163, 166
and Hitler-Stalin Pact 64, 166
Stalingrad, battle of 64
'State capitalism' 163, 171
Surrealism 189, 197
Sverdlov, Yakov 102
Syndicalism 27–9, 32, 36, 37, 38, 44, 202
Industrial Workers of the World (IWW) 28

Tatchell, Peter 210
Thatcher, Margaret 92, 147, 151
Thompson, E. P. 17–18, 40
Ticktin, Hillel 118
Tillon, Charles 66
Tito, Josip; Titoism 67, 68, 70, 76, 122, 174
Togliatti, Palmiro 182

Trades Union Congress 29
Trotsky, Leon; Trotskyism 9, 32,
    44, 47, 48, 50, 55, 58, 59,
    60, 63, 75, 78, 82, 102, 103,
    159–64, 179, 180, 185, 189,
    194, 195, 197, 199, 223,
    246n.
  'uneven and combined
    development' 46
  and 'permanent revolution'
    161ff.
  and 'bureaucratic (degenerate)
    workers' state' 161ff.
  and Fourth International 163ff,
    199
  in Ceylon (LSSP) 167, 168–9
Truman, Harry 138–9
Truman Doctrine 68, 69, 84
Tsarism 33, 34, 46, 60, 88, 101,
    117, 133, 162, 165, 172

Ulbricht, Walter 85

Vietnam War 42, 71, 83, 87, 89,
    144, 194, 196

Waite, Mike 172
Wainwright, Hilary 221, 231

Wall Street crash (1929) 61
'War communism' 58 59
Warsaw Pact 85, 92
Waugh, Evelyn 1
Weathermen 198
Webbs, Beatrice and Sidney 21,
    30, 237n.
Weber, Max 24, 103, 187, 236n.
Webster, Richard 219
Weitling, Wilhelm 17
Weimar Republic 54, 130–1
Wells, H, G. 189
Wilhelm II 24
Wilson, Harold 148, 193
Wood, Ellen Meiksins 215
Wollstonecraft, Mary 202

Yalta Agreements 66
Yeltsin, Boris 100, 101, 116, 117

Zanyatin, Yevgeny 189
Zhdanov, Andrei 69
Zhirinovsky, Vladimir 117
Zhukov, Marshal 96
Zimmerwald meeting 47, 48
Zinoviev, Grigory 50, 57, 160,
    161
Zionism 200